Wounded Warriors
Chosen Lives

Healing for Vietnam Veterans

Howard J. Olsen

Clear Stream Publishing
Box 122128, Arlington, Texas 76012

If this book has been given to you, it was made available following Christ's principles for giving:

Give and it will be given to you, full measure, pressed down, shaken together, running over, they will pour into your lap. For whatever measure you deal out to others, it will be dealt to you in return. Give to everyone who asks of you, and whoever takes away what is yours, do not demand it back. And just as you want men to treat you, treat them the same way. Be on guard against every form of greed; for not even when one has abundance does life consist of his possessions. (Luke 6:30-38; 12:15-21)

I want to be found a "faithful steward" of what God has entrusted to my care. He has given to me freely, and my desire is to reflect His character. The principles outlined in 2 Corinthians 8:11-15 and 9:6-12 govern the distribution of this book:

. . . For this is not for the ease of others and for your affliction, but by way of equality. . . at this present time your abundance being a supply for their want, that their abundance may also become a supply for your want, that there may be equality."

He who sows sparingly shall also reap sparingly; and he who sows bountifully shall also reap bountifully. Let each one do just as he has purposed in his heart; not grudgingly or under compulsion; for God loves a cheerful giver. And God is able to make all grace abound to you, that always having all sufficiency in everything, you may have an abundance for every good deed; as it is written: He scattered abroad, He gave to the poor, His righteousness abides forever.

Now He who supplies seed to the sower and bread for food, will supply and multiply your seed for sowing and increase the harvest of your righteousness; you will be enriched in everything for all liberality which through us is producing thanksgiving to God. For the ministry of this service is not only fully supplying the needs of the saints, but is also overflowing through many thanksgivings to God.

This book is given according to availability. I ask only that you send a donation. I believe God will richly bless those who respond in integrity, and those who give to see this book distributed freely. To share in this ministry, see the response form on page 239.

Howard Olsen

ii

Wounded Warriors Chosen Lives

Healing for Vietnam Veterans

About the Author

Howard Olsen grew up in the small town of Staples, Minnesota.
He volunteered for the draft in 1967 and served in the Vietnam War in
1967-68 with Charlie Battery, 1st Batallion, 8th Artillery, 25th Infantry
Division. He has also authored *Issues of the Heart: Memoirs of an
Artilleryman in Vietnam.*
Howard is a counselor who writes and teaches seminars with his
wife, Myrna. He and his wife also teach and facilitate small group
interaction in FOCUS Retreat Seminars. Howard and his wife live in
Ft. Worth, Texas, and have two sons, Benjamin and Brady.

Scripture quotations are from the King James Version (1970),
New King James Version (1982),
New American Standard Version (1977),
and Good News for Modern Man.

Italics and [ ] in Scripture references are added by the author
for emphasis and clarification only.

Quotes from Vietnam veterans contained in this book have been
included verbatim with no attempt to edit out language which may
be objectionable to some readers.

Cover photo and design by N. Lee Bowman

ISBN # 0-9637741-1-5

Printed in the United States of America
Clear Stream, Inc. Publishing
Box 122128, Arlington, TX 76012
(817) 265-2766   (817) 861-0703 Fax

It is with gratitude and affection
that I dedicate this book to all Vietnam Veterans.

A special thanks to those who helped edit this book:
Hank Slikker, Jim Norgaard, Lee and Carol Bowman,
Judy Henderson-Prather, and especially to my wife Myrna,
who graciously gave of her time to make this book readable.

CONTENTS

Preface

The Vietnam War left an indelible mark on the life of nearly every Vietnam veteran. The severity of the wars impact varies, but few escaped Vietnam unscathed. I am no exception. The Vietnam War produced a great variety of broken relationships which, in the long run, have been damaging and detrimental to our nation. Reconciliation of these relationships, therefore, is one key to the restoration of our nation. Reconciliation in relationships also aids personal recovery. This book travels the uncomfortable path of personal scrutiny required to achieve not only personal wholeness, but reconciliation between veterans and their nation, and between veterans and God.

Underlying the general theme of healing and restoration is the *value* of human life and relationships. Values are a controversial subject. Americans seldom agree on what has value anymore. What is considered desirable, useful, or ultimately of worth has greatly changed. Because of this, agreeing on solutions to problems is thwarted by the increasing polarization of values and perspectives. So although I address the wounds and behaviors of people with post-traumatic stress disorder and why they occur, *I can only suggest* solutions. Only those who agree with the solutions I present are likely to implement them.

Not everyone wants to pay the price of study, self-examination, or change, to sustain a healthy life, or to apply the discipline necessary to maintain emotional and mental fitness. Many are satisfied to sustain their life by siphoning off the strength of others, or by forcing others to satisfy their needs. The road to healing and freedom is often difficult. It is truly the road less traveled. Healing requires growth. Growth requires change. Continual change, like continual growth, is never very easy.

This book reflects my own personal struggle with the wounds I received during and after Vietnam. My journey, drawn as it were by some unseen hand, was in reality a spiritual pilgrimage. I did not always see it that way. Eventually though, it led to a personal relationship with Jesus Christ. It was His ability to reach across time and space that restored wholeness to my life. It was He who unraveled the cord that bound me to my past. Unpolished as it is, this is my attempt to give Him honor. If you read this book with an open heart and mind you will find healing, and insight. You will also discover sound patterns for building and sustaining healthy relationships. In the words of Bob Mumford, "The Bible always handles the essential issues; it seldom deals with peripherals. It continually gives us the enlightened perspective and always presents us with abiding solutions."[1]

Introduction

In November of 1992, after leaving the Togus, Maine, Veterans Administration Hospital after a twenty-eight day stay in its post traumatic stress treatment program, R.D., a Vietnam veteran, immediately drove home where he shot five people to death, including himself. A week later, twenty-year veteran B.A., following a two-week stay at the same facility, shot himself in the head. In January, another Vietnam veteran jumped to his death from an abandoned mill in his home town and less than a week later, M.O. returned from Togus and shot himself to death in his Portland apartment. In March of '93 another Vietnam veteran returned from one of his many visits to Togus and held at least a dozen police officers at bay while threatening to kill himself with a hunting knife.[1] Just what is going on? Are these merely unrelated incidences? They are not! As early as 1971, before the war was even officially over, the National Council of Churches reported that 49,000 veterans had committed suicide after returning from Vietnam. Rough estimates showed that Vietnam veterans were continuing to die at a rate of 800 per year.[3] Chuck Dean says that "more Vietnam veterans have committed suicide since 1975 than were killed in the war itself__by nearly *three times*."[2] Considering over 58,000 men lost their lives in Vietnam, that would be approximately 174,000 men. The deaths of these men have been primarily of a violent nature: hangings, shootings, vehicular accidents, and drug overdoses.

Suicide, however, is only one example of the problems Vietnam vets still face. Lack of quality medical care, homelessness, substance abuse, poverty, unemployment, family and marital dysfunction, crime, and mental health, are all issues faced by troubled vets. To assure the reader that these problems are not unique to *Vietnam* vets, I include this:

> On a tour of the country, in the midst of which I am at the time of this writing, I have visited 18 government hospitals for veterans. In them are a total of about 50,000 destroyed men... men who were the pick of the nation 18 years ago. The very able chief surgeon at the government hospital in Milwaukee, where there are 3,800 of the living dead, told me that mortality among veterans is three times as great as among those who stayed at home.
>
> Boys with normal viewpoints were taken out of the fields and offices and factories and classrooms and put into the ranks. There they were remolded; they were made over; they were made to "about face"; to regard murder as the order of the

day. They were put shoulder to shoulder, and through mass psychology, they were entirely changed. We used them for a couple of years and trained them to think nothing at all of killing or of being killed.

Then, suddenly, we discharged them and told them to make another 'about face'! This time they had to do it on their own, readjusting sans mass psychology, sans officers' aid and advice, sans nation-wide propaganda. We didn't need them anymore, so we scattered them about without any speeches or parades. Many, too many, of these fine boys are eventually destroyed, mentally, because they could not make that final "about face" alone.

Smedley D. Butler, *1936*
Major General, United States Marines
Two-time winner, Congressional Medal of Honor

Most Vietnam veterans made the adjustment back to civilian life successfully. This may be a tribute to their character, ability, or simply the grace of God, for almost all of them had to face and overcome a difficult homecoming. Adjustment rates for *combat veterans*, however, are different. A large portion of combat vets have never finished the journey home. Resolution for them has been painfully slow, and is made more difficult by those who still question and dispute the validity of their struggle. Nowhere is this as blatantly obvious as in the ongoing battle Vietnam vets face with the very organization designed to serve their needs, the Department of Veterans' Affairs (DVA).

Post-traumatic stress disorder

The National Vietnam Veterans Readjustment Study (NVVRS) on postwar psychological problems of Vietnam veterans reveals that 829,000 of the 3.14 million veterans who served in Vietnam, *currently* suffer from some degree of Post-traumatic stress disorder (PTSD). This study estimates that at some point in their lives 30.6% of all male veterans, and 26.9% of all female veterans, will develop *a prevailing lifetime condition* of "full-blown" PTSD. *Additionally,* 11.1% of males, and 7.8% of females, will suffer some degree of PTSD which will profoundly disrupt their ability to function in society, and will warrant professional attention.[4] Veterans exposed to combat are the ones most likely to experience stress symptoms, psychiatric conditions, physical health problems, and postwar readjustment problems. Additional studies suggest that when persistent conditions related to PTSD occur over a lifetime, other conditions like major depression, panic disorder, generalized anxiety disorder, and phobic disorders develop.[5] The Department of Veteran Affairs also says that the mortality rate for veterans with PTSD is 71% higher than for other veterans.[6]

The fact that a significant percentage of Vietnam vets have PTSD or stress-related disorders is sobering. It must command the attention of all who are concerned about the welfare of America's veterans and their families. Major studies warn that as the majority of Vietnam vets enter mid-life crises, dragging along the unfinished business of Vietnam, their problems will intensify. Yet in light of this, only 4% have sought help from the VA. In addition, there are less than 300 hospital beds in the entire country specifically set aside for inpatient treatment of veterans with PTSD. VA Medical Centers (VAMC) that do have beds often have long waiting lists, lack adequate funding, and lack sufficiently trained or experienced staff. Vet Centers, the primary source of help for veterans seeking help outside the VAMC, are often overloaded and understaffed. Current budget cuts and attempts to place Vet Centers under greater VAMC control further inhibit their effectiveness.

Family Casualties

A particularly tragic discovery is that spouses, partners, and children of vets with PTSD, also become casualties. They report more general psychological distress, less happiness and satisfaction with their lives, and more behavioral problems than the normal population. The divorce rate for Vietnam veterans is in the 90th percentile, nearly double the national average. Multiple marriage failures are common as veterans tend to choose mates with emotionally unstable personalities. Aphrodite Matsakis reports that of veterans' children:[7]
- 83% suffer from low self-worth
- 79% have developmental difficulties
- 69% have impaired social functioning
- 22% experience nightmares
- 42% develop ambivalent feelings toward their mothers
- 77% develop aggressive traits
- 65% experience symptoms similar to PTSD
- 57% feel responsible for their parents' emotional well-being
- 28% become preoccupied with power and death
- 14% hate Orientals, and
- 10% practice self-mutilation.

A 1992 survey of the adolescent runaway population in Seattle revealed that 80% of them were children of Vietnam veterans.

Unemployment

The jobless rate among Vietnam veterans is approximately twice that of their civilian counterparts. Veterans with PTSD are five times more likely to be unemployed, and one in four earns below $7,000 annually, half the national rate set for poverty. Male veterans with PTSD are also twice as likely to report work histories characterized by instability. Female veterans with PTSD are four times as likely. Even though 70% of veterans suffering PTSD *are* employed, they are classified as being part of the "downward trend syndrome."[8]

Homelessness

According to national statistics, close to 250,000 veterans are homeless on any given night.[9] That is somewhere between 30-40% of the homeless population. This problem is national in scope and growing. According to the American Legion, 51.7% of homeless veterans are Vietnam veterans, and an additional 25.2% are Vietnam-era veterans. Despite clear evidence of need, sixteen states have no federal programs to serve homeless veterans. Contrary to public opinion, most homeless veterans are well-educated (over 80% are high school graduates and one-third have attended college), yet the vast majority are unemployed. Many vets are homeless because they suffer from post-traumatic stress disorder.

The performance of the VA in delivering services to the homeless at the local level is often inadequate, not necessarily because of staff, but because of a general lack of funding. VA hospitals regularly release veterans who have completed treatment programs to the streets, or to overcrowded shelters. The Veterans' Administration also contributes to the homeless problem by foreclosing on mortgages when veterans get behind on payments. The VA appears to be unwilling to provide the same leniency, flexibility, or loan restructuring that other federal programs like HUD or FHA do their buyers. This increases the likelihood that veterans' families will become homeless. The VA has a program to make foreclosed properties available to groups providing services to the homeless, yet in 1994, of an estimated 6,800 empty foreclosed homes, only six had been released.

Drug and Alcohol Abuse

Research concludes that Vietnam combat veterans also exhibit substantially higher levels of drug and alcohol abuse. Among the homeless, approximately one-half of all vets have problems with alcohol or drugs. Alcohol and drug use is seen by many professionals as an attempt to self-medicate PTSD symptoms, and although professional help may be recommended, long waiting lists for alcohol and drug treatment programs exist in virtually every VA facility.

Legal System

By 1979 over 400,000 Vietnam veterans were caught up in the legal system,[10] often a direct result of the antisocial feature of their readjustment problems. 29,000 veterans were in state or federal prisons, 37,500 were on parole, 250,000 were under probationary supervision, and 87,000 were awaiting trial. John Woods, in his pamphlet *From Felon to Freedom*, says that in 1990 there were still 403,000 Vietnam-era veterans incarcerated. The recidivism rate among vets is above 70%, a tragic reminder of their inability to adjust to society.[11]

Toxic Chemicals

In spite of overwhelming medical and scientific evidence, the Veterans' Administration bucks at providing compensation and treatment for disorders related to the exposure of toxic chemicals widely used in Vietnam.[12] Even though the Environmental Protection Agency clearly says that Agent Orange and dioxin are significantly linked to a large variety of physical and psychological illnesses, the VA stubbornly refuses to acknowledge the facts and glaringly refuses assistance to veterans and the estimated 50 to 70% of veterans' children suffering genetic damage.[13] As a result of this, and other issues, surveys reveal that as many as 46.7% of Vietnam veterans currently rate VA medical services as "poor" or "clearly dissatisfactory."[14]

Lack of Democratic Representation

Veterans are the only group exclusively denied the fundamental principle of representative democracy in the "bill making" legislative process. Bills emerging from the House Veterans Affairs Committee are exempt from floor amendments, virtually denying House members the opportunity to advance the legislative interest of veteran constituents.[15] In spite of lofty rhetoric by politicians to "pay homage to those fallen, by insuring that living veterans are never slighted," national laws which give "equal access to justice" are denied veterans. This is especially true regarding judicial review where a back-log of over 800,000 compensation cases face intolerable delays in adjudication. Appeals take from six months to four years to decide. Veterans are placed in the untenable position of having to outlay substantial sums of money in order to pursue their claims because they are denied the same rights to legal representation by government agencies that every citizen is afforded.[16] Many, frustrated by the injustice or overwhelmed by the bureaucratic process, simply drop their cases.

Summary

Statistics paint a bleak picture of the darkness and despair that many Vietnam veterans and their families face. Is there hope? Who has the solutions? The VA? The government? As you will discover, the problem of PTSD has been around for thousands of years. Doctors, politicians, generals, and priests have sought solutions, yet have often failed to use the One that has been there all along.

Parts I and II of this book examine the traumatic impact of the Vietnam War, and its residual effects. It reflects both the secular and spiritual perspectives of those who fought the war, as well as those of mental health professionals. Part III deals primarily with healing. The solutions I present stress Biblical principles, incorporating the spiritual component often missing from contemporary treatment, but which I believe is essential to the successful treatment of PTSD.

PART I

OVERVIEW

-1-

Looking Back
[EARLIER TO RECENT WARS]

"The older I get, the sadder I feel about the uselessness of it all, but in particular the deaths of my comrades... I thought I had managed all right, kept the awful things out of my mind. But now I'm an old man and they come out from where I hid them. Every night."
–World War I veteran[1]

"You're dealing with complicated psychological states. No man in battle is really sane. The mendacity of the soldier on the battlefield is a highly disturbed mind, and this is an epidemic of insanity which affects everybody there, and those not afflicted by it die very quickly."
–Marine, World War II[2]

"Soldiers may lose body parts, suffer head wounds that leave skull deformities or cause brain dysfunction, or sustain spinal cord injury from bullets or shrapnel that results in permanent paralysis. Witnessing the wounding of others is a major source of war stress. This sometimes reaches macabre realms, as when buddies nearby are blown up by direct hits from grenades, or persons are set afire by napalm. War involves a regular exposure to mutilation and death, agony, and gruesomeness; wounding or blowing up of children or other noncombatants, whether accidentally caused or not, can be a lasting source of stress. The exposure to wounds can be especially intensive in medical personnel, both in the field and in hospitals removed from the field. Many persons deal with dead bodies in war: medivac pilots and medics, hospital corpsman, doctors, nurses, and graves registration personnel who clean up and prepare bodies for shipment home (sometimes for months on end). An immersion in death is also experienced by those who dig the graves and bury the bodies in stateside cemeteries, as well as by those with the responsibility of going to the homes telling families about the death of a relative."
–Arthur S. Blank, Jr.

Post-traumatic stress disorder has been with us for thousands of years, though not always identified as such. Although individuals respond differently when faced with life-threatening circumstances, there have been no wars in which men were not afraid of dying. The earliest historical, classical, and religious literature among all ethnic groups reveals that men often broke during combat. Soldiers experienced paralysis, exhaustion, vomiting, shuddering, fear, mental confusion, depression, and collapse. Steve Bentley and Richard Gabriel, both authors and soldiers who have studied disorders resulting from the effects of combat, say that war has always had a severe, immediate, and long-lasting psychological impact on people.[3]

Early Wars

As early as 490 B.C., Hereditas, a Greek historian, recorded a warrior going permanently blind when a soldier next to him was killed, even though the blinded soldier suffered no wounds. Blindness, severe and uncontrollable trembling, paralysis, deafness, and catatonic withdrawal were all common to early soldiers.

War has always had a severe, immediate, and long-lasting psychological impact on people.

War: The 1600s to the Civil War

In the early 1600s, military physicians among the Swiss, French, Germans and Spanish, began to identify a pattern of behaviors among combat soldiers they defined as "nostalgia," "maladie du pays," "heimweh" (homesickness), and "estar roto" (literally: to be broken). These behaviors included melancholy (depression), loss of appetite, incessant thinking patterns, disturbed sleep and insomnia, weakness, anxiety, cardiac palpitations, gastrointestinal symptoms, heightened excitement, frustration, self-inflicted wounds, stupor, and fever.

During the 1700s, accounts of war experiences from the siege of Gibraltar to the battlefields of the Little Big Horn have recounted severe emotional, psychological, and physiological symptoms following or during combat.

Bentley[4] points out that during the 1800s, Civil War physicians diagnosed many cases of functional disability resulting from fear of battle and the stresses of military life. Civil War physicians reported that soldiers on normal leave often collapsed with emotional illness at home, even when they had shown no symptoms of mental debilitation before leaving front lines. Psychological symptoms became so common that field commanders and medical doctors pleaded with the War Department to provide some type of screening to eliminate recruits susceptible to psychiatric breakdown. Gabriel[5] reports that the number of insane soldiers wandering around after the Civil War was so great, public outcry led to the establishment of the first military hospital for the insane.

World War I

Doctors attributed the large numbers of psychologically wounded in WW I to new weapons, specifically large-caliber artillery. Psychiatric casualties were thought to be caused by disrupted physiology in the brain caused by exploding shells. Thus the term "shell shock." By the end of the war, hundreds of psychiatrists had been sent overseas. They discovered that emotions, not physiological brain damage, were causing the casualties. Symptoms characterized by mental troubles, sadness, weariness, pessimism, repugnance to effort, abnormal irritability, defective control of temper, tendency to weep on slight provocation, timidity, lessened attention, defective memory and will power were all defined as "war neurosis," "combat neurosis," and "neurasthenia." In spite of the military's use of the best available psychiatric testing to screen out possible psychological casualties (they turned away over five million men), 159,000 of those sent overseas developed psychiatric problems. Half of these were permanently discharged.

Other nations had their share of psychiatric casualties as well. Russia was the first to determine that mental collapse was a direct result of the stress of war. 80% of their soldiers diagnosed and treated for "battle shock," were unable to return to duty.

World War II

Although statisticians do not agree completely, Bentley reports that during World War II the ratio of rear-area support troops to combat troops was twelve to one.[6] He estimates that no more than 800,000 soldiers saw direct combat. Of these, 37.5% developed such serious psychiatric cases that they were permanently discharged. All totaled, 1,393,000 soldiers suffered psychiatric symptoms serious enough to impair their ability to fight. Gabriel says, "In World War II American fighting forces lost 504,000 men from the fighting effort because of psychiatric collapse."[7] Other sources report that a *moderate* psychiatric casualty rate of 23% took place.[8] The National Academy of Sciences and National Research Council[9] reported that 25.8% of Pacific Theater veterans, and 13.6% of European Theater veterans were compensated for anxiety neurosis, yet not all who filed were compensated.

Given sufficient combat stress and exposure, virtually everyone becomes a psychiatric casualty.

By World War II a subtle shift in diagnosis had begun and "combat neurosis" gave way to the terms "combat exhaustion," "battle fatigue," "traumatic war neurosis," "anxiety neurosis," and "K-Z Syndrome." These disorders, believed to be caused by *combat stress*, included the following symptoms: breaking out in cold sweats, self-inflicted wounds, frostbite and trench foot caused by the inability to process mental information, vomiting and diarrhea, faintness, weakness in the knees, paralysis of the limbs or vocal cords, deafness, madness, blindness, surdomutism, nostalgia (a cluster of symptoms marked by excessive physical fatigue, an inability to concentrate, an unwillingness to eat or drink, feelings of isolation and total frustration creating an inability to function), acute battle shock, stupor, suicide, lower back pain, musculoskeletal disorders, irritability, sleep disturbance, unusual sensitivity, withdrawal, depression, and mental confusion.

Korea and Vietnam

1,587,040 men served in the Korean War. Of the 198,380 who actually saw combat, 24.2% became psychiatric casualties. Stenger[10] reports that the most prevalent disability among Korean War veterans was "anxiety neurosis." The chances of becoming a psychiatric casualty were 143% higher than the chances of being killed.

Estimates of between three or four million veterans served in southeast Asia during the Vietnam War.[11]

- Approximately one-fourth served in direct combat units
- One-quarter[12] to one-half[13] suffered emotional disturbances
- 39% still suffer from PTSD[14]
- 20% of all vets and 60% of all *combat* vets suffer PTSD.[15]
- 87.5% of 25th Infantry Division Association members who answered a health survey reported having more than three symptoms associated with PTSD.[16]
- At least 18%, and possibly as many as 54%, suffer psychiatric symptoms.[17]

Wars: From the 1970s to 1990s

In the 1973 Arab-Israeli war, almost a third of Israeli casualties were due to psychiatric problems. The same was true among opposing Egyptian forces. In the 1982 incursion into Lebanon, Israeli psychiatric casualties were twice as high as the number of dead and accounted for 27% of the wounded.[18]

Of all Desert Storm troops, 54% suffered significant psychological stress, and 19% suffered severe or moderate readjustment problems.[19] The National Center for the Study of PTSD[20] reported that 76.3% of male veterans, and 79.5% of female veterans, reported significant stress symptoms during or following the Gulf War. The *Disabled American Veteran* reports that "according to a VA survey of 4,500 Gulf veterans, 34% suffered psychological distress relating to marital and employment problems, among others, and 9% experienced symptoms of PTSD."[21]

War and Trauma

Although today's wars change progressively with new technological advances, what has not changed is the number of soldiers who become dysfunctional. Whether this dysfunction is called shell shock, insanity, combat stress, anxiety neurosis, or delayed stress syndrome, it is all the same. The idea that those who suffer symptoms of war trauma are, in fact, malingering (a sentiment which existed during the Civil War and WWI), is a slap in the face. It calls into question the very character and honor of those who served. It is especially disparaging to hear other vets mouth the same condescending attitude as health providers who discount the effects of combat trauma.

Everyone is subject to breakdown in combat. Although there are environmental and psychological factors associated with psychiatric breakdown, *none predict or predetermine psychiatric collapse*. Gabriel says, "It is impossible to predict which soldiers will collapse and which will behave bravely."[22] Bentley points out that the judgmental attitudes of others, combined with veterans' pride and distrust, account for the fact that while a Research Triangle Institute study concludes that 830,000 Vietnam veterans have full-blown or partial PTSD, as of July, 1990, only 55,119 had filed claims. Of those, the adjudication boards had only believed 28,411.[23] The NVVRS study says that while 480,000 vets currently meet the full diagnostic criteria for PTSD, *the vast majority of them have not asked their government for compensation*. As of 1989, only 20,549 veterans had received disability compensation for PTSD. This figure represents only 4.3% of those eligible![24]

Why has the VA been so antagonistic toward veterans? In WW II it became clear it was not just the *weak* in character who were breaking down, yet this has not kept the military belief of "predisposition plus stress equals collapse" from affecting the attitudes of VA health care providers.[25]

In a presentation before the National Vietnam Veterans Coalition, Major David Grossman[26] presented the following:

• Research from World War II demonstrated that given sufficient combat stress and exposure, virtually everyone becomes a psychiatric casualty. Exposure to continuous combat for sixty days resulted in psychiatric casualties to almost everyone involved, no matter how strong they were.

• PTSD casualties among Vietnam veterans are much higher than necessary because of a lack of acceptance at home.

• The Veterans Administration has a vested interest, although unintentional, to keep the numbers requiring treatment down, and the studies are accordingly understated.

Summary

The general population is largely ignorant of the brutality, or of the pain and suffering experienced by combat soldiers. They are rarely affected by weary, broken, rootless, or cynical soldiers. To them they are faceless and unknown. It is hard for all but those who have been severely traumatized to imagine the psychic numbing or detachment necessary for sensitive human beings to rid themselves of the natural bond between all humanity, in order to kill. Yet as society becomes increasingly violent, as people lose their normal affection for their own, as rape and incest and human selfishness increase, more are getting the picture.

Anyone who shuts down emotionally or numbs one's self in order to survive, faces the shaky task of restoring their humanity. It takes time, effort, and courage to overcome such detachment. The truth is, some never do. This leaves us with important questions to answer.

Do all normal people have a breaking point?

Is not wanting to die, "cowardice?"

Is it sane, or insane, to be disturbed by killing, maiming, and death?

Are normal people justly disturbed by war?

Is it stress that produces abnormal behavior or does war open the souls of the walking dead to the dark domain of evil's influence?

Is PTSD simply the result of serving the "Masters of War," as Bob Dylan put it, or the "Prince of Darkness," as others have said?

Victor Frankel wrote in *Man's Search for Meaning,* "An abnormal response to an abnormal situation is normal behavior." Bentley says, "If some things don't make you crazy, then you aren't very sane to begin with!"

-2-

The Wounds of War
[PTSD: ITS DEVELOPMENT]

"My marriage is falling apart. We just don't talk anymore. Hell, I guess we've never really talked about anything, ever. I spend most of my time at home alone in the basement. She's upstairs and I'm downstairs. Sure we'll talk about the groceries and who will get gas for the car, but that's about it. She's tried to tell me she cares for me, but I get real uncomfortable talking about things like that, and I get up and leave. Sometimes I get real angry over the smallest thing. I used to hit her when this would happen, but lately I just punch out a hole in the wall or leave and go for a long drive. Sometimes I spend more time on the road just driving aimlessly than I do at home.

"I really don't have any friends. I'm pretty much dog eat dog, and no one seems to care much for anyone else. As far as I'm concerned I'm really not a part of this messed up society. What I'd really like to do is have a home in the mountains, somewhere far away from everyone. Sometimes I get so angry with the way things are being run I think about placing a few blocks of C-4 (military explosives) under some of the sons-a-bitches. A couple of times a year I get into fights at bars. I usually pick the biggest guy. I don't know why, I usually get creamed. There are times when I drive real crazily, screaming and yelling at other drivers.

"I usually feel depressed. I've felt this way for years. There have been times I've been so depressed that I won't even leave the basement. I'll usually start drinking pretty heavily around these times. I've also thought about committing suicide when I've been depressed. I've got an old .38 that I snuck back from 'Nam. A couple of times I've sat with it loaded. Once I even had the barrel in my mouth and the hammer pulled back. I couldn't do it. I see Smitty back in 'Nam with his brains smeared all over the bunker. Hell, I fought too hard to make it back to the World [U.S.]; I can't waste it now. How come I survived and he didn't? There has to be some reason.

"Sometimes, my head starts to replay some of my experiences in 'Nam. Regardless of what I'd like to think about, it comes creeping in. It's so hard to push back out again. It's old friends, their faces, the ambush, the screams, their faces [tears]... You know, every time I hear a chopper [helicopter] or see a clear unobstructed green tree line, a chill goes down my back; I remember. When I go hiking now, I avoid green areas. I usually stay above timber line. When I walk down the street, I get real uncomfortable with people behind me that I can't see. When I sit, I always try to find a chair with something big and solid directly behind me. I feel most comfortable in the corner of a room with walls on both sides of me. Loud noise irritates me and sudden movement or noise will make me jump.

"Night is hardest for me. I go to sleep long after my wife has gone to bed. It seems like hours before I finally drop off. I think of many of my 'Nam experiences at night. Sometimes my wife awakens me with a wild look in her eye. I'm all sweaty and tense. Sometimes I grab for her neck before I realize where I am. Sometimes I remember the dreams and it's 'Nam; other times it's just people after me, and I can't run anymore.

"I don't know, this has been going on for so long; it seems to be getting gradually worse. My wife is talking about leaving. I guess it's no big deal. But I'm lonely. I really don't have anyone else. Why am I the only one like this? What the hell is wrong with me?"

–Goodwin, 1991[1]

Vietnam vets often know they are broken, but don't always know how to fix themselves. The long-term effects of the war on their health then steadily increase. The various symptoms of PTSD form a tightly threaded, intertwined cord, and it is the strength of this cord that binds veterans to their past. This chapter is a brief, introductory overview of PTSD. It examines the development of the PTSD diagnosis, acute and chronic stress reactions, delayed responses, the difference between Vietnam and other wars, and what often triggers the onset of PTSD.

The Development of PTSD

Post-traumatic stress disorder is a severe reaction to traumatic life events, yet to call it a "disorder" is really misleading. This stress syndrome is really a *normal* response to *abnormal* conditions. For years VA Medical Centers denied the existence of PTSD, in spite of conclusive studies conducted by its own organization linking war and anxiety neurosis,[2] and statistics linking the emotional chaos and suicidal deaths of Vietnam vets to their wartime experience.[3] It took a political maneuver *by veterans* in the late 1970s to get the American Psychiatric Association to include PTSD as a recognizable disorder in their Diagnostic and Statistical Manual.[4] This finally *forced* the Veterans' Administration to begin providing treatment to vets.[5] Still, the travails of accessing the VA's bureaucratic system, perceived indifference, lengthy waiting periods, and less than cordial treatment, keep most Vietnam veterans away.

Although the PTSD diagnosis originated with Vietnam veterans, PTSD can result from any traumatic event that impairs normal functioning. Today this classification includes pathology resulting from natural disasters, rape, child abuse, incest, survival of the holocaust, the bombardment of civilian homesteads, the great fires in London and San Francisco, and to survivors of car accidents, near starvation, and extremes of heat and cold.[6] The broad use of this diagnosis has created debate and confusion about what constitutes events "outside the range of normal human experience." Still, documentation shows that survivors of trauma, regardless of what created it, often experience psychological break-down, sleeplessness, intense startle reactions, irrational fears, periods of depression, incessant thinking patterns, intrusive thoughts, loss of appetite, withdrawal, isolation, anxiety, and other symptoms.

Post-traumatic stress disorder is a severe reaction to traumatic life events, yet to call it a disorder is really misleading. The stress syndrome is really a normal response to abnormal conditions.

What is important to note, is that Vietnam vets do not hold an exclusive contract on PTSD. Consider the black mother of six children who lives in a ravaged ghetto. She may have no husband to help her support or protect her children, and will be burdened with financial pressure. There may be gang killings every day, random violence, metal detectors in the schools, chain link fences with barbed wire on top to keep out drug dealers, and gangs soliciting members. There may be few safe places, perhaps not even in her own building. Her purse may be snatched as she leaves her home; she may see her children mugged in the streets. Does she have some understanding of what life is like in a combat zone? Vets who believe that no one can understand their experiences, simply because they were not in Vietnam, may be believing a subtle lie which keeps them trapped in isolation, pain, anger, or guilt. This can be an excuse to hold on to one's past.

Acute and Chronic Stress Reactions

Behaviors/symptoms associated with trauma can be severe and immediate (acute), repeat themselves over a long period (chronic), or be delayed (post). Positive and negative stress reactions occurring within individuals during life-threatening events are often rapidly suppressed in order to focus on survival. When traumatic events persist or repeat themselves, a *pattern* (habit) of suppression generally develops. To avoid unpleasantness associated with the event, survivors also tend to suppress symptoms associated with the trauma, even after the event passes. Acute stress reactions *always* occur during life-threatening events. If not dealt with, they will affect long-term physical, emotional, and psychological health.

Delayed Reactions

Stress symptoms can persist for days, weeks, or months depending on individual differences and the severity of the trauma. It is not uncommon for symptoms to arise six months or more after a traumatic event. Individual coping styles, circumstances, or a combination of either can prevent acceptable resolutions to trauma. People often delay dealing with inner issues because of:

- sensory overload,
- survival needs,
- a desire to avoid feelings,
- having to sort out confusing, conflicting thoughts,
- or simply because of a lack of support and help.

When threatened, we are bombarded with a barrage of thoughts and emotions. It becomes necessary to make multiple split-second decisions, many of which have fearful and lasting consequences. It is impossible to respond with any healthy reflection while a barrage of internal and external information is being processed. Sensory data unimportant to survival gets garaged. Once a dangerous situation has passed, we can sort out our thoughts and feelings by talking them out. Talking about gut-level issues, however, is difficult for many of us.

Sometimes the situation itself makes communication difficult. In Vietnam, group survival depended on every man fulfilling his duty. Issues that could potentially divide the unit were avoided. Questions of conscience, reasons for what we did, and our purpose in Vietnam were often not voiced. Therefore, pain, internal conflict, and the need to make sense of the war often went unresolved.

Most people maintain some sense of balance *during* traumatic events, integrating sensory onslaught into a healthy response. Others numb themselves, detaching emotionally. Some experience emotional or mental breakdown, or severe breaks with reality (dissociation), developing stupors or becoming catatonic. Later, they may develop split or alternate personalities.

We are susceptible to spiritual forces during times of severe trauma and can continue to experience crippling torment as a result. We can also develop "tunnel vision," blocking out everything else but the task at hand. We can end up directing our anger and rage at others, or even toward ourselves. We can also develop fear and pain-based behaviors which stay with us for life.[7]

Some suggest that the primary reasons Vietnam vets are unable to resolve war-related trauma is because of the unjust treatment they received once home, the lack of opportunity to grieve their losses, and the lack of psychiatric help available on the battlefield.[8] Others say that what was really lacking in their lives was a spiritual foundation.

Differences from Other Wars

There were circumstances unique to Vietnam. Previous wars had battle fronts, with battle lines from which one could withdraw to find rest and safety. In Vietnam, fronts and lines did not exist. The enemy was nearly everyone and everywhere. Exposure to combat was intense, prolonged, and repetitive, lasting almost the entire tour of duty. There were few safe havens for those in the field other than a seven-day R & R outside Vietnam.

To avoid prolonged combat exposure, the military developed a 12-

month rotation system called DEROS (Date of Expected Return from Overseas Service). It appeared to be a great plan, but instead produced isolation, alienation, independence and rebellion. Instead of soldiers being sent to Vietnam as units, men came and went as individuals. In many cases, especially in support units, this produced a lack of unit morale and cohesion. The lack of continuity also created an individualistic attitude. For many, Vietnam became a solitary experience.

Battle-hardened vets (those who survived the first three months) distanced themselves from those who had not yet proven themselves. New recruits, otherwise known as *greenies* or *cherries*, were often expected to be killed during the first few weeks of on-the-job training and thus, were avoided. Few men risked getting emotionally close to them. This sometimes created intense isolation for new arrivals.

The rotation system, and the lack of initial briefing on war strategy prevented soldiers from getting a glimpse of the big picture. Thus they lacked a sense of overall direction. They rarely knew the goals of daily operations, other than to locate and kill *Charlie*. A soldier's tour became a game of survival, counting off days on a calendar. *Short-timers* developed a "hold on" attitude, suppressing their anxiety, guilt, and grief as they held out for leave. This lowered the *reported* rate of men suffering stress reaction.

Eventually, thousands of psychiatric and spiritual casualties who were in 'Nam one day, were dumped on American streets the next. They had no time to debrief, no one to talk to, and no time to adjust. Among these vets were those administratively discharged for using drugs or for insubordination. Discharge eliminated having to deal with them. This also kept the psychiatric casualty count down. Dumping these men back into society without treatment or resolution created a segment of the veteran population ripe for discord. Many committed suicide or ended up in the criminal justice system.

World War II veterans came home on troop ships that often took from fourteen to forty-five days, giving them time to debrief, talk out their experiences in the safety of a supportive environment, and help resolve feelings of guilt or grief. The *freedom birds*, on the other hand, provided quick, 24-hour separation from Vietnam. This left little time to adjust to drastic changes in environment, or to resolve feelings created by leaving friends behind.

The average age of soldiers in WWII was twenty-six. The average age in Vietnam was nineteen.[9] This was our first teenage war. In normal human growth and development, people are not confronted with death and loss, and do not have to deal with the grieving process until they are in their middle to late forties when their parents die. At this stage of life, maturity has more adequately prepared us to deal with loss. For Vietnam's teenage warriors, exposure to death came at a vulnerable and formative period of their lives. This "premature encounter with mortality" literally turned their world upside down.[10] Young soldiers coming back said they felt like ninety-year-old men. This further distanced them from peers who were still living carefree, indulgent lives.

As a whole, the generation that went to Vietnam was one without a firm spiritual foundation. An objective look at the sixties will note the extreme differences in values held by that generation, compared to the previous one. That is not to say the previous generation was perfect, for many of its values were mired in materialism. Yet its spiritual foundation, even though it may have been crumbling, created strong social restrictions that were not evident in the generation that went to Vietnam.

We know that all species have
a profound resistance to killing their own.
This resistance is not overcome without intense
indoctrination or severe hardening of the heart.

Killing human beings at close range, friendly fire which took American lives, secondary injury to innocent civilians, and the unintentional death of friends, all contributed to the trauma experienced by Vietnam vets. In Vietnam virtually all field troops were involved in close combat.[11] Fire support bases, which were safe havens during the day, were always susceptible to mortar and ground attacks at night.

We know that all species have a profound resistance to killing their own. This resistance is not overcome without intense indoctrination or severe hardening of the heart. Was that the purpose of military training? Do hardened hearts result from years of emotional conditioning? Painful childhood neglect or abuse? A lack of conscience due to sin, spiritual death, or separation from the life and love of God? From the natural human instinct to survive? Whatever the reason, the killing left many vets scarred and burdened by guilt.

A Hostile Home Front

There have been dissenters in all wars fought by the United States. Yet since the Civil War, none has been so divisive to national unity as Vietnam. Soldiers contended with a hostile enemy, and a sometimes indifferent ally. They contended with inner conflict and fellow soldiers, also with an ideological battle and controversy at home. Very few Vietnam vets were welcomed home. There were no victory parades, and few informal celebrations. There was little acceptance from the nation, and little empathy for their suffering, sacrifice, and loss. At no other time has the U.S. military been so vehemently turned upon by its own citizens. If Americans were not outright hostile, they were indifferent. Far too many soldiers felt painfully rejected. Those who had struggled to hold on to their sanity in Vietnam, hoping to come home to a place of refuge and safety, found neither.

Many vets, deeply resentful of the treatment they received, returned to Vietnam. Some turned their back on a nation which they believed had turned its back on them. Those unwilling to resolve the pain of rejection, carried their bitterness and lost their sense of belonging. Unloved, uncomforted, and often lacking affirmation, they settled into a life of blame, self-pity, and social and emotional isolation. Vets who had held the power of life and death in their hands, could not stomach inconsequential, meaningless jobs which could not hold their attention. Unresolved issues of betrayal and mistrust circumvented relationships with people in authority, making working for others difficult. Suddenly, life was no longer the same.

Treatment

Veterans who began to recognize and acknowledge personal problems often found it difficult to deal with VA Medical Centers. Unfortunately, the primary agency for helping veterans was a subsidiary of the same system that sent them to Vietnam. It represented the same government. It carried out government goals. VAMC employees were often torn between serving the best interest of vets, or serving the mandates of the system it represented. When Vietnam vets began seeking help, the VA didn't even believe PTSD existed. Some VA employees *still* don't. Veterans were often treated with disdain or disbelief and seen as bums, faking problems for a handout. Vets with emotional or mental difficulties were labeled with unchangeable character disorders or viewed as borderline, anti-social, sociopathic, or paranoid schizophrenics. VA therapists saw veterans as manipulative, unpredictable, and distrustful, so they were rarely helped. Vets quickly lost trust in the system.

The Increasing Rise of PTSD

Recent epidemiological studies indicate rates of PTSD among veterans, and the general population, are on the increase.[12] The good news is, today there is a greater knowledge of post-traumatic stress disorder and an attitude shift among mental health providers. Researchers have made us aware that long buried war-related issues can be triggered by current stress and conflict, such as might occur on the job, in a marriage, or even during mid-life crisis. PTSD can also be triggered by environmental similarities and things as simple as climate, topography, and smells. It can also be triggered by aging. Danieli says:

> The usual occurrences of old age–the loss of gratification, support and distractions, the shift from doing to thinking, from planning to reminiscing, from preoccupation with everyday events and long-range planning to reviewing and rethinking one's life impose the inescapable necessity of facing one's past.[13]

The increase may simply be God's hand forcing unresolved issues to the surface in an attempt to bring healing. Or, to correct behaviors associated with trauma. Just as many fathers use a combination of acceptance and correction to instruct their children, God patiently gives time to His children, letting them discover the effects of their behavior while yet trying to purge, correct, and bring balance to their lives. God's kindness allows us to reap what we have sown in anger and unforgiveness, in hopes it will lead us to repentance, and save us from having to suffer more of what we have set in motion.

God takes an active part in the timing and triggering of all unresolved issues in the lives of His children, surfacing what has been hidden too long in the heart as a part of the cleansing process all believers go through. Once God determines that our relationship with Him is on firm ground and can withstand some shaking without it being destroyed, He puts His finger on issues we have often avoided. God's healing and restoration are designed to bring us to a place of maturity so His life can be seen in us, for how else will the world know His love?

When Memories are Triggered

When an acute episode of PTSD is triggered, it generally starts with a persistent, unwanted flashback or memory. This is often closely followed by a persistent avoidance of Vietnam-related issues, a general withdrawal, and an unresponsiveness to the external world. These behaviors may be accompanied by a collection of thoughts, emotions, and physical behaviors related to increased physiological arousal. Symptoms may include: difficulty sleeping, increased irritability or anger, difficulty concentrating, an exaggerated startle response, and hypervigilance (a state in which all our physical senses are heightened) when exposed to circumstances which are reminders of Vietnam. The intensity of PTSD symptoms vary greatly over time. They can be mildly uncomfortable or completely impair one's ability to function.

The Official Criteria for PTSD

The psychiatric profession's official description of the behaviors associated with PTSD are found in the Diagnostic and Statistical Manual of Mental Disorders, Third Printing, Revised Edition. The following symptoms are adapted to recent changes in the fourth Edition.

DSM-IV
Diagnostic Criteria
309.89 Post-traumatic Stress Disorder

A. The person has experienced, witnessed or been confronted with an event that involved actual or threatened death or serious injury or a threat to the physical integrity of self or others and that person's response involved intense fear, helplessness or horror. Note: In children, this may be expressed instead by disorganized or agitated behavior, e.g., serious threat to one's life or physical integrity; serious threat or harm to one's children, spouse, or other close relatives and friends; sudden destruction of one's home or community; or seeing another person who had recently been, or is being, seriously injured or killed as the result of an accident or physical violence.

B. The traumatic event is persistently reexperienced in at least one of the following ways:

(1) recurrent and intrusive distressing recollections of the event, including images, thoughts, or perceptions (in young children, repetitive play in which themes or aspects of the trauma are expressed)

(2) recurrent distressing dreams of the event. Note: In children, there may be frightening dreams without recognizable content

(3) sudden acting or feeling as if the traumatic event were recurring (includes a sense of reliving the experience, illusion, hallucinations, and dissociative [flashback] episodes, even those that occur upon awakening or when intoxicated). In young children, trauma-specific reenactment may occur

(4) intense psychological distress at exposure to internal or external cues that symbolize or resemble an aspect of the traumatic event

(5) physiologic reactivity upon exposure to internal or external cues that symbolize or resemble an aspect of the traumatic event (e.g., a woman who was raped in an elevator breaks out in a sweat when entering any elevator)

C. Persistent avoidance of stimuli associated with the trauma and numbing of the general responsiveness (not present before the trauma), as indicated by at least three of the following:

(1) efforts to avoid thoughts or feeling associated with the trauma

(2) efforts to avoid activities, situations, or play that arouse recollections of the trauma

(3) inability to recall an important aspect of the trauma (psychological amnesia)

(4) markedly diminished interest in significant activities (in young children, loss of recently acquired developmental skills such as toilet training or language skills)

(5) feeling of detachment or estrangement from others

(6) restricted range of affect, e.g., unable to have loving feelings

(7) sense of a foreshortened future, e.g., does not expect to have a career, marriage, or children, or a long life

D. Persistent symptoms of increased arousal (not present before the trauma), as indicated by at least two of the following:

(1) difficulty falling or staying asleep

(2) irritability or outbursts of anger

(3) difficulty concentrating

(4) hypervigilance

(5) exaggerated startle response

E. Duration of the disturbance (symptoms in B, C, and D) of at least one month.

Specify delayed onset if the onset of symptoms was at least six months after the trauma.

Summary

Post-traumatic stress disorder is said to be life-long and passed on intergenerationally, regardless of what particular style of adaptation or coping survivors choose. Yet we do not have to settle for merely adapting or coping. Healing is available. If you have symptoms associated with PTSD, it is important not to see them as enemies to be avoided. Welcome them instead as opportunities to be healed, comforted, and set free by God.

PART II

PATTERNS OF BEHAVIOR

-3-

It Don't Mean a Thing
[DENIAL]

"I resumed my Clark Kent identity as a family physician as though nothing had happened. I've been carrying the Vietnam experience around in my conscious and unconscious mind since I left Vietnam in 1968. Hardly a day has gone by that flashbacks and confusion about that experience hasn't popped into my mind. But I have conveniently, until just lately, shut out all deep thinking about my Vietnam adventure. I have managed to somehow sublimate all my thoughts and doubts and frustration concerning my involvement in Vietnam, and convinced myself that nothing really happened to me of significance during my 365 days. But I know it did. I have felt it was unhealthy to be preoccupied with the past."

–a Vietnam veteran[1]

"You must look at them carefully. Their appearance is deceptive... they look like the others. They eat, they laugh, they love. They seek money, fame, love, like the others. But it isn't true. Anyone who has seen what they have seen cannot be like the others, cannot laugh, love, pray, bargain, suffer, have fun, or forget like the others. You have to watch them carefully when they pass by an innocent looking smokestack, or when they lift a piece of bread to their mouths. Something in them shudders and makes you turn your eyes away. These people have been amputated; they haven't lost their legs or eyes but their will and their taste for life. The things that they have seen will come to the surface again sooner or later."

–Elie Wiesel[2]

Behavioral patterns associated with post-traumatic stress disorder have become all too familiar to many Vietnam veterans. These finely tuned responses to life, conditioned by repeated self-protective reactions, are rarely challenged by themselves or others. When vets surround themselves with people who are like-minded, or isolate themselves from outside influence, they stay stuck. Of all the behaviors associated with PTSD, perhaps none is so destructive as *denial*. People unwilling to acknowledge their need for change, don't seek healing.

What Exactly is Denial?
Denial, in the psychological sense, is a highly refined defense

mechanism rooted in fear and self-preservation. It is the refusal to believe, acknowledge, or accept something that is true or real. We use denial to escape unpleasantness and avoid responsibility. Denial may involve the selective repression of memories, the conscious suppression of emotions, or refusal to acknowledge responsibility for choices and actions. Refusing to acknowledge dependent behaviors or refusing to grant oneself permission to feel are also forms of denial.

Denial is an avoidance behavior. It is one of the ways we run from issues that are painful, confusing, or those we believe we are incapable of doing anything about. Denial involves rejecting external reality or rejecting self. It may involve doing without, withholding, pretending, or simply telling an outright lie. When denial becomes a *practice*, it leads to self-deception. Self-deception, in turn, leads to delusional thinking and behavior.

Not all denial is unhealthy. We may have an urge to jump off a ten-story building or slug our spouse, but we have a responsibility to deny behaviors which inappropriately inflict harm on ourselves or others. Denial, as a form of self-control, is necessary. Most of us don't go around jumping off tall buildings, although we might easily hide the truth that we might have the urge to. One is healthy, the other is not.

The Effects of Denial

Denial always creates some sort of separation. Separation is sometimes a psychic-splitting (a separation from self, that is, our feelings, memories, or deeply held beliefs), and sometimes a separation from others. In its most advanced form, denial creates a separation from the truth, and ultimately from reality.

Separation from Self

If for any reason we believe a part of our self is unacceptable, we generally deny that part in order to prevent it from being exposed. Our desire may be to hide it from others or to avoid acknowledging it ourselves. Since it is impossible to truly separate our self, we suppress those areas which seem unacceptable. When we deny self, we reject self. Self-rejection creates a lack of wholeness. Our inability to accept ourselves for who we are ultimately results in an inability to acknowledge the truth about ourselves.

Separation from Others

When we reject ourselves, our tendency is to withdraw from others. No matter how hard we try to hide the fact that we see ourselves as unacceptable, that message comes out in subtle, indirect ways. When we send the message that we are unacceptable, people tend to respond to us in ways that fulfill our belief. They avoid telling us things they believe might hurt us or otherwise damage our frail esteem. They avoid giving honest feedback or correcting us. In doing so they may even deny wise counsel or avoid us altogether. We have some accountability for soliciting these behaviors because consciously or subconsciously, we teach others how to treat us.

Separation from Reality

The ultimate separation that denial creates is from truth. Truth is reality. If we know the truth about who we are, or what we see in others, and deny it, we lie. When we consistently lie, we begin to confuse what's true with what's false, what's real with what's not. If we practice deception long enough we lose sight of the truth, and reality. We lose sight of our true character, yet think we see clearly. We think and do what is wrong, but reckon ourselves to be right. The nature and danger of self-deception is that we begin to believe the lie, and that is true delusion. A liar knows his true self but tries to deceive others. An obsessed person deceives himself, and by virtue of his deception becomes obsessed with maintaining the lie. The obsessed live in their imaginations. Such are the proud! They believe those things they imagine themselves to be... and desire others to believe them as well.

The Trap

There may be something sadly familiar and poignant about the beginning quotes of this chapter, yet if we buy into this image too deeply, it can become a trap. We can end up feeling sorry for ourselves because people don't recognize our pain, without understanding that we, in part, are responsible for creating our situation. Our attitudes, behaviors, and our stubborn refusal to examine or change them, often cause others to "turn their eyes away." Those closest to us, frustrated by their inability to penetrate our defenses, or to make any real satisfying emotional connection, often give up trying. When we send direct or subtle messages about wanting to be left alone, we are teaching others how to treat us. We may end up feeling isolated or even misunderstood, but we play a part in creating it.

If this sounds vaguely familiar, you may already be imprisoned by a defensive *perimeter of denial*. Perhaps the behaviors you use to protect yourself help create your imprisonment. Denial can keep us in a state of deprivation, pushing away those who offer love, acceptance, wisdom, understanding, and counsel. We may think of ourselves as vigilant and courageous, while in truth we may be prisoners of fear.

The Challenge to Examine Our Lives

The first step toward healing involves acknowledging reality. Forward movement is created by dismantling old Fire Bases; that is, abandoning defensive positions that once provided a measure of safety. In the artillery, we called this a "march order." In civilian life there is no one giving us orders to move forward. We must do it ourselves. We must tear down barriers that keep us from seeing ourselves as we truly are, or from receiving truthful feedback from others. *Closet vets*, who deny that Vietnam had any affect on their lives, or who deny they were even there, stuff their experiences, using denial as a means of coping. Yet, there really is no escape. Consider the following:

• We cannot change or heal what we are unwilling to acknowledge. Healing and wholeness require recognition and truthful acknowledgment of what we think, feel, and do.

• Truth is reality. People who accept reality live healthier lives. Jesus said, "You shall know the truth and the truth will make you free." Truth sets us free, both knowing and accepting it.

• We *need* others. Mutual support provides strength. We need mirrors. The most accurate picture of ourselves often comes through truthful and loving feedback from others.

• People who never question their attitudes and beliefs often fall prey to deception. Our interpretation of life may be based on faulty input, a lack of factual information, limited perspective, faulty or premature judgment, presumption, or prejudice. Keep an open mind!

• What we keep hidden remains in darkness. If we say we walk in the light, but in reality walk in darkness by denying the truth which is in us, how great is our deception.

Summary
Denial is simply avoiding truth. Denial results in separation from self, others, and reality. Denial is a defense mechanism that must be put aside if we are to grow into maturity. If we have the courage to examine what we spent so many years desperately trying to forget, we can make a clean break with our past. It is highly possible that we experience problems in our life, and in our relationships, because of denial. Denial creates distorted thinking and behaviors.

The Bible says there is a wisdom which comes from *above* which is spiritual, and a wisdom which comes from *below* which is based on a worldly view. A spiritual perspective on life will often differ from that which is natural. Examine both! Recognizing behaviors associated with post-traumatic stress disorder, and understanding their development and affect on our lives, is the initial step toward healing.

-4-

Issues of the Heart
[LOSS AND GRIEF]

"In World War II, pictures and stories about troops at the front were carefully limited, screened so that the civilian population would not be upset by too graphic a view of the realities of war. Americans in particular have received their view of war mostly through motion pictures and television shows. However war is portrayed for mass audiences, soldiers breaking down under the strain of battle are rarely, if ever, portrayed. The simple fact is, that men are crushed by the strain of war."
–Gabriel1

"Those who passed through the long night of 'Nam and still linger in its shadow know above all how painful the ordeal; how deep the wound. In war, some men receive flesh wounds while others are afflicted with more subtle scars. Some came home from Vietnam in flag-draped coffins, some disfigured without arms or legs or eyes, while untold thousands returned psychologically shattered, whole in body but broken in spirit, a quiet company of men and women wounded within.

"The visible injuries are much easier to perceive, but the hidden wounds of the heart and soul are often more difficult to diagnose and harder to heal. During the Vietnam Conflict, a steady stream of unseen casualties trickled home as anonymous servicemen in transit, lugging the residual baggage of war. At a casual glance, they appeared no different than the ever present ebb tide of men in uniform who seem so natural a part of airport lobbies or bus terminals. But to the discerning observer, there was something different about their eyes.

"Outwardly, they may not have manifested the 1,000 yard stare of shell-shocked soldiers straggling back to the rear after grim months of combat, but still, their haggard eyes revealed something deeper, something haunting. They were often darker and older and pained. They were windows to the troubled soul of a wounded generation of adolescent men. They were eyes which betrayed a loss of innocence and a look of knowing beyond their years."
–*Before the Dawn, The Mickey Blocke Story*

It is an indisputable fact that wars are fought to kill and maim. There is no evidence that soldiers in Vietnam were any less fearful of dying or being maimed than those in other wars. War is one of the most threatening, stressful, terrifying experiences people can endure. The horrors of war can create any number of behaviors that would normally be considered complete "madness." Soldiers leave a part of themselves on the battlefield that never gets returned. To understand post-traumatic stress disorder, and the grief that soldiers endured, we must understand the personal cost of war. This chapter examines loss, responses to loss, the effects of loss, and hindrances to healing.

Lost Innocence

Just as war often kills the innocent, it kills innocence. The outcome of any war fought by young adults and teenagers, is the loss of youth and emotional sensitivity. Few soldiers were unaffected by the death surrounding them, and the accompanying emotional pain. Unfortunately, in combat there is little time for grieving. Delayed and prolonged grief lead to emotional detachment, and therefore, some denial of reality.

> We threw a hundred bodies in the Saigon River that flows through Cho Lon. It was a problem. So many VC were killed that it clogged up the river so that the Navy complained to the Army about throwing bodies in the river... The Navy was complaining because the patrol boats would get tangled up with the bodies. Somehow the propeller would get caught on an arm or a leg. You got three or four bodies fall into a propeller, it can really mess up a boat. All this came down and the Army command unit told us to go pull the bodies out... This is a body that's been sitting there for a while. It's swelled up, it turned color, the fish are biting on it. We got bodies out on an embankment and we poured diesel fuel on them and had like a big bonfire.
>
> It was like the lieutenant told us, "This is our world. You went to hell and you're still alive." I understood it. In fact, I started to enjoy it. I enjoyed the shooting and killing. I was literally turned on when I saw a gook get shot. When a GI got shot, even if I didn't know him, he could be in a different unit than me, that would really bother me. A GI was real. Americans get killed, it was a real loss, but if a gook got killed, it was like me going out here and stepping on a rock.[2]

This soldier's attitude wasn't uncommon. Death can harden the softest heart. In war, there is no shortage of death, pain, or loss. Days and months of grinding drudgery and perpetual fear steals both strength and youth. Constant stress and weariness exhaust vitality. Gnawing guilt consumes joy. Body parts ripped apart, scattered flesh hanging from wire and trees, heads dismembered... the horror of war and one's participation in it, slowly erodes innocence. Once you've killed, your life is forever changed. One soldier writes:

> He wasn't stupid. He wasn't misinformed. He just didn't know
> if the war was right or wrong. And who did? Who really *knew*?

So he went to war for reasons beyond knowledge. Because he believed in law, and law told him to go. Because it was a democracy, after all, and because LBJ and the others had a rightful claim to their offices. He went to the war because it was expected. Because not to go was to risk censure, and to bring embarrassment on his father, and his town. Because, not knowing, he saw no reason to distrust those with more experience. Because he loved his country and, more than that, because he trusted it.[3]

As the Vietnam War ground on without resolution, loss of confidence in government and superiors soon became commonplace. Morally smug assumptions about self were quickly shattered in the first few battles. In the frenzy and fear of combat, men stopped at nothing to kill those trying to kill them. How men *thought* they would react was often very different than how they did.

Humanity has a thin veneer. Ideals become mired in cyclical episodes of survival, random violence, exploding revenge, tedium, and deadly combat. Idealistic speculation and sanctimonious presumption vanish with the humbling realization that one isn't always the man he thinks he is. Reality exposes the ugly and sometimes dark core of human nature. Mahedy's words mirror my experience:

> In theological terms, war is sin. This has nothing to do with whether a particular war is justified or whether isolated incidents in a soldier's war were right or wrong. The point is that war as a human experience is a matter of sin. It is a form of hatred for one's fellow human beings. It produces alienation from others and nihilism, and it ultimately represents a turning away from God.
>
> Veterans and victims of war experience the sinful side of human nature as few others do. They come close to sin and are immersed in it. They acquire a pervasive sense of suffering, injustice, and evil... a response to the world's condition that produces a feeling of despair and disgust...[4]

Illusions are rarely possible when life is transformed by harsh, personal experience. The brutality of the human condition is not the pale abstraction we make of it when we live comfortable, morally smug lives. It all changes when *we realize that we are a part of it.* Then our spirits are crushed and our hearts are broken. We despair. No bleakness of soul can compare with the realization that evil lies close to the heart of all that is human, and includes our own. Listen to this vet:

> It was a job. Most of the work was boring, menial labor. GIs were ditch diggers, pack animals and file clerks, slogging through a swamp of their own cold sweat. What little enthusiasm they brought to the task quickly oozed away, with nothing to replace it but the instinct to survive. The only diversion was the possibility of getting killed. I'd pray for a fire fight, just so we could stop walking for a little while. Adrenaline junkies, zom-

bied out on fear, working the assembly line on the nod, they shuffled about the business of the war factory. Anxiety, even death, gets to be routine. They made a life of trying to endure.

War is killing. Killing is the easiest part of the whole thing. Sweating twenty-four hours a day, seeing guys drop all around you of heatstroke, not having food, not having water, sleeping only three hours a night for weeks at a time, that's what war is. Survival!

Home was far away, even farther in mind than in miles. The longer they labored for the American Dream, the more they resented the management. Broken ideals, unattended, began to knit together in a hard cynicism. I remember July 20, 1969. I sat in my hootch and watched satellite relay after-the-fact footage of the astronauts landing on the moon and Neil Armstrong's first step on the surface. When I heard that fuckin-bullshit nonsense phrase, "One small step for man, a giant leap for mankind," I was so angry. I thought to myself, "Come here and step with me for a day, mother-fucker.5

Lost Friends

War has a way of forcing people together, then tearing them apart. Shared experiences force intimacy and when those bonds are broken through death, heartache is inevitable. Many vets watched helplessly as friends died horrifying deaths. They held one another as life slipped away. Friends who were severely wounded were often shipped out of the country for treatment, never to be seen or heard from again. Friends shipped out at the end of their tour often left with just a moment's notice. There was little time for prolonged good-byes. A "change of orders" often separated friends forever. These losses left many feeling detached, empty, and alone. Those who lost close friends sometimes vowed never let anyone get close to them again. Repeated loss left some believing that anyone who got close to them would die, so they distanced themselves from everyone.

Lost Limbs

Physical wounds, although initially painful, generally heal. They scar over and are forgotten. Extensive destruction of the body, however, creates long-lasting emotional trauma as well as disfigurement.

I was shot to shit. I had forty-five holes in me and still I felt guilty. When you see a paraplegic who has no feeling in his body anymore, you feel sorry he's like that. But you don't show empathy for him. (You say to yourself) "You got fucked, but there's a guy who's a blinke, the quadriplegic, and he got worse than you." Nobody cut any slack for anybody else in the hospital. Inside you can. You see a triple amputee, you felt bad, but you didn't let them know it. You could get tremendous hang-ups for not being fucked up enough...

Another buddy of mine, Mark Cole, had been a Special Forces officer that lost an eye and an ear and an arm and a leg.

He'd get drunk in a bar and start banging at the glasses and throwing things. You'd be sitting there drinking beer and you'd feel guilty because you still had everything. Yet the Presidential aspirants were all talking about how we shouldn't be defoliating the trees in Vietnam. Fuck defoliating the trees, how about defoliating us?[6]

Lost Faith

While in Vietnam, some lost faith in God. They forgot or never knew that the very foundation of American political, civil, and religious freedom was based on the moral freedom God gave each one of us to *choose*. For them, the war became a blame game. They blamed God for the choices made by others. They blamed God for not saving them from the consequences of their own choices. Edwin Cole writes:

> War, injustice, greed, betrayal and all the other problems that devour humanity are not God's fault. He does not cause them. We do. Satan does. Sin and selfishness, pride and arrogance, these things destroy the planet, not God. It is because of who we are that God has intervened in our lives, to do for man what man cannot do for himself. We transpose the ills of society from self and Satan to God. The problem is not that God is unfaithful, unkind or unloving, but that we are.[7]

Loss of faith, whether in self, country, or God, results from a loss of trust. When trust is broken by our primary caretakers (parents, government, leaders, or God) we often spend a lifetime "suspecting" all caretaking relationships. Relationships which normally provide comfort and protection, no longer feel safe. Broken trust also creates disillusion, and disillusionment easily leads to a loss of faith in our ability to become more than what we are. We become overly cynical and critical.

Faith, whether in God or others, requires trust. Trust requires vulnerability. Once we believe vulnerability is foolish or detrimental, we close our hearts and become guarded. Vulnerability also requires risk, and taking risks is hard once we have been betrayed or hurt. All the above can create a gradual flight into isolation and withdrawal.

Responses to Loss

Grief, anger, shock, denial, despair, depression, disillusionment, mistrust... all of these are normal reactions to loss. To some degree, psychological shut down almost always follows loss. Shutting down can be as simple as suppressing emotional pain or as severe as dissociation, where there is an extreme separation from reality. It's not uncommon to separate from emotional pain or mental confusion, especially when overwhelmed or severely threatened. When we are unable to make reasonable sense of losses, we tend to shelve those events. We may purposely forget painful experiences by dismissing them from our conscious mind. Later, we may even deny they ever happened.

Survival Instincts

Survival instincts are so strong that in life-threatening situations, all but the intense needs of the moment get shelved. Losses, when they occur, become impossible to grieve immediately. When losses mount, as they did in Vietnam, so does the need to mourn. But, with little chance of emotional release (other than vets taking their pain and anger out on suspected Viet Cong), grief soon becomes impacted. Like a garbage compactor, painful losses get pushed down to make room for even more. Vets learned to say, "It don't mean a thing," but initially I doubt if they meant it. They simply didn't have the luxury, or perhaps even the skills, to deal with the pain and anger. Grieving was a handicap. It got in the way of surviving. So did a conscience.

For many, survival in combat meant a painful process of dehumanization through a slow hardening of the heart. The multiplicity and complexity of pain slowly eroded sensitivity and vulnerability. Constant, repetitive loss pushed *caring* emotions to the background. Emotions which created connectedness with others became a liability and were severed. The tragedy was that once Vietnam was over, caring for others on a deep level never felt safe again.

Broken Trust

The Book of Hebrews says that our experiences can "turn that which is lame, out of joint, rather than bring healing." If our ability to trust was already damaged before military service, then our experiences in Vietnam crippled it further. This *predisposition* is alluded to in the DVA's *Health Care for Homeless Veterans Program: The Fifth Annual Progress Report*.[8] This report found four pre-military variables which had a *direct affect* on homelessness among veterans. They were:
- year of birth
- physical abuse
- sexual abuse
- placement in foster care before the age of 16

Physical abuse, sexual abuse, and abandonment by our biological parents are painful experiences which wound the heart and destroy trust. If these experiences affect homelessness, a life-style characterized by abandonment, hopelessness, alienation and broken trust, then it is reasonable to assume that they also had some affect on the severity of our response to Vietnam, and the development of PTSD.

Loss of trust in others affects our ability to relate, but loss of trust in our emotions can lead to a significant loss of confidence, mastery, and self-worth. If we no longer trust our emotions we will continue to grow intellectually, but will no longer exercise our emotions. Our lives then get out of balance. We lose direction because we end up out of touch with an important element of our nature, our ability to feel. Inner emptiness, loneliness, and unresolved loss leaves us believing life is futile. Unsure of why we exist, disillusioned with our self and others, we eventually end up in despair and our life becomes a disaster.

Unresolved Losses

Lori Galperin says, "What makes an event traumatic is not simply its magnitude or brutality, but also the context in which it occurs, the opportunity or lack thereof for expression of the undiluted affect it engenders, and the possibility or impossibility of redress, such that safety is reinstituted in a profound and comforting way."[9] Put simply, it is not just *what* happens, *where* it happens, or *how often* it happens that has a negative affect. It is our not being able to express its affect on us, or do anything about it. When we lack opportunity, or choose not to resolve painful losses, we lose the opportunity to be comforted in a way that makes us feel safe and secure again. The long-term effects can be:

- inhibited personal and intellectual growth
- emotional retardation and withdrawal
- depression
- impaired stability and insecurity
- a self-protective, guarded, isolated lifestyle
- an inability to change how we see ourselves
- fear-based behaviors
- broken, distant, impersonal and superficial relationships
- multiple dysfunctional behaviors
- alcohol and drug abuse or dependency

If healing is significantly hindered, it ultimately impairs our ability to function with normalcy. This not only applies to Vietnam vets, but to anyone who has been traumatized. Blocking emotional pain and sorrow may have been necessary for survival in Vietnam, but it does little to help us live a full life back in "the world." What worked then will not work now, yet many still live with past fixed behaviors. Vets who have never grieved their losses often remain locked in a time warp, chained to the past in what Parsons refers to as a "frozen identity."[10]

Lack of healing creates chaos in our lives, and in our families. Emotional constriction keeps us from bonding. It inhibits intimacy and produces alienation. Unhealed wounds also lead to psychological depression, which almost always accompanies PTSD. Energy expended unconsciously to suppress pain creates fatigue. We lose motivation. We may turn to amphetamines or energy-inducing drugs (caffeine, nicotine, adrenaline like substitutes) to compensate for chronic fatigue. Depleted emotional energy reduces sex drive. It creates a sense of hopelessness. Hopelessness encourages further isolation and withdrawal, creating a downward spiral. Medical research shows it not uncommon for people to be hospitalized for depression after years of *ignoring the way they felt*. Depressed people also tend to exhibit suicidal tendencies.

Our desire to grieve unresolved losses may lead us to create self-inflicted losses (divorce or personal injury) that then legitimize or give us permission to grieve. We may also become rageaholics, living off the emotional high created by adrenaline. Anger may be a more acceptable emotion than grief. The negative effects of resisting healing are numerous, yet we carry on these games because of an unwillingness to face pain. To be healed, we must see that those behaviors whereby we avoid grief also inhibit personal maturity.

Pain-Based Behaviors

The following behaviors are indicators of unhealed wounds. As you read them over, ask God to reveal any that pertain to you.

Constant irritation or uncontrollable explosive anger: Once we master the ability to suppress pain, we often skip over our pain as though it didn't exist. We can become so adept, that we lose touch with our pain altogether. Anger then becomes a substitute, drowning out pain in the same way a loud noise covers an irritable squeak.

Guardedness and self-preservation: A wounded heart naturally defends itself. Walls of self-protection then produce a guarded lifestyle. We are to "guard our heart with all diligence,"[11] so that it remains tender and sensitive. If we let it become hard, we lose our ability to be sensitive to others. Grief is a mark of compassion. Legitimate boundaries protect us from being violated, but do not make us unapproachable. Hardening our heart makes us insensitive, and though we may still have passion, we most definitely will lose *com*passion.

Denial, shock, and dissociative behaviors: Most of us respond to pain with some degree of avoidance which temporarily enables us to better prepare ourselves to work through it. Yet defense mechanisms like avoidance or denial are not designed to become lifestyles. As we mature, we should become more adept at handling suffering, and life's inconsistencies. Growth should lead us to resolve past pain which we still carry. Avoiding pain hinders emotional maturity.

Mistrust, insecurity, and isolation: Deep seated mistrust is based in fear. Fear prevents us from bonding with God or others, and from *entrusting* ourselves to them. Fear and mistrust keep us from being open, vulnerable, transparent, honest, and truthful, thus preventing intimacy. When we fear rejection or disapproval we keep our lives hidden. We withdraw emotionally or isolate ourselves, and live with the constant fear of being found out or hurt again.

Conflict and strife: Arguing and fighting keep others at a distance. For some, it is more comfortable to be abrasive, antagonistic, or even cruel if it keeps people from getting close. We control our environment by creating emotional distance.

Recurring depression: Depression and reduced activity is normal following loss or injury. We may feel anything from mild discouragement to despair. Some degree of depression generally follows rejection, failure, and illness, and often accompanies periods of major change or transition. When we do not allow ourselves to grieve we never experience relief. Buried emotions eventually create prolonged periods of depression which obstruct normal biological and social functioning. When we choose to bear the unbearable, we are prone to depression and melancholy.[12] Proverbs says, "When the heart is sad, the spirit is broken... The spirit of a man can endure his sickness but a broken spirit who can bear?"[13]

Dependencies, addictions, or compulsive behaviors: Solomon wrote, "laughter cannot mask a heavy heart, when the laughter ends the grief remains."[14] Yet we still think we can mask our pain with a nonchalant, carefree attitude. If that doesn't work, we try drugs, alcohol, sexual gratification, or may even party, party, party. We seek relief through excessive physical activity, compulsive work, over-eating, or a preoccupation with doing everything right. We substitute pleasure (sensuality) for emotional pain. All these behaviors are futile attempts to numb our pain or satisfy unfulfilled needs.

Insensitive or unresponsive to the needs of others: When we suppress pain and deny our need for comfort, we expect others to do the same. We criticize others for what we perceive as weaknesses, and expect them to be self-reliant like us. Pride, arrogance, and self-righteousness reflect a hard heart. We pull away when others go through hard times and justify our emotional aloofness. We avoid listening to others' pain because it activates our own. We feel helpless to fix others because we haven't learned to fix ourselves.

Our conscience is never fully alive in areas where we repeatedly offend others. A hard heart keeps us from being unaware of how our behavior affects people, or causes us simply to not care. When we see needs in others and close our heart to them, we are being self-protective. Scripture encourages us to "not merely look out for our own personal interests, but for the interests of others."[15]

Easily offended: Unhealed wounds are tender to the touch and often produce explosive reactions. Want to talk about the government? The VA? Jane Fonda? POWs or MIAs? Touchy subjects reveal unresolved pain and anger. Do you still have buttons that are easily pushed?

Can't talk about personal experiences: We protect ourselves by shielding or concealing areas of pain, guilt, anger, or failure. We make talking about these areas "off limits," and hide what secretly occupies our life.

Perfectionism and caretaking: As long we keep the emphasis on someone else, we keep it off ourselves, carefully avoiding personal exposure. We emphasize personal performance, outward appearance, ministry, or a self-sacrificing identity to keep our inner fears hidden.

Uneasiness around authority figures: We carry mistrust and fear created by unresolved betrayal, rejection, or abuse.

Easily intimidated by personal criticism: Words prick and stab at unhealed wounds, and awake sleeping insecurities. If someone points out our shortcomings we feel unacceptable or disapproved of. It shakes the self-image we have so carefully constructed. When we are corrected we feel either condemned or rejected, whether the intent is there or not. God's word, and the counsel of others, falls like seed on hardened ground; nothing penetrates or takes root.

Preoccupation with being rejected or abandoned: We feel a compulsive need to please others by performing up to their expectations. We need to win people's love or approval in order to feel we belong, or to feel good about ourselves. Deep seated insecurities cause us to overreact to events over which we have no control. We have difficulty laughing at ourselves or take ourselves and others too seriously.

Personally, I can identify with most of the above behaviors. Growing up, I developed a highly refined system of defenses to protect myself. I used trip flares, concertina wire, booby traps, and claymore mines. If these didn't work, I brought out the heavy artillery or conducted a direct assault, firing for effect. However, these behaviors also worked to my detriment. In the end, they prevented me from receiving the love I needed to live a productive life.

Hindrances to Healing

When a physical wound goes unhealed it festers. A hard scab may form to protect it, but that doesn't stop it from being painful to the touch. Emotional wounds are the same. When treating a physical wound we remove the scab, open the wound, and remove all impurities which keep it from healing. Why do we resist the same process to heal our hearts? Do we still carry self-limiting beliefs like, "there is no safe, supportive place," or "no one really cares." These beliefs keep us stuck in our pain! One vet wrote: "I'm afraid that if I start [to grieve] I don't think I can quit... I will lose control and it [survival] will be all over."

Do we not let go of painful memories because they keep our defenses alive? Do they provide a buffer between us and others? Might resolving pain mean an embarrassing "unmasking?" Does equating pain and vulnerability with weakness rob us of our true masculine identity? Does acknowledging limitations nullify existing strengths? When we choose to live in pretense, stuffing valid emotions, we reflect the schism so prevalent within today's society.

Summary

Physical loss and destruction was rampant in Vietnam, as was emotional loss and deprivation. For many, there has been no resolution. When we resist the natural process of grieving it progressively hardens our heart. This hardening isolates us from others and keeps us from being healed. Resolving our losses and working through grief is difficult, but possible. A strong commitment to healing can bring lasting comfort and wholeness if we truly desire and seek it. It was for our healing that God sent us His Son.

-5-

A Barbed Wire Perimeter
[ISOLATION AND WITHDRAWAL]

"Man, I had some real trepidation. I was genuinely concerned over how I was going to be accepted. I had been in 'Nam only a few hours earlier and had thought about it on the flight all the way home. What were people going to say? How would my friends act? Would I be an outcast? Man, I didn't know. The soldiers at Ft. Ord said there was a huge crowd of peaceniks protesting at the main gate and that we had better wait until after dark before leaving the base if we wanted to avoid confrontation. I waited. So did a bunch of other guys.

"There was no sweeter feeling than being free from that hell hole, but it was mixed. I had felt like a hostage for thirteen months and now that I was finally home, I was hiding out on base. I had anxiously anticipated my homecoming, but now it felt bittersweet. That night, when we took a cab out of the base, the driver said the main gate was still surrounded by protesters. He said he knew another way out, but personally I didn't trust him. I thought he just wanted to take the long way so he could make more money, but you know... I mean, who could you trust? Anyway, I just shrugged it off and went along with it.

"The exit we took wasn't far from the main gate, and I could see the protesters bathed in the floodlights mounted on both sides of the barbed wire fence. The scene created an eerie, familiar feeling. It reminded me of the entrance gate to the compound in Cu Chi, only these weren't gooks we were keeping out, they were Americans. And here I was, sneaking back into my own country."

–the Author

"He loves you, but he doesn't trust you and he wants to run away from you, that's the double message you get from someone with PTSD. Looking back on the early years of our marriage, I don't know what was harder for me, Jim's anger or his depression and his numbing. That numbing, it was and is, one of the biggest problems we have. Sometimes I can't get through to him no matter what I do.

"At first I tried to pierce the wall gently. No success. So then I tried rejection and anger. Maybe if I rebuffed and scorned him, he would come around. That worked... sometimes. But if his wall was really up, I could throw a first-class temper tantrum and he'd just shrug his shoulders and walk out the door. I soon discovered that pressuring Jim for a response, whether I used loving tactics or not, was self-defeating.

Either way, I'd usually drive him further away from me."

–wife of a Vietnam veteran[1]

"There is one great fear in the heart of every serviceman and it is not that he will be killed or maimed, but that when he is finally allowed to go home and piece together what he can of life, that he will be made to feel that he has been a sucker for the sacrifices he has made."

–WW II soldier[2]

Jim Goodwin writes in *The Etiology of Combat-Related Post-Traumatic Stress Disorders* that, "Combat veterans have few friends."[3] Research supports this statement, and although research findings cannot always be generalized, a Vet Center study revealed that 95% of all therapists working with vets observed problems with emotional numbing, detachment, withdrawal, isolation, and a reluctance to share on a deep emotional level.[4] Studies show that vets exposed to high levels of combat stress also experience greater social isolation, homelessness, and vagrancy[5]. These tendencies indicate a lack of vulnerability, transparency, and openness among the Vietnam veteran population, and demonstrate the underlying difficulty combat vets have trusting others. This chapter examines the roots of emotional and social isolation, the specific ways these behaviors manifest, how they affect vets and those close to them, and the difficulties of restoring trust.

Creating Isolating Behaviors

Combat veterans who experience multiple losses, deep emotional wounds, terror induced stress, betrayal, and a myriad of life-threatening situations, carry deep emotional scars which propel them to distance themselves from people and situations which appear unsafe. Social isolation is simply an expression of emotional guardedness and is characteristic of a lifestyle of self-preservation and fear. These behaviors are normal reactions to painful events and are often reinforced within our culture.

When losses, betrayal, or offenses create emotional wounds, we build protective walls around our hearts to prevent future vulnerability and pain. When we are hurt repeatedly, we become habitually guarded. We learn to protect ourselves with a *layer* of defenses. The more pain, the thicker the wall.

Walls *may* keep us from being hurt, but they also keep pain, anger, and fear locked inside. They prevent us from being open and transparent. They keep others from getting close. When we generalize these learned behaviors, we often end up mistrusting everyone. The more guarded *we* become, the harder it is for others to get to know us. That can make it hard for them to trust *us*. When we are driven by a compulsive need for safety, we often choose safety over anything else. We stop taking risks and settle for what's familiar. When we withdraw and isolate, the residual effect is loneliness.

The following familiar pattern then emerges:

Emotional loss, betrayal, and life-threatening events
lead to
Broken trust, pain, and fear
lead to
Preoccupation with safety
lead to
Self-protective, guarded behaviors
lead to
Emotional withdrawal and social isolation
lead to
Egocentric (self-centered) lifestyle

Trauma and Combat Stress

Traumatic, stressful events produce emotional numbing. Previously mentioned as one form of denial, emotional numbing is both a natural reaction and a learned behavior. It is a form of emotional anesthesia which protects us from being overwhelmed by intense feelings which can cause temporary mental confusion and keep us from normal functioning. Disorganization and confusion are life-threatening in the face of combat, therefore, some feelings *need* to be shut off during battle. The repeated internal and external stress of combat, the loss of life and other emotionally painful experiences, cause soldiers to suppress normal feelings. This is often necessary for their survival and for the survival of others. Young men who may have already learned to shut down emotionally before military service, had this behavior deeply reinforced in Vietnam at a very formative period in their development. It became fixed in their lives. Unfortunately, when we shut down emotionally we deny an important part of our humanity.

The damaging effects of combat trauma and emotional numbing are often linked to individual differences. Although all humans have the *same biological reaction* to stressful stimuli, we react in varying degrees. And, because we are unique as individuals, we often *respond* to the same situations differently. What is traumatic for one person because of temperament, personality, predisposition, or personal history, might not be traumatic to another. Likewise, the same experiences do not always have the same lasting effects.

Betrayal and Rejection

Isolation and withdrawal are natural responses to betrayal and rejection. We limp away from painful experiences to lick our wounds, but sometimes we never fully recover from them. Betrayal and rejection break trust. Self-protection and guardedness are reasonable responses when trust has been broken, or when we have been violated through painful vulnerability. Solomon, the writer of Proverbs, says:

> A merry heart produces a cheerful countenance but by sorrow of the heart the spirit is broken. A broken spirit dries up the bones. The spirit of a man will sustain his infirmity but a wounded spirit who can bear?[6]

When the sanctity of trust is violated, our hearts are painfully broken. Life-long consequences follow. Deep wounds impair our *capacity* to trust and severely damage our ability to bond with others. The more trusted and highly esteemed the trust breaker, the deeper the breach of trust and the more lasting and destructive the results. The earlier betrayal or rejection occur in an individual's development, the greater it undermines security and therefore, fundamental stability. When a breach of trust occurs between parent (or primary caretaker) and child, a child's ability to bond with others in the future can be destroyed. Future caretaking relationships never feel safe again.[7]

Solomon wrote, "A brother offended is harder to be won than a strong city, and contentions are like the bars of a castle."[8] An emotionally injured person creates defenses similar to the walls around a guarded city. When you try to get close to them, conflict occurs. Contention is a part of their defense system. Conflict is used to keep people at a distance. It is often difficult to get past the defenses of those deeply wounded. It takes time to establish trust. Fear, like pain, gets lodged in the heart. Both these emotions reinforce self-protective behaviors.

When we shut down emotionally, we deny an important part of our humanity.

Betrayal in the Military

Many of us took to heart the values taught during Basic Training. These values, conveyed as a Code of Conduct, were drilled into us. We were told we were representatives of America and, as ambassadors, we were to esteem honesty, justice, fairness, moral integrity, loyalty, courage, equality, honor, respect, and dignity. Yet our own military leaders (including the Commander in Chief, the President), made a mockery of these ideals.

• Black-marketeering and theft of military supplies were common among non-commissioned officers and field officers alike, often to the detriment of needy soldiers in the field.

• Officers traded favors, recommending one another for medals they neither won nor deserved, while those who truly laid down their lives for others received little recognition.

• Officers were cycled through combat units, often a month at a time, just to have on record they had served in combat. The common (or uncommon) soldier spent an entire year grinding through hell.

• Military leaders lied to the press, lied to the American public, and lied to soldiers in the field.

• Most high-ranking officers made sure they enjoyed the best of everything: servants, liquor, whores, good food, and air-conditioned comfort. They visited the field in the comfort and safety of their helicopters while most soldiers slept in the mud and rain, and ate C-rations.

• Racism permeated leadership, and although rare in front line combat units, it deeply affected duty assignments in both combat and support units.

• Upwardly mobile officers sometimes risked lives unnecessarily to put another star on their uniform, build their reputation, and climb the military ladder of power and success.

• We expected military and political leaders to make decisions which protected our well-being. We trusted them to do so. Yet many policies and restrictions guiding the war often left us with our hands tied, unable to protect ourselves or others.

• Soldiers were humiliated, threatened, and sometimes jailed by a system that robbed them of dignity, choice, and respect.

• The high ideals which often drew men into service through a sense of loyalty and duty, were later discovered to be untrue. In reality, political and economic opportunists saw Vietnam as a chance to increase personal power and bank accounts at the cost of soldiers' lives.

Betrayal in Vietnam

Many veterans were told by Vietnamese civilians that they didn't even want them in their country. Combat units were told not to associate with or trust the very people they were sent to protect. South Vietnamese Army (ARVN) soldiers were known to trade in their uniforms at night for black pajamas (the Viet Cong uniform), to attack American forces. ARVN units often ran in the midst of battle, leaving American troops to do their fighting. ARVN's often refused to go into areas where there were known hostile forces, leaving Americans to root out the enemy at the high cost of American lives. Vietnamese military and civilian officials were notoriously corrupt, yet *we* were expected to support them and lay down our lives for them if necessary.

Betrayal and Rejection at Home

While serving in Vietnam, soldiers expected their nation as a whole to take care of their best interest.[9] When they began to see that the policies affecting the war were not in their best interest, trust was broken. This letter conveys the wounds many experienced:

> Dear Editor, this letter is not only from me, but quite a few of my friends... You can believe me that a lot of our descriptive phrases and obscenities are being omitted. This outburst of malice spontaneously occurred when the following quotation was read aloud to them from a letter. "We've had some memo-

rial services for them at school and there's a movement for a strike." The quotation was in regards to the recent killings at Kent State University. We are sorrowful and mourn the dead, but it grieves us no end and shoots pain into our hearts that the biggest upset is over the kids who got killed at Kent. So why don't your hearts cry out and shed a tear for the 40-plus thousand red-blooded Americans and brave, fearless, loyal men who have given their lives so a bunch of bloody bastard radicals can protest, dissent, and generally bitch about our private and personal war in Vietnam, and now Cambodia? During the past 18 months in hell I've seen and held my friends during their last gasping seconds before they succumbed to death. And not once, I repeat, and not one goddam time did they chastise our country's involvement in Vietnam.

And how the hell do you think we in Vietnam feel when we read of the dissension and unrest in our country cussed by young, worthless radicals and the SDS. This is what we feel like: We have an acute hatred, an unfathomable lust to maim, yes, even kill. Last month my company lost 12 good men and five more were torn up so bad that they have been sent back to the States. What did you do? Protest. In your feeble and deteriorating and filthy degenerate minds you have forced and caused these men to die for nothing. Do you place such a low value on our heads?[10]

The inner sense of *unfittedness* that characterizes the social isolation of Vietnam veterans is partly due to their homecoming. America should have provided the support necessary to aid individuals returning from Vietnam with a shattered psyche, but it didn't. Parsons writes, "no containing, facilitating, nor support can occur in a reception of cold hostility, abandonment, and blaming (of the soldier), which *for the most part,* was a characteristic experience for these veterans."[11] Individuals need family, friends, and the support of others to assist them in making sense of tragedy and to resolve personal pain. Vietnam veterans needed their country to give sanction, meaning, and recognition to their sacrifice, yet they were often hated, ignored, ridiculed, and treated with dishonor. They were told to forget what happened and to keep quiet about their experience. Soul searching questions that examined American involvement in Vietnam were unwelcome, and often seen as unpatriotic.

The lack of support from fellow Americans has been difficult for many veterans to forget. As Figley and Leventman point out, "the home we returned to, was not the home we left."[12] It seemed no one was really interested in an experience, which for many veterans, was integral to their identity, values, and perspective on life. One veteran wrote:

I felt like a total stranger in my own home. I told her I was her son; that I was just back from fighting for my country, an important family value she and pop had instilled in me. I thought she had read all those letters I wrote to her, my dad, and brother... telling them how happy I was going to be when I came home. I was not happy at all. "Tell me, mom, what is going on." "Well I'll tell you," she began. Now, I wasn't sure I wanted to hear it, I'd been traumatized already since I was back home, and I didn't need anymore. She went on, "I want to feel proud of you but I don't. I just keep hearing those awful things on TV about what you guys are doing over there, just killing innocent people." She said that was why she was so distant from me... that her problem was what she kept hearing from the media about the soldiers in Vietnam.[13]

In the face of rejection, veterans began isolating themselves almost immediately. Many veterans took off to live in the wilderness. Some returned to Vietnam, where they knew they would be welcome. Some burned, buried, or discarded their uniforms, believing that by discarding their identity they could bury their past. Those who did adjust to the mainstream often withdrew emotionally.

Influences Affecting Isolation

Dominant behavioral patterns are acquired early on in our primary school of learning, our homes. Behavioral patterns are then reinforced by widespread cultural influences in religion, education, the arts, the media, entertainment, government, extended family structures, and peer relationships. Emotional numbing and social isolation are predominant patterns in our society, especially among men. These patterns are reflected and reinforced in the media through stereotypical gender roles and passed down generationally within families.

Dominant behavioral patterns are acquired early on in our primary school of learning, our homes.

Family Influence

Consider the historical and cultural influences of the extended family. John Sandford[14] writes that before WW I, family members were less isolated from one another. Society was less mobile and it was a more affectionate age. Even when fathers went off to fight in the war and were gone for long periods of time, there were still extended families left behind where other men filled the nurturing role of a father. After the war, the entire nation became mobile. Families traveled greater distances and lived farther apart. The stock market crash and years of depression created further disintegration of families as hundreds of thousands of people migrated, seeking employment.

During World War II, fathers again went off to war, only this time mothers also went off to work in war plants. Children grew up in child care centers or in the care of friends. Men were away from their families for two or three years, then came home to an entire generation of toddlers who had never known them. These children missed out on the essential kind of nurturing that only fathers can provide. Then came the Korean War.

When troops came home from these wars they found themselves often "psychologically wounded, and so far behind in their education and careers that, in many cases, they just got their wives pregnant and went off to bury themselves in school or in the work force."[15] Men were unable to nurture their children as normal fathers should because they had not known nurturing themselves. Like their fathers, they learned to numb their feelings. Mothers were left to raise the children and yet another generation grew up without close relationships with their dads. They grew up looking to peers, television, and movies for role models. This is the generation that went off to fight in the jungles of Vietnam.

Media Influence

How we interpret life, and what we expect of life, is often formed for us in 1/2 to 1 1/2 hour sound bites. The media provides sources of role-modeling which are especially influential on those whose fathers are emotionally or physically absent. The last generation said to have had any real heroes was the generation prepared for the draft. I had my own heroes, but they were also the movie stars of my generation: John Wayne, James Dean, Marlon Brando, Victor Mature, Humphrey Bogart, Alan Ladd, Glenn Ford, Richard Boone, Randolph Scott, and even Elvis Presley. These men portrayed heroes who were loners. They were self-sufficient, self-contained, self-controlled, independent men of steel who needed no one. These men could be angry or violent, but were rarely forgiving or tender, except towards women. Many of us went to Vietnam with the "John Wayne American Syndrome," an identity formed by the media and reinforced by cultural standards.

Cultural Influence

Society has taught us that men must always be strong, sufficient, supportive, able, and ready. This makes it difficult for men who are victimized to receive any kind of healing, because society also teaches that *victims* are weak and powerless. Men who are legitimately victimized are then left in turmoil. After all, if *real* men cannot be victimized, victims cannot be *real* men. Yet in Vietnam, under the shadow of incriminating cultural pressure to always react heroically, many men did feel victimized and inadequate. Feeling unacceptable, many vets hid their experiences in shame.

Our present cultural preoccupation with autonomy and independence has also greatly affected us. Since the 1950s, American youth have increasingly been asking, "What's in it for me?" We tend to consider others, or even the welfare of our nation, only when we can personally benefit. Self has become the center of our values and of our involvement. Perhaps John F. Kennedy saw this trend when he said, "Ask not what your country can do for you, but what you can do for your country!"

> Attitudes of selfishness, self-centeredness,
> and self-preservation are hostile to social bonds.
> They focus on rights and freedoms,
> rather than on responsibility and obligation.

The American "cult of self," which emphasizes individualism above that of community, has created an obsession with self that is pathological. We are encouraged to break relationships with others to pursue what *we* want. Personal happiness has become the goal, replacing personal loyalty, responsibility, integrity, duty, or honor. Self-centeredness has created what Bob Mumford calls an *atomistic* society, where everything is designed to disintegrate. Our divorce statistics, the general breakdown of corporate ethics, the abandonment of loyalty between employers and employees, and the desertion of families by both mothers and fathers are but a few examples. This narcissistic attitude of being solely preoccupied with one's self, ultimately results in a society that is isolated from itself. Attitudes of selfishness, self-centeredness, and self-preservation are hostile to social bonds. They focus on rights and freedoms, rather than on responsibility and obligation. They overlook the role commitment plays in developing accountability, maturity, and personal fulfillment.

Identifying Isolating Behaviors

It is not enough to know *why* veterans withdraw and isolate. It is also important to identify a *lifestyle* of withdrawal and isolation as unhealthy. Only then will we seek to identify these behaviors and willingly give them up. Sometimes our unhealthy behaviors are obvious to others, but are oblivious to us. We may even believe them to be normal. The following are examples of isolating behaviors:

- compulsive feelings of needing to get away
- driving around endlessly to escape the pressures of life or to evade vague, unsettling feelings
- dropping out of sight for days
- abandoning families, jobs, and careers to live in the woods
- choosing solitary pursuits
- imposing social restrictions on family members
- passively responding to life and interpersonal relationships[16]
- choosing philosophical/religious beliefs (from Quakerism to Hinduism) that embrace passive, separatist lifestyles
- physical or emotional absence from home life
- unwillingness to communicate with any degree of intimacy
- unwillingness to form social and emotional attachments
- denial of natural affection or feelings
- unresponsiveness to needs of family members

- deep seated attitudes of self-sufficiency and independence
- workaholism, alcoholism, or drug dependency
- preoccupation with control and safety
- egocentric behavior

The Effects of Isolating Behaviors

Emotional detachment and isolation has a devastating affect on family relationships. Parenting, which requires an enormous amount of energy and commitment, is extremely difficult when either spouse is emotionally or physically absent. Veterans with PTSD often lack the emotional energy to parent because of stress depletion, depression, and preoccupation with the past. Fulfilling parental roles also requires emotional bonding, which many veterans are unwilling to do. When parental roles feel one-sided, either spouse can easily become resentful.

When our isolating behaviors are rooted in beliefs like, "I don't need anybody else," or "I need to take care of all my needs," we readily transfer these same beliefs to our children. These beliefs, often developed during painful childhood experiences, are rooted in mistrust. When we believe *we* don't need anybody, then we expect others not to need *us*. Without ever voicing our beliefs, our family picks up these messages in our actions and attitudes.

We attempt to be self-sufficient and independent because we don't want to need others. Needing others means admitting we are incomplete in ourselves and thus, in some way, still vulnerable. If we see vulnerability as weakness, we deny "needs" exist. Denying our own emotional needs eventually leads us to deny the emotional needs of others. As I mentioned before, denial opens the door to self-deception and obsession, and many of us are obsessed with our independence.

Emotional isolation and guardedness are sure signs of egocentric behavior. We want the world to revolve around our needs. We think of each new encounter in terms of how it will affect *us* rather than others. Our behavior centers on how we can best protect ourselves and keep from being hurt. Everything revolves around *our* pain, *our* safety, and *our* need to control *our* environment.

The Flip Side of Isolation

Emotional withdrawal and guardedness don't always produce social isolation. Emotional withdrawal may lead to compulsive activity to fill the void created by lack of personal relationships. The compulsive need to fill this void can motivate workaholism or even religious and civic service. We may think we are motivated by unselfish devotion, when in reality we are simply using our activity as a means of avoiding pain and loneliness. Our real attitudes, however, are rarely hidden from those who know us well. We can be actively involved in the lives of others while still avoiding intimacy and transparency.

Those who live with a guarded inner heart are often there for people, but won't let people be there for them. By refusing to acknowledge their own needs, they avoid vulnerability. Fear, independence, and self-reliance keep them from asking for support; however, they may still secretly carry resentment because nobody is there for them. They think people should know their needs without them having to ask. They fault others to avoid accountability for their fears. They have problems saying no, and are unable to draw healthy boundaries. They wear the mask of being strong and having it all together, while secretly fearing disapproval for not being so.

Mistrust and Isolation

For most people, connection with others holds the promise of comfort. For those who have been deeply wounded and know all too well the predatory nature of humans, connecting interpersonally only means pain. For them, trust is dangerous. Vulnerability is foolishness! Although a guarded lifestyle may feel safe to such individuals, eventually it impacts their life in a negative way. Their *indiscriminate* mistrust deprives them of the love and fellowship that makes life enjoyable. Instead, their lives resemble solitary confinement.[17] For these people, fear becomes a dominating, controlling influence.

Betrayal is most painful when it involves someone we trust, for it is only those close to us who have the capacity to deeply wound us. David, the Psalmist and Biblical King of Israel, wrote:

> It is not an enemy who criticized and denounced me, then I could bear it; nor is it one who hates me who sets himself against me, then I could hide from him; but it is you, a man my equal, my guide, my familiar friend.[18]

David's response is familiar to many of us:

> I am restless in my complaint and am surely distracted... my heart is in anguish within me, fear and trembling come upon me... I feel overwhelmed... I would run away and be at rest, I would wander and lodge in the wilderness, I would hasten to a place of refuge.[18]

David, like many Vietnam veterans, was wounded and bruised by those he trusted. He became critical and cynical. He felt overwhelmed because he perceived himself as being alone. Confused, bewildered, and distracted by an array of conflicting thoughts and emotions, he struggled to make sense of his situation. In doing so, he isolated himself. Not knowing whom he could trust, he withdrew to the wilderness, a place of safety and refuge. Does this sound familiar?

Summary

Isolation and withdrawal are normal reactions to painful betrayal or rejection. They are means by which we guard our heart. They are also clues that we have been unable to restore broken trust. Cloud and Townsend say, "Our ability to give and respond to love is our greatest gift. The heart that God has fashioned in his image is the center of our being. Its abilities to open up to receive love, and to allow love to flow outward are crucial to life."[19] Yet those with crippling emotional pain have great difficulty giving or receiving love, and self-protection often leaves them alienated, lonely, and empty.

The longer wounds remain unhealed, the deeper dysfunctional behavior is imprinted. Research shows that individuals with chronic PTSD become more resistant to treatment. When there is nowhere to turn for comfort, safety, or support, as was the case for many returning from Vietnam, problems get worse.

When we got in over our heads in Vietnam, we called in support. We can still call in support today by calling on brothers who have been there and want to see us through. The choice is *ours*. Freedom from a guarded lifestyle comes through emotional healing and restored trust. We must ask whether our guardedness is working to meet our heartfelt needs, or hindering us. Only then can we begin to take responsibility for changing. Are we allowing ourselves to get close to others? Are we allowing others to get close to us? Much of our loneliness results from choices *we* make.

-6-

Strangers in a Strange Land
[ALIENATION]

"After a short while, my girlfriend told me she didn't know how to relate to me; honestly, I didn't know how to relate to her either. She also said I wasn't the loving guy she used to know and love; that something horrible must have happened to me over there to change me so completely. I told her I didn't know what she was talking about. She said that the look in my eyes was the look of a deeply terrorized person, with a long-distance stare, not into the present, with her all the time. She also mentioned my frightened look and pallid complexion, my uptight way of sitting, talking, walking, you name it, my aloofness and all that, it made it too uncomfortable for us to continue our relationship."

–a Vietnam veteran[1]

"As the years pass, veterans realize that the experience of war is open-ended. Wars do not end: they have aftermaths, which are in some cases excruciatingly painful."

–*Parallels* [2]

The book, *Strangers at Home: Vietnam Veterans Since the War,*[3] did an excellent job documenting the separation of Vietnam veterans from their country, yet this detachment was deeper than mere social isolation. Veterans experienced a breakdown in their ability to relate to peers, fellow soldiers, women, themselves, and God. This left many feeling like strangers in a strange land. The tear in the fabric that once knit veterans to others has been difficult and slow to mend. This chapter examines the origins of alienation, areas of disengagement, the effects of separation on self and others, and finally, a call to reconciliation.

The Beginnings of Alienation

For many vets, coming home was a mixed blessing. Along with the exhilaration of leaving 'Nam was a sense of foreboding. The *shorter* they got, the more questions they had. The escalating anti-war movement created great uncertainty and although no one expected a hero's welcome, few were prepared for outright rejection.

I had no idea that my experience in Vietnam would create such a gulf between myself and others, and I was little prepared for it. I felt out of place almost immediately. The longer I was home, the more it became evident that I was different. I was not only a stranger to my friends, but to myself.

Unlike many, I had close friends who stuck by me in spite of a rough reception in Oakland. They made attempts to get me to talk about Vietnam, but I wouldn't. I knew that no matter what I said they just wouldn't understand. Mere words could not describe what I had just been through, so I said nothing. They tried to pry it out of me, but it was too painful. The emotions stuck in my throat and all I could express were the tears that ran down my face. With no way to say it all, I didn't even try. I felt inadequate to convey the impact Vietnam had on my life, and wasn't even fully aware of it myself. Yet I was convinced of one thing; I had a unique understanding of life and death that my peers didn't, and I was no longer concerned with the same pursuits. Their interests, once mine, now seemed immature and trivial. One vet wrote:

> My best friend and I grew up in Brooklyn, this really pisses me off when I think of it, my best friend stole my girl when I was away in 'Nam, and now works in a topnotch law firm making "boo-coo" bucks... We were like brothers, you know. You name it, we did it... together! But our similarities and friendship ended when I went to 'Nam; he didn't go. He went to Canada... It burns me up inside; it tears at my guts when I think of this. I came back with nothing; he came back with a profession. He is now a lawyer; I am a bum. I lost out on it. I hate to admit it, but I hate him. I feel ripped off. I am so angry it eats me up inside.[4]

Many vets thought war protesters weren't true patriots. They saw the protest as a personal rejection of their sacrifice and service, and in many cases their perception was right. Because people their age were caught up in the protest movement, a gulf grew separating "them" from "us." Vets were particularly at odds with those who could not separate their political or moral indignation about the war, from those who had served out of loyalty, obedience, and duty. Rejection, criticism, and condemnation from protesters created a deep invisible wound.

I was convinced of one thing; I had a unique understanding of life and death that my peers didn't, and I was no longer concerned with the same pursuits. Their interests, once mine, now seemed immature and trivial.

Alienation from Fellow Soldiers

Ironically, it was common for Vietnam vets to disengage from fellow soldiers, some during the war, others after it was over. Soldiers who bore the brunt of hardship withdrew from "slackers" who didn't pull their weight. Career soldiers, who saw the war as an opportunity to increase rank and pay, often disdained those thought to be less committed. There was sometimes a deep gulf between draftees and those who had enlisted. Enlisted men also resented those who, by virtue of commissioned rank, had special privileges. Commissioned officers, on the other hand, weren't *supposed* to affiliate with common soldiers, an attitude sorely despised in the field. There were also factions between black and whites; between those who went "by the book" and those seen as anarchists or trouble makers; between "juicers" and "druggies;" and between "jocks" and "hippies." The following story is a good example:

> The first day I saw him, he stuck out like a sore thumb because he had no rifle. Everybody seemed to treat this guy like shit. The commanding officer would make him go on all the shit details. If they send squads out on patrols around "vill'es," they made him stay in and burn the shit and walk the perimeter. If he did go out with the squad, everybody cursed him. He would be loaded down with all their stuff, twice as much as most people carried. I turned to one of the squad leaders and said, "What's the matter with him?" "He's a conscientious objector." "What does that mean?" "It's against the guy's religion to kill." That struck me as odd, because I thought it was that way for everybody.
>
> I still remember his face. A very sad expression that never changed. Wire-rimmed glasses and really burning eyes that caught you off guard. When we could go through the vill'es and burn them down on Search and Destroy, all he would do is carry everything. Nobody bothered about him. He spoke to no one and just did what he had to do.
>
> This guy must have had something on the dome, because he took all the shit. Everybody hated him. I never said anything to the guy, I just thought, "Wow, he's got a lot of balls!" I liked him even more because although he objected to killing people, he had no objection to going and serving his country. Most people in 'Nam weren't there serving their country. They were just there for their own personal reasons.[5]

Alienation from the Sexes

I do not exclude women as veterans, but I do not profess to understand how their experience in Vietnam *uniquely* affected their relationships with males. Male veterans sometimes distanced themselves from women following Vietnam, loving them to a point but never trusting them completely. They found it hard to carry on genuine relationships with those they perceived as nurturers. They often saw themselves as unworthy or unlovable because of the things they did in Vietnam, and therefore avoided those who by virtue of their gender, evoked intimacy.

Vets who marry often deny their spouse the opportunity to care for them in any meaningful way. Their periodic need for emotional nurturing or sex draws them into relationships, but they are often unwilling to bond emotionally, and usually keep a certain distance. Thus, they often end up sending a mixed message which says, "Come close–stay away."

They indulge their own sexual needs, but fail to return emotional intimacy. This can leave their wives feeling defiled because they intuitively sense the lack of emotional content and commitment. They know there is no genuine emotional exchange and feel used!

Some combat veterans will go years without social contact with women, other than with prostitutes or through casual sex. In a society which condones, or even encourages, casual sex without intimacy, responsibility, or commitment, it is increasingly possible for one's sexual needs to be met without any emotional exposure. The military, with its long history of encouraging or accepting the use of prostitutes during war, also bears some responsibility for creating and sustaining a mentality which encourages sexual exploitation.[6]

Alienation from God

Rejection, broken trust, alienation, isolation, guilt, shame . . .the same issues which plague interpersonal relationships also caused many vets to abandon God. When they walked through "the valley of the shadow of death," some believed God went AWOL. Others felt caught in a spiritual vacuum, torn between the irony of serving their country or remaining true to their faith. Plunged into a situation which was often perceived as absurd and evil, many vets were unable to make sense of the betrayal they felt by their country who, as Bob Dylan sang, "had God on its side." In the end, many vets abandoned both.

Other vets had serious problems accepting themselves for what they did, or didn't do, in Vietnam. They were reluctant to believe that God would accept them either. Like Adam and Eve, they hid from God, believing their transgressions were beyond God's ability to forgive. Like the disciple Peter after his denial of Jesus, vets carried guilt and shame for what they thought was unpardonable behavior. Some vets had problems integrating their behavior in Vietnam with their faith. The destruction and carnage they participated in or witnessed was incompatible with their understanding of a loving and kind God. As a result, they dismissed His existence.

Battlefield pleas and foxhole prayers often confused fear with need. Even those who had prayers miraculously answered, often forgot about them after the threat was over.

Some, out of fear or desperation, wanted visible assurance that God was real. They pleaded for that assurance with unrealistic, self-serving prayers. When their prayers weren't answered in a way which satisfied their expectations, they dismissed God altogether. "Where was God when I needed him?" they said. Battlefield pleas and foxhole prayers often confused fear with need. Even those who had prayers miraculously answered often forgot about them after the threat was over. Some resented God for not keeping them from suffering.

When we believe there are some things God will never allow to happen and they do, faith is shaken. Sometimes it crumbles. Such thinking is presumptuous, and ultimately dangerous. Perhaps that is why some vets who say they went to Vietnam as "Christians" lost their faith. Maybe their faith wasn't really in God, but in their "traditions." Maybe they didn't have a *personal* relationship with God, but related to a church or a religious belief system. Religious systems, rites, and rituals quickly crumble in the face of death.

Whatever the reasons, many vets abandoned their ideologies and "isms" in Vietnam and in their place, substituted faith in Self for faith in God. Faith became self-reliance. Belief in the unseen or in the intangible was too risky for those who wanted immediate relief from the ever present, clearly visible danger. Trust in the institutionalized church failed as readily as trust in other institutionalized systems. Unfortunately, the church fell far short of its mission to bring acceptance and reconciliation to veterans after the war. Thus, many veterans saw the Christian community as phony and hypocritical.

Alienation from Self

One of the most damaging effects of the war, and of our discordant homecoming, was alienation from self. Even those who went to Vietnam with good intentions often ended up at odds with their own ideals. Philip Caputo wrote, "When we marched into the rice paddies on that damp March afternoon, we carried, along with our packs and rifles, the implicit conviction that the Viet Cong would be quickly beaten and that we were doing something altogether noble and good. We kept the packs and rifles; the convictions, we lost."[7]

The loss of convictions, rejection by others, perceived irreconcilable differences between conscience and actions, the inability to resolve inner conflict and guilt, separation from feelings, hiding ones identity as a Vietnam vet... all of this led to a gradual, if not immediate, dissociation from the war, our identity as veterans, and therefore from self. This self-splitting created a pattern of inconsistent, divergent behavior and an inability to further deal with reality. This, in turn, left a schism which slowly destroyed emotional, mental, physical, and spiritual health.

Summary

The Vietnam War produced a widespread fracture in society. None were so torn, nor so alienated from the fabric of social and personal unity, as the warriors who fought it. Uncomfortable with their own identity, unsure of their acceptance from a nation they once esteemed, struggling to understand and put to rest changes forged in Vietnam, many vets ended up disillusioned and alienated from self, others, and God. If we let it, alienation can have a stranglehold on our life. It can separate us from relationships intended to make our life fruitful.

-7-

Living with Rageaholics
[ANGER, RAGE & BITTERNESS]

"For the most part, at least during the initial years, I hid my pain and anger. I was happy just to be back alive. Eventually, I began looking for outlets for the deep-seated hostility and outrage I felt. I joined other Vietnam vets to march against the war, speaking in every public arena I could. I poured relentless anger-fueled energy into political and social action, trying to develop an alternative society. I openly defied authority. For years I could not talk about my personal pain and was often cold, distant, and withdrawn. My anger seethed beneath the surface, but I simply refused to acknowledge it. I thought I was hiding it, but people could see it in my eyes. Even though I could sometimes be sparked by the slightest provocation, I kept my rage under control until I could unload it somewhere safely. Sometimes I used words like knives, sending all but the most hardy scattering. Those with vulnerable hearts, like my wife and children, were repeatedly wounded in the process. Still, I did whatever I had to do to keep people at a distance. My wife put up with it for years, whether out of love or her own emotional needs, I don't know. It didn't matter. She suffered for it either way."

–the Author

"I am going to level with you: I hate the war. I have hated the war since the day I walked off the battlefield. I hate it now even as it works its way up my throat and slips across my tongue... to you. I hate the war so much I can no longer think of it in any terms other than personal. I no longer give a damn about its political legacy, about its cultural vicissitudes, its historical aftershocks, its literary revisionism, its misapplied lessons, its frauds and fakes and Johnny-come-latelies. My hate, my unbridled passion, sweeps all that away. For me Vietnam now is first person singular. I am, I always will be, what I was... a boy pulled from his time, a man who left something essential behind him."

–Michael Norman

Anger is a well documented characteristic of Vietnam veterans with PTSD. Vietnam theater veterans, as well as those exposed to high war stress, commit significantly more violent acts than their civilian counterparts.[1] Goodwin says that our rage occurs with frightening frequency, often leaving us as alarmed by our violent behavior as those around us.[2] Our anger often appears without reason. We may have an exaggerated response to minor situations, or blow-up when we feel out of control. Unfortunately, those nearest us then suffer the brunt of our hostility and rage.[3] This chapter examines what creates anger, what sustains anger, its expression and suppression, and the effects of unresolved anger.

Why Anger?

Anger is a progressive, natural reaction to injury and painful emotional wounds. Emotional wounds are created by behaviors we consider offensive; that is, they violate our sense of justice or trespass the boundaries of love. Jesus said, "Woe to the world because of its offenses! For it *must needs be* that offenses come, but woe to him who brings them." Offenses are *inevitable*. They are an inescapable part of the human exchange because of sin, and our inability to love perfectly. The natural progression of emotions following an offense is:

OFFENSES > INJURY > PAIN (OFTEN FEAR) > ANGER

We are all created in the image of God. We all instinctively carry something of His nature and character. This inherent quality, especially alive in children, gives us our innate sense of love, and forms the moral basis for what we later rationally define as "right and wrong." We instinctively know what love is, even though as adults our intuition may be sublimated by a hardened heart and by contradictory messages we receive growing up.

When we are treated in ways that do not affirm our value and inherent worth, it injures our spirit! We intuitively sense that we are worthy of respect, not because we have necessarily earned it, but by virtue of the fact that we are God's creation and belong to Him. God has put this in our heart. When we respect others, and are treated respectfully, we know it's *right* because it's an expression of *love*. It is therefore *just*. When we are treated disrespectfully, our innate sense of justice is offended. God respects our boundaries and choices, and wants others to do the same. When we do not respect people's beliefs, choices, emotions, or their bodies, we violate God's intent for us to honor one another. We break *His* rules. What is offensive to us is established by what is offensive to God. Unjust, unfair, unloving acts anger God!

Sources of Anger for Vets

Veterans carry anger from their military duty, their tour in Vietnam, their homecoming encounters, and events prior to military service. Eisenhart says, "Military training equated rage with masculine identity in the performance of military duty."[4] Simply put, our military training taught us to be angry in order to carry out our duty. Anyone who remembers charging through the basic training course screaming "kill... kill," as we thrust our bayonets into lifeless human dummies knows this. I was forced to repeat this exercise again and again because the Drill Instructor didn't think I was angry enough when I attacked the dummies. Military life was demeaning, degrading, and often infuriating.

Personal humiliation, prejudicial treatment, callous indifference, biased favoritism, physical deprivation and injury left many wounded, angry, and resentful.[5] Insubordination could lead to imprisonment so most soldiers kept their mouth shut and stuffed their anger.

Injury was compounded by injury as soldiers left stateside training to fight in Vietnam. Even those who loved military life and were never bothered by their tour of duty, came home to an abusive, hostile reception. As one veteran put it, "When I returned from my tour of duty in Vietnam, I tried to go to the university where all of my friends were but I couldn't enjoy the ridiculous parties, games, and childish fun they were caught up in. I didn't understand their world and they didn't seem to understand mine. It was a depressing experience to know that I just didn't fit in, particularly since I had been looking forward to it when I was in Vietnam."[6] Some of us will have to concede that we were carrying a lot of anger before we entered the military. For us, Vietnam was simply the straw that broke the camel's back.

Holding on to Anger

Those who have not resolved their pain, or those who obsess about the injustice done them, have the greatest problem with anger. They tend to bounce between one of two extremes, either venting their anger or holding it in. Those who vent often fly into fits of rage. Those who suppress their anger tend to seclude themselves and fall prey to depression.

When we hold on to offenses, it is like carrying an emotional duffel bag. As we add to it daily, this load becomes increasingly unbearable. A bag has its limits. When it becomes full, something *has* to give. The resulting overflow generally spills out in rage.

We also carry unresolved offenses in our mind by compulsively replaying injustices. When we are obsessed with our injuries, we hammer away at those who have hurt us through critical, condemning, imaginary conversations. We entertain revengeful fantasies. These behaviors keep our pain and anger alive.

Responses to Anger

What follows anger varies, depending on our choices. The natural response to being hurt is to hurt back. This is our attempt to right an injustice by taking justice into our own hands. Seeking justice through revenge is called *retribution*. However, true justice seeks to balance injury through *restitution*. Restitution means restoring, through reconciliation, what has been lost, stolen, or broken through offense. True justice seeks to heal both victim and offender and does this by requiring restitution, not retribution. However, it is not just *things* that are to be restored, but *trust*. Our present judicial system seems to have lost sight of this. It uses its power to apply mere punitive action. This neither satisfies the need of the victim, rehabilitates the offender, nor restores broken trust.

Anger is normal, but our behaviors are often inappropriate. Unresolved anger expresses itself in destructive patterns, either internally when suppressed or externally when expressed. The following behaviors are indications of unresolved pain and anger:

Anger expressed
- a conflictual lifestyle characterized by excessive arguing
- outbursts of rage
- verbal abuse: cursing, shouting, or threatening
- dumping anger on family members where it is perceived as safe
- physical abuse: pushing, grabbing, slapping, kicking, hitting
- destroying inanimate objects: throwing things, putting one's fist through the wall, trashing the house, or smashing up vehicles
- attempting to control others

Anger suppressed
- periods of silence, emotional withdrawal
- depression, hopelessness, despair, self-pity
- unspoken hostility (wearing anger in a set facial expression)
- a flat affect (showing no emotion at all)
- separation or isolation
- anxiety
- problems with alcohol and drugs, physical illness, chronic muscle tension and backaches, chronic fatigue, depression, ulcers, high blood pressure, etc.
- obsessive, compulsive thought patterns
- callousness and a lack of sensitivity to others

Bitterness
Anger can never be completely suppressed or repressed. As long as we carry it, consciously or unconsciously, it eventually surfaces. When it does, it usually creates additional conflict. People who suppress anger for years often become depressed. Suppressed or repressed anger is ultimately expressed in a myriad of physical, emotional, and mental problems. Inevitably, it affects the lives of everyone with whom we have contact, creating an unnecessary strain on our relationships.

No one can live in a constant state of anger. It is draining, emotionally and physically. When anger smolders day after day, it becomes resentment. Resentment eventually gives way to *bitterness*. Bitterness produces a heart *set* in anger. A heart, so hardened, affects every aspect of our life. This is the pattern that generally emerges:

---

offenses > pain > anger
carried anger > resentment > bitterness > hard heart
a hard heart > self-preserving, self-protective lifestyle

Bitterness Affects Our Attitude and Identity
Bill Gothard says, "We become like whatever is the object of our emotional focus."[7] By focusing on those who have injured us, and con-

tinually reviewing their offensive action, we invariably become like them, developing similar behaviors or attitudes. We become critical, judgmental, condemning. We develop unhealthy attitudes of selfishness (self-centeredness), superiority (smug self-righteousness), and a "get them before they get me" attitude. If confronted, we are generally defensive and quick to rationalize and justify our behavior, believing we have a right to feel or behave inappropriately because others deserve it.

Bitterness Affects Relationships

Anger gradually shuts people out, making it difficult to socialize. We end up directing deep-seated anger against politicians, authority figures, family, the people next door, Jane Fonda, war protesters, countrymen who rejected us, and those who do not support us now. We project our anger on those who place demands on us, on those who threaten our independence, on those who criticize us, and sometimes just strangers who happen to get in our way. We keep our anger alive through fantasies of retaliation against the government, politicians, the Veterans' Administration, VA Medical Centers, or any institution that treats us unjustly. Our circle of hatred and mistrust gradually broadens to include just about everyone.[8] If we can't find a legitimate place to focus our anger, we'll create one. We'll find a scapegoat and dump our anger on it. The scapegoat could be blacks, whites, women, politicians, Jews, the IRS or anyone who gets in our way. Then, when no one can be trusted, we escape to the country and isolate ourselves.

The Bible says that when we do not forgive the offenses of others, it establishes a root of bitterness in our life. When this root springs up it eventually troubles us, and leads to the defilement of others. Most people tend to avoid bitter people, unless of course they are one of *us*. Bitter people end up hurting others, if not by what they do, then by what they say. *Webster's Dictionary* describes bitterness as:

a) having a sharp, often unpleasant taste,
b) causing or showing sorrow, pain, etc.,
c) sharp and disagreeable; harsh, and
d) resentful, cynical.

We get the word bitter from the root *bitan*, meaning "bite." Anyone who has been around a bitter person knows what it's like to have their "head bit off." Things said in bitterness have a sting to them that penetrates, piercing the heart in a cutting manner. A bitter person's words are critical, demeaning, and defiling. They destroy every good thing.

Bitterness Affects Our Body

Baum says, "Conflict, both real and imagined, is a highly charged emotional experience accompanied by predictable biochemical, physiological, and behavioral changes."[9] Anger stimulates the nervous system and produces a multitude of biochemical and physical changes. A number of studies have shown that hostility and anger boost stress hormones, accelerate blood pressure, increase production of that sticky component of blood that blocks arteries, hinder successful angioplastic surgery, and promote ulcerative colitis and toxic goiters.[10] Anger activates hormones which produce an "adrenaline rush," and it is easy to become addicted to this *rush* because it makes us feel alive. Yet the excessive release of the above hormones also create chemical imbalances which eventually injure the body.[11] Adrenaline activation also robs us of sleep, creating added physical fatigue.

How we cope with anger and stress affects our health. People who respond to conflict and pressure by withdrawing, isolating, or shutting down emotionally are also shown to be prime candidates for the development of cancer. Research shows the following characteristics to be indicators of potential cancer victims.[12] They:

- tend to see themselves as powerless (as victims)
- tend to be depressed
- tend to be reserved or stoic (appear unemotional)
- are generally pessimistic
- tend to rationalize away their hurts or problems
- avoid conflict

Another familiar phrase taken from the root word *bitan* or bitter, is "to bite the bullet." This means to confront pain without letting it show. In other words, to *suppress* it.

Bitterness Affects Our Emotions

A heart full of anger and bitterness has little room for anything else, especially mercy or compassion. It requires significant emotional energy to maintain a grudge and to live a guarded, hypervigilant life. We can exhaust emotional resources just like we exhaust physical resources. Carried anger depletes emotions, leading to depression.

When our heart becomes hard it becomes set like concrete in anger. When we tire of pain and anger and the loneliness our protective walls create, we often turn off all our emotions until we feel nothing. Once we stop feeling, we become insensitive and callous. It becomes difficult to sense the emotional needs of others. This affects our ability to nurture our families because it destroys our ability to give or display affection. Tiring of feeling nothing and wanting to feel good, we turn to "things" which create *sensual* pleasure, and we eventually develop dependencies.

Bitterness Affects Our Mind

Bitterness affects our mental processes... our comprehension, understanding, perception, and insight. The moment we become *set* in our anger, hating another, we become linked to that person in a way which slowly enslaves us. Anger overpowers our thought life. It develops a tyrannical grip on our mind. Our thinking becomes deliberately, intrusively, and obsessively critical and revengeful. Our thoughts either justify or excuse our behavior, while condemning theirs. We can become so obsessed with our wounds that we are unable to concentrate our energies on anything else. We become so fixated, we are unable to see events from any other viewpoint than our own. Our interpretation becomes set, making us closed minded and unteachable. Thus, bitterness dulls the mind and inhibits our ability to learn.

The relationship between hardness of heart and understanding is repeated throughout scripture. In the book of Mark, following the miraculous multiplication of bread and fish to feed a hungry multitude, Jesus' followers got into a boat to cross the sea of Galilee while He stayed behind. On their way, Jesus appeared to them walking on the water. It says of the disciples,

> They were greatly astonished, for *they had not gained any insight* [understood] from the basis of the incident of the loaves, *for their hearts were hardened* [or, their mind was closed, made dull, or insensible].13

Jesus' followers had witnessed a miracle, yet were unable to process the event in a way which either built their faith or gave them insight into Christ's identity. Their "understanding" was hindered by their "hardness of heart." Later, Jesus overheard the disciples questioning a warning he had given them, "to watch out for the leaven [yeast] of the Pharisees and the leaven of Herod."14 The disciples thought he was talking about bread. Aware of this, Jesus said, "Why do you discuss the fact that you have not bread? Do you not yet see or understand? Do you have a hardened heart?"

The apostle Paul also makes reference to this connection, saying, "Walk no longer just as the Gentiles also walk, in the futility of their mind, being *darkened in their understanding*, excluded from the life of God, because of the *ignorance* that is in them *because of the hardness of their heart*." Paul links the intellectual state of the Ephesians, and their spiritual relationship to God, to hardness of heart, encouraging them to put away "bitterness, wrath, anger, and clamor."15

Bitterness Affects Our Will

We grow in knowledge and understanding by our ability to reason and process new information. We can be hindered in this process by our will. Our willingness or unwillingness to open ourselves to new ideas has to do with trust. When we carry anger and mistrust, we are less willing to lay aside beliefs which justify and bolster self-protection. A will *set* on self-protection (created by inner vows or habitual choices), like a mind *set* on revenge, is generally not open to change. When we become set in our ways, we are unwilling to acknowledge or entertain ideas different from ours. We *will* not move our position. It's not that we *can't*, it's that we *won't!*

Bitterness Affects Our Spirit

We all have a body, a soul, and a spirit. Our mind, emotions, and will function on an interrelated basis. So does our body, soul, and spirit. Although we can talk about our mind, emotions, and will as having separate, distinct functions, they are not separate entities; one affects the other. So it is with our body, soul, and spirit. Anyone who does not nurture his spirit goes through life incomplete, like a person who is missing a leg or who is emotionally shut down.

God is *Spirit*. We meet God spirit to Spirit. Bitterness pollutes our spirit, thereby hindering our communication with God. Watchman Nee says, "the main functions of our spirit are intuition, communion, and conscience."[16] *Intuition* is the means by which we receive spiritual revelation. All we know, all we are able to comprehend about God, comes by revelation. By revelation God speaks to our mind. "Understanding," Scripture says, "comes from God." Our spirit is not just the means by which we *perceive* the things of God, it is the means by which we perceive the motive and intentions of others.[17] It enables us to see past the words people speak, the *context* of their conversation, to the *content* of what is in their heart. *Conscience* is the means by which we are able to discern the heart (desire) of God. This enables us to intuitively determine what is right or wrong in a situation where we have trouble determining on an intellectual level, what is appropriate. A knowledge of the law, coupled with an intuitive sense of right and wrong, keeps us on course in life. *Communion* makes communication and exchange with God possible. This creates intimacy. Intimacy allows us to know God, and to be known by Him.

When the gospel was first spoken to the Jews, Scripture says, "They were *pierced to the heart*." The literal translation is "smitten in conscience." God's Spirit touched man's spirit, convincing them that their lives were going in the wrong direction. This caused them to turn to Him. Had their spirit not been penetrated by God's Spirit, their conscience would have remained dead. Hardness of heart blocks crucial sensitivity to our spirit, and therefore to God's. This not only keeps us from perceiving the virtue of God, it keeps us from receiving His love. It prevents us from discovering His purpose and direction. It hinders crucial insight into God's nature and character. If we fail to perceive God as good, loving, or all powerful, it affects our ability to trust Him. Trust, or a lack of it, affects our daily lives.

We can grieve and alienate God's Spirit by harboring bitterness.[18] We insult God's Spirit by hardening our heart toward Him.[19] Even believers can be separated from the activity of the Spirit by bitterness. Luke, a physician and the writer of the Book of Acts, records this experience in Samaria:

> Now they believed Philip's message that Jesus was the Messiah, and his words concerning the Kingdom of God; and many men and women were baptized. Then even *Simon believed* and was *baptized* and began following Philip and was amazed by the miracles he did. Now when the apostles in Jerusalem heard that the people in Samaria had accepted God's message, they sent down Peter and John. As soon as they came down they began praying for these new Christians to receive the Holy Spirit, for He had not yet fallen upon any of them; they had simply been baptized in the name of the Lord Jesus. When Peter and John

began laying their hands on them they received the Holy Spirit.

When Simon saw that the Spirit was given through the laying on of the apostles' hands, he offered them money saying, 'Give this authority to me as well, so that everyone on whom I lay my hands may receive the Holy Spirit.' But Peter replied, 'May your money perish with you, because you thought you could buy the gift of God with money! You *can have no part or portion in this matter*, for your *heart* is not right before God. Therefore turn from this wickedness of yours, and pray the Lord that if possible, the *intention of your heart* may be forgiven you. For I see that you are in the gall of *bitterness* and in the bondage of *iniquity*.' [20]

Simon was a water baptized believer, but the condition of his heart (bitterness) kept him from receiving the "part and portion," which was his rightful inheritance (the Holy Spirit). *It also prevented him from understanding* that God's Spirit was a "gift," not something he had to purchase.

Bitterness Affects Our Behavior

Simon's bitterness also produced "bondage to iniquity." The Hebrew word *iniquity* means, "to make what is straight, crooked." It is used in scripture to denote lawlessness, or the propensity toward sinful behavior. Today we call iniquity *dysfunctional behavior*. When Peter refers to the *gall* of bitterness, he speaks directly to its distastefulness (such as the bile from the gall-bladder). Gall is a sore on the skin, a cancerous growth in the body which results from chafing, rubbing, or continual annoyance. We have all heard the expression, "He rubs me the wrong way." It means someone's offensive behavior grates on us. It makes us angry. The constant annoyance of anger also has a grating, cancerous effect on our body. It eats away at our demeanor from the inside out, eventually affecting our attitudes, behavior, and health.

Is Anger Wrong?

Anger is one of a broad array of normal human emotions. We may, however, believe anger is unacceptable because we associate it with angry *behavior*. Or, we may have grown up in a family where it was not acceptable to express anger, and developed the perception that anger itself was wrong. When we suffer abuse at the hands of angry people who are not controlling their tongue or their *actions*, we often associate their *actions* with anger, and therefore see anger as wrong. However, it is not the anger that is wrong; it is the abusive behavior. It is not anger that needs to be controlled; it is *abusive behavior*. Scripture says, "*Be* angry and do not sin."[21] It clearly distinguishes between the emotion, and sinful behavior (or attitudes). The Bible encourages us to be truthful about our anger, but not to sin. We are to honestly acknowledge our anger, yet resolve our feelings daily... before the sun sets.

The Example Jesus Set

Jesus said, "When you see me you see the Father." Jesus revealed both the true nature of God, and the true character of man. *Jesus got angry.* He was especially grieved by people's hardness of heart, their stubbornness, and their self-righteous attitudes. Jesus was in touch with his feelings; he did not hide them. Neither did he displace his anger on the innocent. He had the courage to confront those who offended him. He was assertive, forceful, and challenging, yet did injury to no man. He communicated his position clearly, took action to bring about changes, and did not carry grudges.[22]

When we lay aside our anger, or are slow to anger, we reflect God's character. We prevent injury to others just as Christ did.[23] Jesus clearly understood that unresolved anger (internalized) soon gives way to destructive behavior (externalized). He taught that bitterness produces the following:

- wrath (rage) and anger
- clamor: complaining about others (one's country, leadership, authority, spouse, etc.)
- slander: making false statements about others that damage their reputation, name-calling, gossip
- unwholesome words (swearing, derogatory statements)
- callousness, sensuality, lust, greed, and moral impurity
- depression, fear, anxiety, worry, and jealousy
- selfish ambition, arrogance, and lying.[24]

Who creates this mental and emotional torment? We do! We allow it by holding on to grudges and carrying the offenses of others, letting anger become set in our life.

Summary

Emotional wounds, like physical wounds, can become painfully crippling. Anger generally follows pain. It is a normal, natural result of being offended or treated unjustly. Anger carried day after day becomes resentment. Resentment turns to bitterness. Bitterness affects our attitudes, our identity, how we relate to others, and how others relate to us. Bitterness destroys our health, our ability to feel, our ability to learn and develop our full potential, and our ability to be spiritually in tune with God. God encourages us to lay aside our grievances. Nobody benefits when we hold on to our anger.

-8-

Yoked Under
a Heavy Burden
[SHAME, BLAME, AND GUILT]

"The torment started almost immediately. As much as I tried to put it out of my mind or harden myself to keep it from affecting me, it was always there. When I wasn't aware of it consciously, it surfaced in my dreams. I kept seeing the same fragmented bodies, heads detached with horrible grimaces, faces shattered, arms and legs blown in disarray, gaping chests and torsos totally dismembered, and they were all just kids... not much older than my brothers and sisters.

"The nightmares continued on R & R. They followed me home to the states. For years I kept quiet about what I had done, but I couldn't shake the guilt. I thought, if people only knew they would never accept me. On top of this was the constant overriding guilt of having come back at all, for leaving my brothers behind. I felt I had deserted them. I couldn't listen to the radio for fear they would talk about the war. I couldn't watch television for fear I would see some buddy. If by accident I did hear anything, I had to fight back tears. And crap, there was hardly anyplace you could go where the war wasn't being broadcast."

–the Author

There is a pervasive individual and collective guilt about the Vietnam war, and the means by which it was fought. Even the means by which it was lost. Guilt left an enduring mark on those who fought the war and sealed the lips of thousands who hid dehumanizing acts committed in Vietnam. Sometimes guilt is so great veterans cannot even face one another. When asked why so many veterans still suffer from post-traumatic stress disorder, Brende and Parson say *guilt* is the issue.[1] But what is guilt? How is it created? How has it affected our behavior? How have we dealt with it? And, have we been successful?

War and Guilt

War is always ugly. Combat is filled with tragedy and horror. Although men may rise to glorious heights of compassion and courage, they also plummet to the depths of human degradation. There is nothing about war that makes it envious. It leaves a trail of destruction and death, carnage and decay, and in some way those who participate in it always feel partly, if not wholly, responsible. As in any war, men do things they never imagined they would do in any other circumstances. War and guilt are like lovers, they walk through life hand in hand.

What is Guilt?

Guilt has mental, emotional, and spiritual components. It is a *feeling* of self-reproach which comes from the *inner conviction* or *belief* that we have done something wrong. Our thoughts either condemn or excuse us. When they condemn us, we may feel shame, remorse, sorrow, embarrassment, regret, disappointment, dismay, humiliation, or disgrace. Even Christ's apostles struggled with guilt. Paul compared himself to one guilty of premeditated murder. Edwin Cole writes:

> The punishment during that period [Paul's life] for someone tried, found guilty, and convicted of deliberately plotting murder, is unusual to us but fits the crime. The body of the victim was chained to the guilty and wherever the convicted murderer went, he dragged the dead body with him. Ostracized by the community, he found it difficult to survive. Eventually the weight of the dead body, the guilt of the deed, exclusion from society, the isolation from normalcy, and the separation from family and friends, killed the condemned person.[2]

Many veterans live like this. They are chained to past deeds through guilt and shame. They drag them around wherever they go, with no hope of escape from the vivid imagery or oppressive feelings. Like the stench of a dead body decaying, guilt is an ever-present reminder of our deeds. I was unable to rid myself of the smell of death for nearly twenty years. I could smell it on the sick, and on those in hospitals. I could even smell it on people who walked by. When I did, it sent me running. Like the stench of death, guilt easily becomes unbearable.

Guilt is a feeling of self-reproach which comes from the inner conviction or belief that we have done something wrong.

What Creates Guilt?

Guilt is created in both spirit and mind by conviction. It comes from *knowing* or *sensing* that we have violated *external* or *internal* standards. External standards are what we have been taught by parents, society, or religious institutions. Internal standards are those we integrate into our heart by way of a functioning conscience. Guilt can be either deserved or undeserved. *Valid* guilt exists to guide us. It turns us from attitudes and behaviors which are destructive to ourselves and others. If guilt does not produce a "turning," then we end up hardening our hearts, continuing in destructive patterns, and carrying tormenting sorrow. This eventually produces death.₃ The oppressive burden of guilt is generally *self-induced*. We carry shame and condemnation, criticizing and chastising ourselves over the things we do or fail to do, and burden ourselves with the judgments of others.

Acts committed

Recalling the things we participated in can be tormenting.

This Vietnamese woman came out of the edge of the woods, like out of nowhere. We had just been in a firefight and we were all edgy as hell. I fired on her almost immediately. Just as the bullets started tearing her apart, I noticed she was pregnant. God, her body just flew to pieces. Flesh and guts went everywhere! Even today I still see it. (Rich)

We were coming around the bend in a river in our patrol boat and spotted this little village on the river's edge. As we began our approach I saw a couple of sampans quickly load up. One had this old mama-san in it and it was full of little children. As they pulled from the bank the first shots rang out from the village; then all hell broke loose. It was a VC ambush! I don't know why, but that sampan headed straight for our boat. Maybe they were seeking shelter. Maybe they were just trying to get out of the way, I don't know. I don't even know who hit them, whether it was enemy fire or ours. All I know is that I saw that boat explode right before my eyes. I was peering out the rifle slots in the armor covering the side of our boat when I saw the boat lift in the air, then suddenly sink. Damn, it happened so quickly there was nothing I could do but watch. No one survived. They were so close I could clearly see the grandmother's face. For one short moment, our eyes met. I could see she saw me. The look in her eyes was devastating; it was like she knew she was going to die and all I could see in her eyes were resignation and hopelessness. God, I felt helpless to do anything about it but at the same time I sure felt guilty. After that, I just didn't care any longer. I lost all feeling about the war. (Larry)

Acts Omitted

Sometimes it's not what we do, but what we didn't do that haunts us. Curt, an ARVN advisor, stood by while others were tortured.

I should have done something. Instead, I just watched as they strung up suspected VC by their thumbs. Some were women and some old men. I can still hear the sound of a two-by-four smash into their skulls. I can still see the splatter of brains and blood on the hootch walls where they hung. I can still smell the blood and the putrefying flesh. God... it was my job! What was I to do? After awhile I just became hard to it. I laughed like they did, just to show them I wasn't some American pussy.

Some vets carry guilt because they succumbed to fear. They either did something they believed was cowardly, or something which compromised their integrity. The belief that they acted in a manner unbecoming a man haunts many. If there *were* soldiers who never yielded to fear, even during their first exposure to combat, I wasn't one of them. I was too ignorant to recognize the first time my life was in danger, but after that, and long into my tour, I always experienced momentary panic created by fear. Many soldiers did things to get out of the field or to avoid potentially dangerous duty. As fighting escalated during the Tet Offensive in '68, so did self-inflicted wounds. Bob and Jim told me:

> When I first arrived in country, I didn't understand what was going on. I was new in country, green as a lima bean, and here were these guys shooting themselves in the feet to get out of the field. One of the guys I was stationed with purposely inhaled tear gas and ended up severely burning his face and lungs. He said he just couldn't take it any longer. It got him out of the field for a couple of weeks but they just sent him back. One night, under an intense mortar barrage, this guy pulled out his 'sixteen', pointed it at his trigger finger, and blew it off. That was the last time I saw him.

> I had this rash that I would get in the crack of my butt and it would start me hemorrhaging. When it did, I could always get permission to leave the field and go back into base camp to have it looked at. The thing was, I could also purposely make it bleed and often did whenever I got to feeling like I wasn't going to live through the next battle. After the battle I would return to the field, but I began to notice that some of the men in my platoon started avoiding me. I knew why. It was because I wasn't sticking around to pull my weight. Man, sometimes I felt like shit but I didn't stop doing it. I was too scared not to.

Surviving

Survival guilt is common among all survivors of catastrophic events. It expresses itself in a variety of ways, but most often in the question, "Why them and not me? Why did I survive and they didn't?" People who carry survivor guilt also tend to see themselves as less deserving of life.

It was difficult to leave men behind who once stood arm-in-arm through the toughest of times; who saved our lives or carried us through heartache and the terror of battle. Combat created a marriage of heart and soul. Separation felt like abandonment and betrayal. We felt we owed one another a debt. No man begrudged another for leaving, but those leaving sometimes felt disloyal.

Goodwin[4] reports that corpsmen/medics often suffer the most painful survivor guilt. With only minimum training and knowledge they frequently performed heroic deeds on the battle field, delivering aid that saved countless lives. Still, their duties brought them into constant contact with the dead and the dying. While other soldiers had to leave the wounded to fight for the survival of the group, medics stayed to patch up bodies torn apart by war. Combat doctors and nurses who served in the Evacuation Hospitals often blamed themselves for being incompetent, even though many of the wounded were beyond medical help.

When combat units were severely decimated, lone survivors were deeply affected. John S. had been a platoon leader. During his tour he was relieved of his role by a new replacement with higher rank. He ended up walking last on a patrol he generally led. On a night mission he knew they should not have undertaken, his entire platoon was killed. Seriously wounded, he hung on to a rice paddy dike in darkness while the NVA (North Vietnamese Army) walked down the line and sliced the throats of all remaining wounded. For years he struggled with guilt, believing he was responsible for their deaths.

Although there is not always a readily available, logical explanation for why some survived and others didn't, survivors are almost always left feeling there was something more they should have done.

Combat created a marriage of heart and soul.
Separation felt like abandonment and betrayal.
We felt we owed one another a debt.

Other Issues

Combat vets are not the only ones who struggle with guilt. Vietnam Era vets feel guilty for being stationed somewhere other than Vietnam. Vietnam vets who were stationed in Vietnam, but in rear support units, often express guilt for not being in the "field." Men who escaped military service altogether feel guilty because they *didn't* serve, while others feel guilty for protesting the war. Civilians experience corporate guilt for the way they, or others, treated returning vets. Some vets also carry the guilt of a nation unwilling to bring out every soldier left behind. This kind of corporate guilt, from which there can be no realistic release, often comes from individuals transferring personal guilt to a broader cause, thus avoiding personal issues.

The Effects of Guilt

Unresolved guilt always has a devastating effect on human behavior. Research on survivors of trauma shows that those who carry guilt:[5]

- have poorer general psychological functioning during subsequent negative life experiences
- have less control over memories associated with war experiences
- suffer from frequent self-blame, shame, and condemnation
- distance themselves emotionally, socially, and physically, and live more isolated and secluded lives

- display behaviors which reflect emotional callousness
- experience a lack of social support
- have lower self-esteem and a greater sense of worthlessness
- experience more fear and paranoia
- suffer greater depression, hopelessness, helplessness, despair, rejection, and dejection
- have more compulsive, addictive, or self-medicating behaviors
- have higher rates of suicide and premature deaths
- experience an unconscious need to punish themselves
- are more sensitive to criticism
- tend to be more angry and violent

Guilt creates a false expectation of the way others will see us, thus tainting our interpretation of life. It can drive us to serve others to make up for past sins. It can lead to performance-based behaviors and addictions. Unfortunately, none of these behaviors alleviate guilt.

Bob is a vet who struggles with unresolved guilt. Even when he sleeps, he cannot escape condemnation. Haunted by repeated nightmares and intrusive memories about abandoning a young girl to the Viet Cong, he sees a therapist at the VA, takes antidepressants, antianxiety medication, and sleeping pills. Plus, he drinks heavily and uses marijuana. When he can no longer bear the pain he heads for the bars, looking for a fight he believes he can't win. This is the way he vents his frustration, and momentarily escapes pain. It is also a way he punishes himself. Although these behaviors may temporarily change the way he feels, or even compensate for feelings of powerlessness, they do nothing to resolve his guilt. In fact, they create additional guilt.

Dealing With Guilt

All the training in the world does little to prepare for the shock of taking another person's life. Nor does it prepare us for the loss of close friends. In spite of intense training, the instinct to survive often rules the moment. Considering that split-second reactions often meant the difference between life and death, mistakes in combat were all too common. There *are* reasonable justifications for many of our actions, but rationalization, an intellectual process, rarely eases heart-felt pain. Justification offers little comfort for guilt. It's hard to excuse taking an innocent life, especially the life of a woman or a child. Reared to be providers and protectors, it goes against everything men are taught.

Many humanistic psychologists and therapists say that guilt is just a problematic carryover from America's Judeo-Christian heritage. To erase guilt, they say, one needs only to erase wrong thinking developed during childhood training. Guilt, however, is more than just an emotional disturbance resulting from wrong thinking or from breaking socially agreed upon standards of behavior. Guilt results whenever we violate the sanctity of life.

As I mentioned earlier, we all have an intrinsic sense of life's value, providing our spirits with an *internal* sense of what is "right and wrong." An *external* knowledge of right and wrong is acquired through social or religious law. Scripture says:

> For when Gentiles, who do not have the law, by nature do the things contained in the law, these, having not the law, are a law to themselves; which shows that the work of the law is written in their hearts, their conscience also bearing witness, and their thoughts the meanwhile accusing or else excusing one another.[6]

When we violate our conscience we feel guilty, and rightfully so. Without the inner conviction of wrong behavior we would continue in destructive patterns. Guilt should lead us to change. Unfortunately, we have all become adept at different ways of denying, disguising, or trying to alleviate our guilt. There *is* a cleansing process, however, that sets us free from guilt and condemnation. It is called forgiveness.

Summary
There is no shortage of guilt over Vietnam. Acts committed or omitted during combat, the judgments of others, and even the fact that we survived, often created a burdensome legacy of guilt, shame, and condemnation. With this legacy has come a variety of self-destructive, hiding behaviors which have helped to create spiritual, emotional, mental, and physical death. Although true guilt creates just conviction and sorrow, inviting us to change our behaviors, unresolved guilt tortures our soul. This can drive us away from God and others. Justification and rationalization neither excuse our behaviors nor free us from guilt.

In spite of the welcome home given Desert Storm veterans, and to Vietnam veterans tacked on to the end of the parade, this issue has yet to be fully resolved in the national conscience. A reconnaissance officer, finally facing responsibility for his actions in the war, said, "I hated what I did, and I hated the war because it made me do those things. But most of all, I hated myself for doing them. *Only when I could forgive myself and my leaders* who sent me there, *did I start getting better.*"

-9-

Hooked, Line and Sinker
[ADDICTIONS]

"He found himself sliding alone into a kind of limbo, with nobody around he could talk to and no confidence left in himself. He was confused. He was smoking a lot of hash, a hit or two here and a hit or two there, buying peace on the installment plan a quarter-hour or half-hour at a time till the amount he was smoking began to worry him... he sank into depression and dreamed of suicide, a reverie that ended when he caught himself lying in bed one day wondering how he could go about doing it. A spasm of fear coursed through him. What the fuck is wrong with me?"

–David Bean[1]

"By 1977 he was drunk more often than not. He drank at home, he drank on the road, he had charge accounts at more than a dozen liquor stores. His drinking day began early. He and Patti had a daughter now, Amy, and he would get up in the morning to see her off to nursery school. By 9 a.m. he was loaded. Sometimes he would stay home and drink, sometimes drive to a beer joint. In the afternoon, he would take a nap until his family returned. Shortly before dinner, he'd start the happy hour. After the meal, he would drink until bed. He began to have blackouts; turned ugly. Once, when someone offended him at a party, he retrieved his .38 from the closet and put the gun to the man's head."

–a Vietnam veteran[2]

"Oh, so young and oh so dumb, I sold myself to fame and glory. I went alone to give myself up to war and peace, but only to miss the mark. I found myself in a river of blood, and parts of those whom I loved. Chaos and confusion was the order of every day. Don't think, don't think, just act and drink... and it will go away."

–Jim Norgaard

Addictive behavior is common among Vietnam veterans. By 1970, the Army had initiated approximately thirty-five drug and alcohol programs in stateside installations, all oriented toward prevention and rehabilitation of returning Vietnam veterans.[3] Although 76% of all veterans using hard-core *narcotics* ceased use within one year of discharge, and 90% quit later, by 1978 Vietnam veterans with *alcohol* dependencies accounted for 43% of all VA Drug Dependence Treatment Programs.[4]

This chapter examines the pervasiveness of addictive behavior among Vietnam veterans, reasons for addictive behavior, various forms of addiction, complications associated with PTSD, and some of the characteristics of people who develop addictive behaviors.

Pervasiveness Among Vietnam Veterans

Vietnam *combat veterans* exhibit substantially higher levels of alcohol consumption than any of the following: light combat vets, Vietnam era veterans, military veterans from other wars, and non-veterans. They engage in more continuous sustained drinking patterns, engage in frequent binge drinking, and drink to change mood.[5] The NVVRS Study reported: "for the nine specific psychiatric disorders assessed, other than PTSD, those that occurred most frequently among male Vietnam veterans were alcohol abuse or dependence." Lifetime rates for alcohol abuse are also significantly higher for women veterans. The *Washington Post* (1995) printed the results of a preliminary study conducted at the Washington University School of Medicine in St. Louis, which found that by their mid-40s, former enlisted men who used drugs in Vietnam were *nine times more likely to have died* than non-veterans. Even non-drug users had mortality rates three times higher than non-veterans.

For the nine specific psychiatric disorders assessed, other than PTSD, those that occurred most frequently among male Vietnam veterans were alcohol abuse or dependence.

Reasons for Use

Extensive drug use is relatively new among soldiers, although alcohol has a history of use as a combat-zone coping device. In fact, there has always been a subtle encouragement in the military to indulge in heavy drinking, particularly in rear areas removed from combat.[6] Many vets were introduced to drug use during military service.[7]

Post-traumatic stress disorder is often accompanied by polysubstance abuse. Alcohol, marijuana, barbiturates, tranquilizers, opiates, and a variety of stimulants and prescription medications are used to:
- suppress or mask symptoms of PTSD
- control pain through emotional numbing
- ward off intrusive thoughts, anxiety, and depression
- provide stimulation to overcome lack of motivation and fatigue
- combat sleeping disorders or insomnia
- escape negative feelings
- control underlying impulses toward anger and rage
- turn down the body's stress reaction response

Addictive and dependent behaviors result when people look to *external* coping mechanisms to provide relief from or mask negative *internal* issues. Drug use, however, inhibits emotional growth and character formation, and when used to avoid issues, actually delays resolution and prolongs problems.

Forms of Addictive Behavior

Addictive behaviors used to mask deeper pathologies *may* include, but are not limited to:

- workaholism and exercise
- habitual masturbation
- sexual fantasies, pornography, and sexual compulsion
- cigarettes and coffee
- overeating
- materialism, excessive or compulsive shopping
- habitual lying
- building self-esteem through excessive self-accomplishment
- television
- gambling
- religious activities

Addictive and dependent behaviors result when people look to *external* coping mechanisms to provide relief from or mask negative *internal* issues

---

Complications Associated With PTSD

What starts off as a form of self-medication can turn into a vicious cycle of abuse and dependency. Over time, drug tolerance decreases, so consumption increases. Attempts to control dependence by reducing consumption often lead to increased arousal or resurfacing of PTSD symptoms. When unwilling to deal with the issues that surface, people return to heavier drug use or try something different. The cycle of drug abuse is then renewed.[8] Drug use, which sometimes works to suppress symptoms of PTSD, eventually begins to have an opposite effect. Increased consumption produces the necessary inhibition for dissociative breaks with reality [flashbacks], and intensifies recollections of suppressed events.[9]

Characteristics of Dependent Behavior

Behaviors are the end result of a sequential process. This process is an orderly one, built on a hierarchical level. Beliefs form the foundation for all behaviors. The Bible makes reference to this pattern when it refers to "the law of the mind." Beliefs are conclusions. Often formed in infancy, they are carried throughout life. Beliefs create feelings. Feelings create desires. Desires lead to choices, and choices to behaviors/action. To understand addictions, we must understand the role each of these play in sustaining habitual behaviors.

BELIEFS > FEELINGS > DESIRES > CHOICES > BEHAVIORS

Thought Processes

We make choices based on beliefs. Sometimes choices *appear* to be based on emotions because we are overwhelmed by their intensity, yet beliefs create emotions. We may believe that:

- we must deny certain feelings because they are unacceptable,
- we can't handle our feelings or problems because we believe our selves to be inadequate,
- we will become overwhelmed by our feelings, problems, and circumstances, or
- we must rely on external rather than internal solutions to overcome our problems.

Our true beliefs are most evident in our behavior, regardless of what we say or think. Our beliefs become *rooted* in our inner being, often on a subconscious level. That is why scripture says, "As a man believes *in his heart*, so he is." Thinking and believing are not the same. Beliefs are not merely mental concepts to which we agree. We may *choose* to believe something, but that does not mean we do. We may *want* to believe, or think we *should* believe, but that doesn't mean we do. If we think we believe something but our behavior is not consistent with what we say, we are only deceiving ourselves. We may think positively or make positive confessions but little will change in the long run if neither are based on heartfelt beliefs. We often profess certain truths in order to appease our conscience, or to appease others, but if we do not *live* our lives in agreement with our statement, it is because our beliefs are entirely different.

What we truly believe is a *gut* issue; it is a part of our inner being formed early on, from which we are often far removed. Most gut reactions are learned behaviors, they are just so deeply ingrained that we believe they are instinctual. These behaviors are usually rooted in conscious choices repeated so often they are second to nature. It requires diligent self examination and the work of God's Spirit to root out our true beliefs. True beliefs become evident by examining inconsistencies between what we say we believe, and how we behave. For most of us self-examination is frightening.

Emotions and Feelings

The need to mask, deny, or in some way hide our emotions is often at the core of addictive behaviors. If we do not take steps to expose our emotions, regardless of what they are, we will never be free from them. Henry Cloud and John Townsend, in their book *Boundaries*, say:

> Feelings have gotten a bad rap in the Christian world. They have been called everything from unimportant to fleshly...

However, feelings play an enormous role in our motivation and behavior...they cannot be ignored nor placed in charge.[10]

Emotions are necessary *indicators* which exist to make us aware of the state of our life, and of our relationship to others. They help us to identify and focus on areas of need, whether for health, safety, protection or provision. We cannot heal wounds by denying they exist.

Drug use inhibits emotional growth and character formation. When used to avoid issues it actually delays resolution, prolongs and increases problems.

We are responsible for our emotions. They are created by our perceptions, whether right or wrong. Our emotions can be triggered by people or circumstances, but the truth is that they are ours, and are often activated by the choices we make. In other words, people or things do not *make* us feel anything. People who have difficulty taking ownership for their emotions generally hold others responsible for their behaviors as well. In doing so, they see themselves as victims, controlled by others. This fosters the illusion that we are not active agents of our choices. Any belief that unduly puts others in power over us, suggests to us that we are powerless. We are then able to blame others, thereby absolving ourselves of responsibility. This is called *victimization*. We always have the power to choose. If we are tied by strings to others, it is only because we allow it. We choose to be subservient to others because we want to be dependent, generally because we live in fear.

Desires

Addictive behaviors are commonly motivated by our *desire* to escape. We may want to escape fatigue, pain, boredom, anger, fear, anxiety, helplessness, hopelessness, inadequacy, and even a sense of worthlessness, all of which are *internal* conditions. *External* conditions may cause hidden emotions to surface, but they are not always the *cause* of them. Our desire to run from pain, or to substitute sensual pleasure for unpleasant emotions, originates with us.

Desires are not wrong, but how we act on them can be. For desire to be conceived, it must first find fertile ground. Then it must be watered. When desire is nurtured in our thought life, generally through fantasy, it eventually produces action. When our actions fall short of what God expects, it is called in Biblical terms, sin. Sin results in conviction. When we refuse to respond to conviction, we experience guilt. When we willfully continue in sinful behavior, whether it's because it feels good or because we believe it's necessary to our survival, we turn from inner conviction. We harden ourselves to our conscience, and to God's Spirit. When we do this, *the mind rules*, but it is motivated by our desires. When we habitually allow our mind or emotions to rule our behavior, eventually we become insensitive to God's Spirit. Insensitivity to God leads to insensitivity to others. Alienation from God produces spiritual darkness.

Walking in darkness has its pitfalls. We may not be able to find our way out. That is the trap of addictive behaviors. When we depend on external substances while suppressing internal emotions, our ability to get in touch with our self becomes like a muscle that wastes away due to lack of use. We become emotionally numb. We may lose touch with our emotions altogether. Dissociating from emotions leads to mental confusion, because in some significant way we lose touch with reality. We lose our way in life because we shut down important sensors.

We may have a predisposition toward chemical dependency but a *leaning* toward, no matter how strong the leaning, does not dictate our behavior. Choices do.

Will and Choice

Whatever the reason for our addictions/dependencies, they are *ours by choice.* Habitual behaviors are produced by repeating choices. We choose what we *will* allow to occupy our mind, what beliefs we *will* hold on to, and what behaviors we *will* do. We also choose our dependencies. We cannot rid ourselves of addictions if we *will* not. We may say we *can't,* but the truth is we *won't.* It is not an issue of powerlessness, it is one of belief. "I believe I'm unable, therefore I can't." We may be powerless, but we are never without external resources if we trust God. We may deceive ourselves, or even try to deceive others, but in the end we *do* what we want! We may have a genetic (or a spiritual) predisposition toward chemical dependency, but a *leaning* toward, no matter how strong the leaning, does not dictate our behavior. Our choices do! Once we are aware that drugs have a negative affect on us, we are free to choose whether we will continue to use them. Drugs are usually not our initial problem; they are simply used to avoid the problem. They do, however, create additional problems when we choose to take refuge in them.

Personality Characteristics

Individuals with addictive behaviors share certain characteristics. They tend to be self-reliant, mistrustful, guarded, and have problems delaying gratification. They often believe that "they must take care of their own needs, because nobody else will." Alcohol, drugs, and sex are just a few of the means used to take care of emotional needs. These same individuals can appear to be very giving. They can be sensitive and discerning. They often recognize and respond to the needs of others, but have great difficulty recognizing or admitting their own needs. Rather than ask for help, they tend to withdraw when they are in need. They are loners... if not socially, than emotionally. They suffer quietly, settling for self-pity when what they really want is to be genuinely loved. They comfort and console themselves with *things* because they are unwilling to risk painful vulnerability and allow people to comfort them. They tend to confuse walls with boundaries.

Drugs are usually not our initial problem;
they are used to avoid the problem.
They do, however, create additional problems
when we choose to take refuge in them.

Christians with addictions often hide their behaviors because they fear the judgments and rejection of other Christians. They do not fully understand grace, and they fear others will perceive them as hypocrites. They bring their performance orientation into their Christianity and transfer a lifestyle of pleasing others into pleasing God. They may look solely to God for help when what God wants is for them to humble themselves and *learn to receive* comfort and support from others. They often substitute a theology of works for God's unmerited favor, and they confuse self denial with the denial of reality. They keep their needs (perceived as weaknesses) hidden or simply struggle along alone. They may appear to have it all together. They often carry a heart-felt belief that they are unacceptable if they are anything less than perfect.

Biochemical Influences

Contemporary thought is that biochemical deficiencies in the brain are a major factor *in the development* of compulsive disorders and addictions. An imbalance of chemicals is said to result in abnormal, uncontrollable cravings for substances such as alcohol or cocaine. These neurotransmitter or neuromodulator deficits are believed to result from a number of sources, including genetic defects, toxic environmental conditions, and stress. However, recent research also shows these same deficiencies are created by the destructive effects of alcohol and drugs.[11] What is uncertain is whether critical degrees of genetic defects exist prior to alcohol and drug abuse or are created or aggravated by drug and alcohol use. It is not yet proven which comes first.

Alcohol and drugs, as well as some vitamins, minerals, and foods, are thought to provide chemicals which interact with the nervous system, blood, and brain to either stimulate or inhibit biochemical reactions which, in turn, create good "feelings" through stimulation of the reward center in the brain. Diet, nutrition, vitamin supplements, relaxation, and exercise improve brain function by supplying chemicals which build up missing supplies of serotonin, phenylalanine, dopamine, tyrosine, and norepinephrine. Although diet alone will not sufficiently restore major imbalances, certain nutritional supplements like amino acids are said to help. Individuals trying to control addictive behaviors can use nutritional supplements and should strive for a balanced lifestyle.

Summary

Statistics reveal a significant correlation between combat duty, post-traumatic stress disorder, alcohol and drug abuse, and premature death. Although the primary reasons for alcohol and drug use are associated with avoidance behaviors, drug use may also be influenced by biochemical deficits and genetic factors. In addition, drug and alcohol abusers tend to share common characteristics which further enhance unhealthy dependencies.

Whatever their underlying motivation, addictions and dependencies are fixed behaviors which further destroy confidence, self-worth, emotional peace, and relationships. We can remain stuck in our addictions or we can change. It is our choice. To be free we must examine our lives and develop an honest appraisal of our needs. We must also purpose to set aside unhealthy beliefs, thought patterns, attitudes, choices, and behavior. Although this takes courage, risk, and determination, the choice is always ours.

-10-

Bubble, Bubble,
Toil and Trouble...
[STRESS AND ANXIETY]

"I still dream about it. My wife hears me screaming in the middle of the night. I swear to God, it's so real sometimes. I feel like I'm in my dream and can't wake up. It's got to be a dream. But, God, it's here again. I'm back in Vietnam. I'm on my third tour. I only got two more months to go. Then, I'm getting shot at again, getting hit again. My rifle won't work, and then I don't have a rifle. I'm standing by myself and I don't have nothing and these fuckin' gooks are coming at me. I wake up and my stomach will be real funny-feeling. I get headaches and things."

–a Vietnam veteran[1]

War *is* hell. Fighting for one's life, with people trying to kill you every day, is extremely unnerving. War creates periods of severe deprivation, often pushing men beyond their limits. The war may have officially ended at the end of one's tour, but the lessons of war didn't. Vets carried home anxieties, fears, and deeply ingrained survival patterns. Behaviors learned in combat became automatic responses that were not easily discarded. Responses necessary for survival perpetuated a lifestyle known as the stress syndrome. What helped vets to survive in Vietnam, began to cause them to self-destruct at home. This chapter examines the stress syndrome. It explores stress and stressors, causes of stress, individual reactions to stressors, the effects of stress, the relationship of stress to clinical disorders, stress and society, and what alleviates stress.

War, Stressors, and PTSD

The cord that binds veterans to their past, is interwoven at both a conscious and subconscious level. The strength of that cord is determined by behaviors and biological reactions tied to our perception of danger. *It is threat, or the perception of threat, that creates stress*. Life for the combat vet, and in ever increasing amounts for the whole of society, is highly affected by stress.[2] It is said to be the disease of the 90s. Understanding the relationship between threat and stress is critical to understanding post traumatic stress syndrome.

PTSD is officially classified as an "anxiety disorder," yet as I have said, *disorder* is a misnomer. War, although *seemingly* normal throughout history, creates abnormal circumstances called *traumatic stressors* which induce stress. *Disorder* is created when we carry learned responses to stressors beyond the circumstances that create them.

I had never been pressed so hard, nor stretched so tight as I was in Vietnam. I lived severely exhausted: emotionally, mentally, and physically. I not only had to learn an incredible array of new skills under duress, I had to master them. As team leader for the Fire Direction Control Center of a 105mm artillery battery, the life and death of hundreds of men depended on my performance. I could not make mistakes. Besides being hard pressed by threatening circumstances, I pressed myself mentally and emotionally, trying to sort through conflicting beliefs and feelings. Even during brief periods of external calm, I often remained in turmoil. Kurt Paur, a Vietnam vet, wrote the following poem which appears throughout this chapter. It conveys the stress of combat.

It's within me, consuming me, I feel the threat of death all around. The sky flashes, the earth shakes, my heart pounds. I become a breathing sound, screams and crying all around. Is death coming to call? Is it my turn this time? I sense I have no control over this situation, life is no longer in my dreams, death is all around.

It's the dark of night, there's both comfort and fear in the darkness. I can hardly see my hand in front of my face. What's coming at me next? Will I see them before I'm seen? Flares light up the sky, shadows flashing back and forth, everything moving fast with little control, surrounded by screams, death is all around, bombs keep pounding the ground.

My life flashes before me, a million times in a second. Life is reduced to my immediate thoughts and feelings. I become each breath, each pound of my heart, my ears feeling like they'll explode with each beat. Has death come to call this time around? The earth erupts from beneath me, I feel myself lifted into the air, I hit the ground. I'm dazed, more rockets and bombs explode. Am I still in one piece? I'm covered in blood, it's puddled beneath me, scream within my ear, death is all around.

We're overrun, Charlie's come to call, it's the dark of the night. The earth shakes again, tracers flash above my head, flares light up the sky. I turn toward the screams and look into the eyes of death, I see his lungs pump. They're coming at me, I watch them fall. The earth shakes again, I hug this foreign ground.

What am I doing here? What is this for? I believed a lie, I believed I couldn't be killed, I couldn't die, that only happens to the other guy. I'm confused and consumed by hate, hate keeps me going. I can't take time to feel, I must be hard. I'm living on life's edge, death I realize is but a breath away. Only a few days left and I'm homeward bound.

Stress and Stressors

So as not to create confusion, I want to define how I am using the terms "stress" and "stressors." *Stressors* are *external events.* They are outside conditions which affect us by stimulating both internal reactions and external responses.[3] *Stress is an internal reaction,* while *behavior is an external response.* Stress reactions are often automatic. Behaviors are frequently chosen.

It is threat, or the perception of threat, that creates stress.

When we say we are under pressure, we may mean external conditions appear to be threatening or that we feel anxious and fearful. We have to clarify what "pressure" means to know where it originates, and whether we are talking about stress or stressors. Behaviors are responses to internal conditions, as well as external ones. I say this because we do not all respond the same way to the same external conditions. Neither will the same external conditions surface the same internal reactions. *It really depends on how we interpret them.*

The Stress Syndrome

Hans Selye[4] developed the concept of the stress syndrome. He called it the *General Adaptation Syndrome* (GAS) He divided it into three distinct stages: alarm, adaptation, and exhaustion. W. B. Cannon[5] later developed the concept of the "flight or fight" response, a reaction similar to Selye's *alarm* stage. These concepts are crucial to understanding the enduring effects of combat on the lives of veterans.

Selye defined stress as "the *result* of any demand upon the body," be it mental, emotional, or somatic (chemical or biological changes in the body). He said that a variety of dissimilar situations... emotional arousal, physical effort, fatigue, pain, fear, rage, concentration, humiliation, loss of blood, or even great and unexpected success, were capable of producing the same *result* (stress). Thus, no single factor could be pinpointed as the cause of the body's stress reaction. However, his research showed that regardless of the type of stressors, we all experience *identical biological changes which enable us to cope* with any type of increased demand on activity vital to our survival.

It is reasonable to assume that if there are identical biochemical changes which occur in our body in response to disturbing influences, then there are also identical emotional, mental, and spiritual responses. I say this because in creation, for every principle or law governing the visible universe (the law of gravity, physics, etc.), there is a paralleling law governing the invisible spiritual universe (faith, morality, etc.).

Not All Stress is Harmful

There are two types of stress... distress and eustress. *Eustress* is a term describing seemingly harmless or even beneficial stress. An example of eustress is tensing or stretching our muscles. When our muscles are exercised they grow in strength and mass. Human cells also grow through a process of stretching, tearing apart, and dividing. That is how they multiply. Some people excel and produce best when they are under pressure. Stress, in all of these cases, is beneficial.

When we talk about negative stress, we are talking about *distress*. Physical distress occurs when we push our muscles beyond a healthy limit. Emotional distress also occurs when we are pushed beyond normal limits of endurance.

Stress can lead to gain or loss. Its affect on us is mitigated by our appraisal, its duration, its severity, and how often it happens. Although we generally talk about stress as being unpleasant, the body's biological reaction is almost identical for pain as it is for intense pleasure.

Reactions to Stressors

Identical *external events* affect people differently because emotional temperaments, biological and psychological predispositions, personality patterns, physical characteristics, learning, history, upbringing, lifestyles and cognitive skills, differ. *Internal stress*, on the other hand, is a biological reaction which affects us all identically, although not always to the same degree. The internal effects of stress are identical because we all share common biological characteristics.

All demands on our adaptability (stressors) set in motion the same internal biological reaction (stress). Yet the primary difference in our *response* to stressors is thought to be in how we appraise, interpret, or perceive them.[6] Therefore *the meaning we assign to an event is the determining factor for how any situation affects us*. For instance, if you walk out in the dark and step on a garden hose with your bare feet and believe it to be a snake, your reaction is quite different than if you believe it to be just a garden hose. *What we believe about a situation essentially controls our feelings, and our reactions to it.*

In addition, our ability to adapt (cope) to stressors depends on our strategies, our beliefs about our capabilities, and on availability of resources. Again, individual predisposition and ability play a key role in coping. Resources can be those intrinsic to self (mental, emotional, or physical abilities) or those external to self (finances, family, friends, tools, weaponry, etc.). If the transmission on your car fails and you don't have any money to fix it, need it for work the next day, and don't have friends to help you out; then both the amount of stress you feel, and your response to it, may be totally different from someone who has the same experience but has another car to use, has the money to have the first one towed and fixed, or has friends to help him out.

Stress: A Psychophysiological Reaction

Stress is a *psychophysiological* response, meaning that it has both psychological and physiological components. Psychological components both trigger and regulate our physiology; that is, the body's numerous biochemical and structural changes. Psychological components include:

- habitual ways of viewing or interpreting events (fixed beliefs),
- habitual emotional responses, and
- habitual choices and behaviors.

Our physiology is regulated through the central nervous system which consists of the brain and spinal cord, and the peripheral nervous system which consists of the somatic and the autonomic nervous system. These systems carry sensory and motor signals to and from the brain and spinal cord to various body organs through a complex system of nerve cells and chemical messengers called neurotransmitters (catecholamines, acetylcholines, serotonin, adrenaline, noradrenaline).

Sensory receptors (eyes, ears, nose, etc.) pick up and transmit events to the brain. Thought processes retrieve stored images, memories, and interpretations of prior experiences in order to correctly interpret the event. This is all sifted through a complex soup of biologic predispositions, personality patterns, learned behaviors, and a list of available resources. Once thought processes are integrated, emotional tone is added. Once the cognitive (thinking) area and affective (emotional) area are integrated, the autonomic nervous system is activated. The nervous system then activates the hormonal and immune systems. The release of overlapping hormones like adrenaline affect all other organs in the body. These processes are interrelated and feed back into each other, often accelerating the stress response and working to prolong it. The sequence is as follows:

Stress Sequence

an event happens
v
sensory receptors transmit event to the brain
v
the brain triggers images, memories, and prior conclusions
v
fixed beliefs lead to an interpretation of the event
v
our interpretation triggers either positive or negative emotions
v
emotions trigger the hypothalamus, a small regulatory center in the brain
v
hypothalamus triggers nervous System, vascular System, and glands
v
glands release chemicals which activate body organs and tissue
v
If the event is interpreted as life threatening, the body responds with a coping behavior, either fight or flight. When extreme fear is triggered, immobilization or death may result.

The Effects of Stress

We can see that stress is more than an emotional reaction, muscular tension or a biological, chemical event. Stress influences every area of our life. While some of the *effects* of stressors are clearly measurable, especially biological reactions, many lie outside the realm of objective, scientific measures. Mental confusion, emotional pain, or spiritual bankruptcy, although clearly observable in expression and behavior, are impossible to measure in any tangible way.

Although physical well-being is not the primary indicator of health, perhaps stress can be best measured by what goes on in the body. The absence of disease is a limiting, unsatisfactory measure of how well we are doing. It does not measure the degree of peace or joy we experience or how well we get along with others. Nor is it an indication of the quality of life we experience in spite of physical illness.

The unique feature of stress is that when it produces dysfunctional behavior, the behavior needs to be specifically and clearly identified in order to clearly identify internal effects, and their cause. When work performance (behavior) deteriorates, it could be caused by anxiety, depression, conflict, fatigue, indifference, or possibly even fear (emotional and mental features). Determining what is going on internally is thus essential to altering its effect (behavior). *To alter what goes on internally, we must identify and alter our perceptions.*

Stress produces immediate and long lasting identifiable effects. You may recognize some of them as I go through Selye's stages. Perhaps they will help you determine whether you are experiencing acute or prolonged stress. They may also help you determine to what extent you may be suffering from PTSD.

The meaning we assign to an event is the determining factor in how any situation affects us. What we believe about a situation essentially controls our feelings and our reactions to it.

The Alarm Stage

Selye called the body's initial response to "disturbing influences" the *alarm* stage. When external events are seen as threatening, *whether they are or not*, the body activates itself to neutralize or repair the disturbance (thinking the garden hose is a snake, the body reacts as if it were a snake). This activation is a general *call to arms* of the body's defense mechanism. It speeds throughout the body like an electric shock, activating the autonomic nervous system, the neuroendocrine system, and the psychoimmune system. The autonomic nervous system (ANS) mobilizes the body through the sympathetic nervous system (SNS), to prepare it for muscular activity.

The SNS, thought to be sympathetic to our needs, prepares and sustains our body for fight or flight. Activation of the SNS takes place within 1/100 of a millisecond in an explosive reaction which might be compared to a shotgun blast or a beehive round. Over one-thousand different physical reactions occur within this time frame. What the body experiences is an adrenaline rush which feels like an electric shock.

Toxic substances (poisons), regardless of their source (disease, food, stress, chemicals), produce an autonomic response. Excess cold or heat, infections, hemorrhage, nervous irritation, trauma, stress, and stimulants produce the same autonomic response as toxins. Different situations have the same potential to be toxic because they produce identical patterns of change in the body. When repeatedly faced with demands to ward off disease or perceived threat, invariably the body develops specific *signs of damage*. These signs of damage are now recognized by the medical community as leading *indicators of stress*. During the alarm stage the body reacts in the following ways:

Pituitary Gland
releases:
> endorphins (for pain control), chemicals which signal adrenal glands, antidiuretic hormones (causes kidneys to retain water), and growth and reproductive hormones

increases:
> blood volume, blood pressure (more oxygen), thyroid stimulation, and calcium, potassium, and sodium levels

Adrenal Gland
releases:
> adrenaline (epinephrine), noradrenaline (norepinephrine), and ketone

increases:
> heart rate, cardiac output and respiration, sugar and fat in the blood, and protein metabolism

decreases urine formation and reduces immune system responsiveness

Brain
alters the immune system

releases neuropeptides (important in pain reduction)

causes release of adrenaline and noradrenaline (think more clearly)

Cardiovascular System
constricts:
> arteries (less blood lost if we become wounded or injured), and muscles around blood vessels (making them smaller)

increases:
> heart rate, force of contractions, blood pressure, blood flow to deep muscles in the legs, heart, and brain, cholesterol and fatty acids in the blood, and blood coagulation (to prevent blood loss)

increases:
> risk of coronary spasm, thrombosis formation, hypertension, and sudden death from arrhythmia and myocardial ischemia/fibrillation

reduces:
> blood flow to kidneys, intestines, and extremities (face may turn white, hands turn cold, skin temperature drop)

Kidneys
decreases:
> urine formation (to prevent infection if abdominal injury occurs)
> blood volume through kidneys (decreased cleansing of toxins)

Digestive System
increases:
> motility, acid secretion, and constriction of intestine (urge to defecate)

decreases:
> muscle movement responsible for digestion, normal bowel movement (reduces risk of infection from abdominal injuries), appetite, and mucus secretion (stomach/intestinal walls less protected from acids)

constricts:
> blood vessels in the lining of the stomach and intestines (prevents deep internal bleeding)

Immune System
increases:
> suppression of the immune system, activity in lymph nodes, tonsils and Peyer's patches in intestines, interferon production, and antibodies to Epstein-Barr virus (mononucleosis)

decreases:
> responsiveness of the thymus, spleen, and bone marrow, response of T lymphocytes, suppression of herpes virus, natural killer cell activity, immunoglobulin production (suppresses bacterial/virus infections), phagocytosis of bacteria, and white blood count (alters response to viruses and cancer cells)

Musculoskeletal System
increases:
> muscle tension without muscle movement, muscle contraction (fortifying "body armor"), muscle tension which pulls on vertebra and which constricts sensitive nerve endings (inflames nerve tissue), muscle strength, and glycogenolysis

Nervous System
increases:
> activation of central nervous system (brain/spinal cord) and peripheral nervous system (activates nerves to skeletal muscles and sensory systems of skin), activation of the sympathetic nervous system (releases adrenaline, noradrenaline, acetylcholines, serotonin, neuropeptides, endorphins, and substance P: chemical transmitters which stimulate or shut down body organs) and parasympathetic nervous system

Other
increases:
> dilation of pupils (aiding vision) and sensory capabilities (hearing, touch), dilation of bronchi in lungs and rate of breathing (provides more oxygen), conversion of glycogen to bile in liver, the release of glucose in the liver, bladder contractions (stimulates uncontrolled urination), sweat gland production (clammy hands, profuse sweating), and basal metabolism (provides strength and energy)

decreases flow of saliva in mouth (dry mouth)

Besides the immediate reaction of the body's nervous system, we also react on an emotional, intellectual, and behavioral level. During the alarm stage we may experience any of the following:

Emotional Reactions
anticipation, excitement, euphoria, calm
anger, frustration, edginess, irritability
fear, anxiety, hyperalertness, hypervigilance, panic
grief, hopelessness, helplessness, depression, despair

Mental Reactions
clarity, concreteness, increased concentration, alertness,
rapid processing of thoughts
dissociation, breaks with reality, forgetfulness
confusion, disorientation, and insomnia

Willful Reactions (choices)
stand, fight, resist
run, avoid, deny, suppress, withdraw, isolate
yield, follow, give in, give up

Adaptation

Following the alarm stage the body enters a stage of *adaptation* or *resistance*. A continual state of alarm has severe consequences. Selye's research showed that when external situations are so drastic that continual exposure to them becomes incompatible with life, the organism being attacked dies. This is what occurs during a heart attack, stroke, heat exhaustion, or death by fright. During adaptation, the body works to bring itself back to a state of homeostasis (normal balance, stability).

To prevent "burn out," and to help the body recover from stress, the parasympathetic nervous system (PNS) is activated. The PNS works to bring the body back to normal. Unlike the shotgun response of the SNS, the PNS acts like a rifle shot, shutting down body organs one at a time, slowly bringing the body back to its normal state. Whereas the SNS acts automatically, without purposeful direction from the mind, the influence of the PNS on the body can be assisted through thought processes, choices, and modifications in behavior. The natural process of recovery can be speeded up by exercises that help us to relax, by assigning different meaning to circumstances, and by controlling obsessive thinking. These behaviors also help change the way we feel.

During adaptation the reactions of body organs, and their chemical manifestations, are often exactly *opposite* of what occurs during alarm. This is a result of the body's natural tendency to resist destructive changes which occur during extended states of *hypervigilance*. If your breathing becomes rapid and heavy when alarmed, it will slow down as the body begins to adapt. Deactivation of the SNS is experienced in the following ways:

Body Systems
increased:
flow of saliva, liver function, production of urine, release of bile in liver, and appetite, stimulation of peristalsis and secretion of stomach acids
decreased:
adrenal cortical and sympathetic nervous system activity, heartbeat, contraction of bladder and constriction of pupils, medulla oblongata in brain, and bronchi in lungs

Emotional, Mental, and Willful Reactions
peace, calm, rest, organized systematic thought pattern, clarity

It is important to remember that we can intervene at this stage to help our body recover from hypervigilance and increased arousal. If we feed the stress reaction, allowing our mind and emotions to sustain a state of hypervigilance, we will eventually exhaust ourselves.

Exhaustion

We go through alarm and adaptation stages repeatedly during the normal course of life. But, when the human body is continuously exposed to life-threatening events, *or even perceived threats,* the body's ability to adapt begins to break down and crumble. At this point the body enters a third stage called *exhaustion.* When repeatedly exposed to real *or imagined* stressors we eventually begin to use up our adaptation energy. We wear down emotionally, mentally, and physically. Our body can literally wear out as body organs break down. We call these breakdowns diseases. Disease occurs because organs become dysfunctional.

Prolonged, severe stress doesn't just affect the body, it also produces dysfunctional emotional and mental conditions. Extreme or continuous stress puts life in jeopardy. Once we lose the ability to return to normalcy, stress becomes chronic. Adrenaline and noradrenaline levels remain high and the excess stimulation damages body organs and tissue.

Exhaustion *always* follows when demands on the body are severe or prolonged. Because exhaustion always occurs under constant stress, Selye believes that the body's adaptation energy is limited. We do not know precisely what the body loses, but we do know it's not just caloric energy. Just as any inanimate machine gradually wears out, so does the human body. Our reserve of adaptable energy can therefore be compared to a bank account from which we can make withdrawals, but to which we cannot make deposits. Sleep and rest can nearly restore adaptability, but Selye says *complete restoration is probably impossible.* Every biological reaction to stress leaves some irreversible chemical scar, and prolonged, severe trauma can forever alter one's coping ability. Although normal wear and tear on the body accumulates to constitute aging, the aging process can be rapidly accelerated by excessive stress. Perhaps this is why so many veterans came home feeling like they had aged beyond their years. Indicators of exhaustion are:

Physical Breakdown
diminished range of breathing, dizziness, and nausea
weight loss
exacerbation of hypertension and hyperactivity
deep, bleeding ulcers in stomach and upper intestines (colitis)
long term elevation of adrenaline, noradrenaline, cortisol, and
other steroids (produces blocked arteries, enlarges adrenal
glands, and destroys heart muscle tissue)
increased fat deposits, cholesterol levels, and blood clotting
(increases risk of stroke, coronary artery spasms, heart disease)
musculoskeletal disorders (arthritis, back pain, fatigue)
shrinking of thymus, spleen, lymph nodes, lymphatic structures
immune system impairment (increased vulnerability to disease)
sleep disorders (associated with adrenaline overstimulation)
oversleeping (caused by depression or exhaustion)
impotence and low sexual arousal
decreased estrogen production and irregular menstrual cycles
tremulousness (trembling of the hands)
persistent physical weakness due to adrenal burn-out
evolving disturbances in neurotransmitter functioning
(depletion or increased sensitization of receptor systems created
by chronic adrenal activity)

Emotional Breakdown
deterioration of coping skills, low confidence and self-worth
absence of ambition, apathy, low motivation, passivity, and
hopelessness
restlessness, distractibility, irritability, low tolerance of emotions,
crowds, noise, and movement
emotional numbing, withdrawal, despair, and clinical depression

Mental Breakdown
mental confusion/disorganization, inability to concentrate or
process information, loss of problem-solving, and reduced deci-
sion-making ability
attention-deficit, memory loss, and accident-prone behavior
intrusive thoughts, images, sensations or feelings (flashbacks),
nightmares,
preoccupation with traumatic memories, and fear of recurrences
dissociative breaks, catatonic stupors, suicidal ideation, and psy-
chosis

Breakdown of the Will
give up, quit trying, passivity

The Influence of Stress on Clinical Disorders
Because physical, emotional, and mental reactions occur under
severe stress, all illness has a psychological component. No disease is
exempt from psychological influence, and all disease has some influence

on how we think and feel. John Sandford writes, "When we abuse our bodies through over-work, stress, fatigue, drugs, or poor hygiene we suffer more than physically. Our body 'on tilt' affects our entire system."[7] The functions of our being are inseparably linked and thus influence one another. This cross-influence cannot be measured entirely in laboratory experiments, but medical research does point to a number of stress-related or stress-induced clinical disorders. These disorders are classified into four major areas: somatic (physical), affective (emotional), cognitive (mental), and behavioral disorders. Somatic disorders also have three subgroups called: psychosomatic, psychophysiologic, and tissue and organ pathologies.[8] Stress either induces or contributes to the following disorders:

nocturnal dyspnea and severe dysphoria
chronic brain syndromes
sudden cardiac death, heart arrhythmias, heart "fluttering"
contraction band necrosis (damaged heart muscle)
migraine headaches and muscle contraction (tension) headaches
Raynauds Disease (spasms in hands and feet)
musculoskeletal disorders, chronic back pain, and arthritis
angina pectoris (pressure and pain in chest which radiates to
    neck, jaw, left shoulder and left arm, occasionally right arm)
coronary artery spasm (a result of constriction of blood vessels)
atherosclerosis (weakening of arteries caused by fatty deposits)
essential hypertension (non-organic high blood pressure)
platelet aggregation (increased blood clots)
gastrointestinal disorders (highly responsive to stress and abuse,
    they account for 40% of all medical appointments)
stomach ulcers and duodenal peptic ulcers
irritable bowel syndrome (stomach pain, constipation, bloating)
colitis (inflammation or swelling of colon)
esophageal spasm (difficulty swallowing, eating, some choking
    due to leaking of stomach acid back into the esophagus)
globus hystericus (having a "lump" in the throat)
asthma
rheumatoid arthritis (destruction of cartilage and bone)
systemic lupus erythematosus (destruction of DNA, blood ves-
    sels, skin and kidneys)
myasthenia gravis (destruction of muscle cell receptor)
multiple sclerosis (destruction of nerve myelin sheath)
juvenile diabetes (destruction of insulin-producing cells)
clenching and bruxism (tightening of jaw muscles and grinding
    of teeth)
muscle tension and spasms (increased tension disorder)
torticollis (head chronically rotated to one side by contraction
    of neck muscles)
phobias and ego-alien aggressive thinking patterns
obsessive-compulsive disorders, excessive checking behaviors
clinical depression (manic depression, major depression, endog-
    enous depression, and suicide)

chronic anxiety neurosis, generalized anxiety, panic disorders

affective psychoses, antisocial personality development, and schizophrenia

alcoholism, drug dependency, extreme defensive avoidant behaviors, and post-traumatic stress disorder [9]

The Relationship of Spirit to Health

If disease and wellness has a psychological component, then both have a spiritual component as well since our inner being consists of soul and spirit. The Bible makes many references to the influence of our spirit, and God's Spirit, upon our well-being. The Book of Hebrews says:

> The word of God is living and powerful, and sharper than any two-edged sword. It pierces deep enough to discern and divide between the soul and the spirit, even to the joints and marrow. It knows and reveals the thoughts and intents of our heart.[10]

God's Spirit (the living word) acts in our life to help us differentiate between the influence originating from our soul, and that of our spirit. The inner working of our being is not hidden from God, even to the point that He sees its influence on our body. You can look no deeper than the marrow of the bone. It is inside the inside of our insides.

The implication is that both soul and spirit influence our physical health. The reference to bone and marrow is important because the bone marrow affects every area of our physical health. It is the bone marrow which produces millions of blood cells each second. Blood cells, in turn, are responsible for carrying all the oxygen and nutrition the body needs for cell growth and reproduction. They also carry hormones, distribute body heat, and carry off all toxins produced by waste products. White blood cells undergird our immune system. They resist disease by fighting infections. They kill germs, viruses, bacteria, cancer cells, parasites, and other harmful organisms. When blood cells break down, the body breaks down. David, in the Psalms, correlates the condition of our bone marrow to the health of our soul. Job does the same, contrasting a healthy soul to a soul made unhealthy by bitterness. Proverbs equates trust in God to health, and equates health to the marrow of the bone.

Spiritual Influence

Our spirit not only influences our life, but can itself be influenced. Our spirit can be willing, perceptive, moved, troubled, provoked, fervent, purposeful, bound, knowledgeable, disquieted, faithful, a source of wisdom, revelation, and love, and can rejoice, sigh, and worship.[11] Our spirit can also be sorrowful, broken, wounded, crushed, unclean, and asleep.[12] It can remain unawakened due to lack of love and nurturing from our primary caretakers. It can also be crushed through abuse and trauma.

A wounded spirit is dysfunctional just like anything *else* that is crippled. A wounded spirit does not fully perform the way God intended, and that has a negative affect on our health. If our spirit knows we were unwanted at birth, it may send an internal message to the rest of the body to shut down and resist life. Because our spirit resides in the inner man, these messages first influence the innermost structure of our body. We may function much of our life on the strength of our own human will and intellect, but invariably, when our strength gives out, our body can begin to break down and our health can quickly deteriorate. We may develop major life-threatening diseases or emotional and mental disorders. We may end up despairing of life.

God gives to each believer a new beginning by renewing our spirit with His. When our spirit is regenerated (regened, so to speak), we have *the potential* for the rest of our life to be reshaped. However, our spirit can remain in a state of infancy because of continual willful behavior contrary to God's purpose, or because we do not allow ourselves to be loved or nurtured. Sandford says that a "slumbering" spirit is evidenced by: one's neglect of prayer or a devotional life, an inability to worship or praise God fully, repeated patterns of falling into sin, lacking a true conscience, an inability to gain understanding or insight from one's past experiences, and an inability to see into the future with any degree of hope.[13]

The Effects of Stress on Specific Features of PTSD:

Hypervigilance

Doctors at a hospital in a violent New York City neighborhood reported that children who were victims of random violence, had witnessed violent crimes, or had lived in a place where gunshots were constant, developed a heightened sense of hearing and could hear gunfire from long distances. To protect themselves, these children had become hyperaware of loud sounds. Thus, they were easily startled and constantly on guard. However, their hyper-awareness created an inability to tune out background noises which soon interfered with their ability to sleep, concentrate in school, and function normally.[14] These children, to some degree, are like Vietnam veterans.

Research shows that even among the most stable personalities, hypervigilance temporarily follows involvement in events which produce emotional shock.[15] Recovery is usually slow for survivors, and many exhibit symptoms of hypervigilance for weeks following. Prolonged periods of extreme watchfulness, alertness, or the jitters, also reoccur each time the victim is reminded of how close he came to being badly injured. Studies indicate that the most intense, prolonged symptoms of hypervigilance occur among:
- survivors who were close to actual danger
- those who narrowly escaped serious injury
- those who lost close relatives or friends
- those who saw maimed bodies, and
- people with defensive or avoidant behavior patterns.

Once hypervigilance occurs, it is easily sustained by:

- deadline pressures
- a lack of contact with family members or other supportive people
- restricted activities
- lack of perceived control over events
- sudden unexpected events
- a failure to act vigilantly about early warning signs, and
- not developing coping skills.[16]

The primary factor in mediating hypervigilance seems to be a change in attitude concerning personal vulnerability. Simply put, once you open up, stop isolating, and receive comfort, you get healthier quicker.

Intrusive Thoughts and Imagery

Intrusive thoughts and imagery, often called *flashbacks*, are recurrent, persistent, involuntary ideas, images, recollections, or impulses associated with traumatic events which invade one's consciousness. Horowitz says, "One experience of a single, very intense image is similar in effect to multiple experiences of less intense, only mildly disturbing images. Those who experience bereavement (significant loss), experience intrusive recollections relatively similar to those who suffer personal injury or who have had near fatal experiences."[17] Intrusive symptoms are virtually universal among survivors of trauma. Distressful conditions lead to significantly higher levels of intrusive/obsessive thinking which, in turn, create additional stress.

Dr. James L. McGraugh, a psychologist at the University of California, Irvine, reports in his studies of compulsive and addictive sexual behavior, "When the body is intensely stimulated, either by pornography, masturbation, or a combination of these, it releases epinephrine from the adrenal gland which imprints an intense memory of the experience on the person's mind."[18] Images imprinted during heightened sexual experience are retained, and tend to recur in the form of fantasies. If an "imprinting" takes place when epinephrine is released during heightened body stimulation, it is logical to assume that combat experiences are imprinted in the same manner.

Because of the overwhelming, intense feelings which generally accompany intrusive memories, intrusive experiences often lead to avoidance behaviors like suppression or denial. Trauma survivors often go through a "period of latency" where recollections are suppressed because of an inability to tolerate emotional pain associated with them. Months or years later, intrusive thoughts can be triggered by relatively minor events. Intrusive experiences are known to persist for years following trauma.

Intrusive thoughts may be a result of incomplete healing. We may think we have left the past behind, but if there is unresolved conflict associated with an event, we remain tied to the emotional residue, attitudes, and meaning (or lack of meaning) we attached to it. We can flip-flop between periods of intrusive recollections and denial, if we have never taken the necessary steps to confront the past and work through it. Healing takes time. Working through trauma takes courage.

It's fifteen years later, I'm in the States. I carry the wounds of our country's insults. Don't they know the price that was paid? I stay awake at night, I relive in my mind the horrors of walking through mine fields of wounded and dead, the twisted bodies, the rolling eyes. How could God allow such cruelty? Don't they realize? Don't they care? Don't they know?

It's the dark of the night. I sit in fear, adrenaline pumping. It took this long for me to realize I should have been afraid, I should have feared more, but only now I realize how many times I could have died. I sit in awe and wonder why... why I'm still alive. *How many times do I have to relive those nights*?

-Kurt Paur

Sleep Disorders

Sleep disorders are common among survivors of trauma and those who experience high levels of distress. Chronic sleep disturbances are divided into two categories: 1) disturbances in the amount, quality, and timing of sleep: insomnia, hypersomnia and sleep-wake schedule disturbances and, 2) abnormal events occurring during sleep or between the threshold of sleep and awakening: nightmares and sleep terror.

The first category of sleep disorders (insomnia) is generally associated with increased states of arousal, such as hypervigilance. These disorders stem from chronic stress patterns developed in Vietnam. Night was a time of heightened vulnerability and often required vigilant guard duty. It was prime time for assaults on fire bases and rocket or mortar attacks. It was not uncommon for combat vets to stay awake all night and sleep when the sun came up.

The second category of sleep disorders (parasomnia) includes nightmares and recurrent dreams of a traumatic nature: being shot at, being back in Vietnam, being pursued but unable to run, having an empty weapon in battle, or, they may not be combat specific, but often contain themes of general dread or helplessness.

Studies comparing poor sleepers to good sleepers, note that poor sleepers show elevated levels of heart rate, respiration, and electrodermal activity, all signs of elevated physiological arousal associated with distress.[19] The inability of veterans with PTSD to shift from a state of arousal to a state of rest, either asleep or awake, keeps them from replenishing necessary energy resources. Lack of sleep and rest eventually leads to exhaustion and depressed mental and emotional states.

Michael Irwin, a psychiatrist at the San Diego VAMC, discovered that 80% of the men who did not get a regular, good-night sleep, suffered a subsequent drop in the production of "natural killer cells." These white blood cells root out and destroy viral infections. People who suffer chronic insomnia go through life with their immune system defenses strained, and do not rebound easily from sickness. The good news was that for those studied, the deficit was short lived and restored following normal sleeping patterns. *Chronic* sleep disturbance patterns, however, were not evaluated.

Sleep disorders, like intrusive experiences, are invasions of our conscious mind by issues carried on a subconscious level. They are generally associated with hypervigilance and unresolved trauma. Disturbances tend to increase during periods of crisis or distress, but also occur during war-related anniversaries and seasonal changes paralleling war-time experience. Like intrusive experiences, they often occur in cycles. Scripture contains several examples of individuals with sleep disturbances similar to those experienced by Vietnam veterans.

In the Psalms, David struggled with some unresolved issues of his own, saying, "I will not give sleep to my eyes or slumber, until I find a place for the Lord." Perhaps worry, anxiety, or even fear, led Solomon to say, "The sleep of the working man is pleasant, whether he eats little or much; but even the full stomach of a rich man does not allow him to sleep." Solomon, troubled by his subconscious, wrote, "I was asleep, but my heart was awake." And Daniel wrote, "Now in the second year of the reign of Nebuchadnezzar, he had dreams, and his spirit was troubled, and his sleep left him." You cannot run from your past anymore than you can run from yourself, for wherever you go, there it is.

Exaggerated Startle Response and Avoidance Behaviors

Exaggerated startle responses and avoidance behaviors are also associated with stress and physiological arousal.[20] Startle responses result from learned conditioning. In combat, explosions, gunfire, booby-traps and a myriad of other noises were associated with loss, or near loss of life. When combat ended, the conditioning continued. Vets still pair loud and unexpected sounds with danger. This makes them uncomfortable in environments with too many sounds. They feel vulnerable as the result of sensory overload. Overstimulation causes fear of not being able to identify warning signs. As a result their stress level rises, adrenaline begins stimulating sensory awareness, and they soon find themselves in a state of hypervigilance. An aversion to crowds develops, and therefore an avoidance of apartment stores, sporting events, or other areas where people congregate.

Research concludes, "The degree to which environmental stimulation is perceived to be *predictable and controllable,* influences the extent to which it induces stress in the individual."[21] For each person there is an optimum level of stimulation beyond which task performance, cognitive functioning, aesthetic pleasure, and physiological health begins to deteriorate. For combat vets, this threshold can be very low. Many vets *feel* unsafe in any situation not under their control. Their need for space, socially and environmentally, is tied to their need for safety.

Although space and safety are important to mental and emotional health, distancing ourselves from others, and from our own feelings, has negative effects. People with silent ischemia, stress-related heart diseases and some forms of cancer, also tend to create significant distance between their feelings and experiences, and between their thoughts and feelings.[22] These people also have a distinct inability to get in touch with feelings. If you ask them what they are *feeling,* they generally tell you what they are *thinking*. These same individuals often have additional problems with addictive and compulsive behavior, both of which are associated with lifestyles of denial, avoidance, and social or emotional isolation.

Janis and Mann[23] say that when under stress, people who have been traumatized often feel compelled to take immediate protective action even if they are unaware of anything directly threatening them. Their increased physiological arousal leads them to engage in *unwarranted* fighting or reactionary violence. Excessive physiological arousal also causes them to respond to minor threats with excessive force.

> It's twenty years later, the first ten years passed away and are but a haze. I bought the lie. That conflict between love and hate, it's been with me now for twenty years. My heart too hard to love or trust; only a few people that I would consider a friend. Afraid to let go or afraid to have a soft heart. I think if I let the hate go I will lose my edge, the instinct to react won't be there if needed. I build walls around me and bunker myself in with sandbags, afraid to feel, afraid to love. I'm consumed by pain. Is life worth living? I bought the lie. It's the dark of night.
>
> -Kurt Paur

Stress and Society

We live in a society preoccupied with material success and its stressful lifestyle. In addition, we experience stressful biological influences common to us all: aging, noise, genetic disorders, pollutants, physical injury, lack of exercise, improper diet, mental retardation, and insufficient rest and relaxation. We also experience common psychological stressors like: anger, guilt, loneliness, depression, anxiety, mental illness, poor self concept, real or perceived loss of control, poor cognitive skills, low tolerance, high frustration levels, an unwillingness to delay gratification, and a growing inability to cope.

Combine PTSD and environmental and social stressors and you have an explosive situation. Our society is stress ridden with: unemployment, lack of social and family ties, poor job skills, poor education, insufficient funds, higher prices, the demands of a success-oriented society, dysfunctional families, time pressures, deadlines, increased violence, gang warfare, drive-by shootings, growing sexual and physical abuse, increase in divorce, intermarriage, moving, changing jobs, finding new careers, loss of spouse or children, imprisonment, natural disasters, and an unending list of daily hassles. Even with strong spiritual, social, and family resources, the most healthy among us are not immune to stress. How much more the combat vet whose coping mechanisms may have been irreparably damaged. Where is their hope?

Alleviating Stress

The Veterans Administration has tried a number of therapies, programs, and philosophies in an attempt to treat PTSD, some with merit, many without. A number of stress-reducing methods are used in the medical and therapeutic community to treat anxiety: drugs, communication skills, cognitive restructuring, self-help techniques, self-talk, altered self-perception, hypnosis, behavior modification, exercise, diet, weight loss, biofeedback therapy, meditation, breathing techniques, progressive relaxation techniques, guided imagery, exposure therapy, humor therapy, didactic, group and individual therapy, and others. Many of these treatment methods have overtones of humanism, the occult, and eastern mystical, metaphysical religions. They also have limited results. What has proven to be the cheapest and most effective means of *preventive* medicine is a person's ability to minimize stress and maximize relaxation. This generally requires environmental and lifestyle changes, which are not always possible. What then?

Moving Toward Healing

The information discussed so far may be new to you. Then again, it may not. You may identify with some of the issues, or with so many that you feel overwhelmed. You may simply be saying, "I've heard all this before, so what?" So decide what action, if any, you want to take. Knowledge is of little use *if it is not applied*. Applying what we know is the hard part, but it is well worth it if it leads to our healing.

If you are uncomfortable being labeled, put into the diagnostic box of PTSD and left without working solutions, there is an answer. I struggled with PTSD and the VA for nearly twenty years trying to make sense of the bondage I was in. I have four inches of medical records documenting my struggle. In some ways these records represent twenty years of pain, self effort, stubbornness, self-reliance, rebellion, and unbelief. But, in spite of myself, God patiently waited for me to turn to Him for healing. And, when I was willing He always showed up. I could have chosen to avoid God's plan for my life by living with chronic emotional pain, anger, and stress, but I didn't. Although healing doesn't come easy, and freedom doesn't come cheap, I chose both.

We can carry the baggage of Vietnam or we can actually experience a change of heart... heart surgery if you will. God said that he would take from us a "heart of stone," and replace it with a "heart of flesh," if only we would let Him. Kurt's poem, like my life, remains unfinished, but it does hold the key:

I lay drunken on the floor, I can't drink enough to remove the pain. I call out... Jesus, God, please help me! It's twenty-one years later and life has just begun. I remove my foot from the door and let Jesus enter my perimeter...

Summary

Stress is a complex combination of external stressors and internal reactions which interact to affect us all. People who live in constant danger, or in a state of distress, live on the verge of constant physiological activation. The application of Selye's research to PTSD is unquestionable. The very nature of war produces conditions which subject soldiers to repeated, severe, prolonged life-threatening situations. When stressful events are repeated above a critical level, they always have a damaging effect.[24] It is highly unlikely that any combat veteran was not emotionally, mentally, or physically affected in some way by their tour of duty. Many veterans still live with those effects today. The VA may say that PTSD is incurable, but it is not. *Nothing is impossible with God.*

PART III

HEALING

-11-

About Face!

[A NEW DIRECTION]

"I thought about that day, and other such times of help coming from the most unexpected sources, when I was asked to tell about my faith in the summer of 1973 after Red came home. I wondered, how do you put into a few words that gradual awareness of God's voice speaking, of God's hand working, until it becomes a sure, steady knowledge of His love? How do you explain His power to work best when we feel most helpless? Just before my part on the program the soloist sang, 'Through It All.' I thought the words expressed my spiritual experiences far better than anything I had planned to say, and so I began my testimony: 'Through it all I learned to trust. . . I would underscore the word *learned*.' There were times when God seemed far away."

–wife of Red McDaniels, POW[1]

"In the game of life there are no substitutes. The path that we voluntarily take must be lived out by our self, and the road we choose must be seen as the ministry we have to offer to other men."

–Martin Luther

Post-traumatic stress disorder does not go away with time! Research suggests that symptoms associated with chronic PTSD get progressively worse. They also become increasingly independent and self-sustaining. When PTSD goes untreated it creates concurrent or delayed emergence of other disorders. At particular risk are: obsessive-compulsive disorders, dysthymia, major and manic depression, panic disorders, generalized anxiety disorder, phobias, alcoholism and drug dependence, antisocial personality disorders, somatization disorders, and endogenous depression. As PTSD symptoms get worse, other disorders are sustained apart from PTSD.[2]

Healing for any disorder requires treatment, yet not all treatment produces satisfying results. If the methods we try are unsuccessful, we should try something else. Successful people maintain the same basic qualities *they had as infants*... they take risks, don't fear making mistakes, and try new behaviors. We need to be more like children, while not being childish, and take the necessary risks to find our healing.

Existing Treatment

The NVVRS reported in 1990 that only 4% of those suffering from

PTSD made use of programs offered by the Veterans' Administration. There are a variety of reasons for this. The VA's philosophy has been, the best you can do is learn how to modify your behaviors... PTSD is incurable. The VA offers education to alter thinking, antidepressants and psychotropic medications to alter feelings, and programs to help control behaviors, but they offer nothing that changes the spirit or alters one's nature. That is why PTSD never goes away.

I believe in biomedicine and the use of psychotropic medications to combat destructive behavior. Chemical imbalances in the body affect mental and emotional processes, just like mental and emotional imbalances create destructive chemical changes in the body. Food and nutrients are chemicals. They change mood and energy, and therefore alter behavior. But not all change promotes healing. Drugs sometimes reduce the severity of symptoms associated with disorders, making it easier to promote internal changes that must occur, but they also produce disabling side effects and mood changes which sometime make treatment difficult. Drugs, without internal change, only create chemical dependency. If you are not committed to self-examination, or to working through your issues, drugs only prolong the problem and ultimately make it worse. Prolonged drug treatment only results in a lifetime of dependency. That is bondage, not freedom.

The Path to Effective Treatment

Invariably, we all come to forks in the road where we are given the opportunity to change direction. When faced with the choice, saying yes to one path always means saying no to the other. Some paths, like some choices, create insignificant change. Other times, the results of our choices are monumental. When Eve ate from the Tree of the Knowledge of Good and Evil, she was essentially believing that she could determine for herself, by acquiring knowledge, what the best path was for her. When Adam ate of the fruit she presented him, he was also deciding that he knew what was best for him. Rather than either of them depending on God for direction, moral guidance, or whatever they needed to live a full and satisfying life, they determined to rule their own destiny. We have inherited their self-reliance and the insecurity and self-centeredness that goes with it. Had they known only good, God would have appeared less distant and His path seemingly less fearful. We too can live as Adam and Eve, relying on our perspective and the accumulated wisdom of our own intellectual pursuit. Or we can turn to God for His.

Consider one of the lessons we were taught in Vietnam. Because the VC understood human nature, they knew that grunts who were dead tired from humping through the bush all day would be tempted to take a well-worn path when they came across it. A well-traveled path is easier to walk down. That's what makes it attractive! Knowing this, the VC planted trip wires, mines, and booby-traps. It was also a good place to set up ambushes. When a patrol leader came to the well traveled path, he had to make a decision. He knew a less-traveled path was harder; it required sustained perseverance and endurance to walk it. But he also had enough experience to know that the easy path was often the most dangerous, and sometimes the road to tragedy. Experienced Pointmen sometimes learned the hard way. Are you looking for the best way or the easy way? God wants you to choose the path that will lead to the greatest reward. This path, often known as the narrow way, always requires some kind of change. *Squeezing* through it generally requires dropping some of the baggage we carry.

Shifting Our Position

Following God requires both a turning *from* and a turning *to*. Turning a new way always means leaving old ways behind. When God changes us, He does not just modify behaviors... He produces lasting internal change. *We* can modify our behaviors by willful determination, but those changes rarely last. *We* can also alter our mind, changing our way of thinking by making what is called a *paradigm* shift. This simply means approaching life from a different philosophical model or framework. For example, we can choose to believe that eating meat is harmful and therefore become a vegetarian. But paradigms change frequently and therefore so do behaviors. Behaviors modified as a result of internal change last longest. Change at the *core* of our being produces the greatest external change.

For our very nature to be altered, something must change on a spiritual level, not just a mental level. When God transforms our life by joining His Spirit to ours, a new spirit is formed. God makes a "paraclete" shift. *Parakletos,* a Greek term meaning "called to one's side" is used in Scripture to refer to the Holy Spirit, who is given to provide aide, instruction, and comfort. Parakletos also referred to the Messiah, who was to be "the consolation of Israel"[3] and our comfort. A paraclete shift means *turning from* self-reliance *to* dependence on God. It is an "about face" which turns us from self effort to the transforming power of the blood, the cross, and the life of Jesus Christ. This shift produces enduring solutions because of the abiding life of Christ.

Getting to the Roots

Enduring solutions to the problems associated with post-traumatic stress disorder are found by focusing on the underlying roots and causes, not on the symptoms. Mahedy[4] and Dean,[5] both Vietnam vets, say the underlying cause of PTSD has a lot to do with spiritual darkness. In part, they say this darkness is an overpowering awareness of human frailty, failure, callousness, and sin. Hank Slikker, another Vietnam vet, sees sin existing as a power outside us, a power within us, and as a condition which we can spread by our actions toward others. Sin is not only a personal act of free will, it is the enduring condition of humanity apart from God. Sin, however, is a notion largely denied by our present therapeutic culture.

Mahedy believes Vietnam veterans were overpowered by their exposure to, and participation in, the ultimate effect of sin... war. He describes war as "the ultimate failure of humankind to reach God-given objectives of maintaining relationships based on love and justice." He believes it has nothing to do with whether a particular war is right or wrong; it is simply a form of inhumanity and hatred for fellow human beings. To him, war destroys everything and creates nothing, and even when directed by God is ultimately a consequence of turning away from God. Whether this is true or not, because of war Vietnam veterans experienced the sinful side of human nature in its most perverse form, and in a way few others in their generation have. During war, there is, as Peter Marin describes, "a pervasive sense of suffering, injustice, and evil"[5]... conditions that produce overwhelming despair and disgust.

I knew the pain of injustice and inhumanity before Vietnam, but it was nothing compared to the carnage I experienced there. I tried to deny that I was as much a part of the brutality as anyone else, but my daily participation left little room for illusion. I clearly saw my own degradation, selfishness, and fear, and although I did not believe in God at the time I was certain of one thing... that mankind unbridled would surely self-destruct. Seeing this forced me to examine my rigid stance against God, and I began a search for truth. My journey took me through many religious beliefs and practices, but eventually God brought me to a knowledge of Himself through Christ. And, it was Jesus who brought about my healing. I also discovered that sin was far more than a therapeutic problem; it was primarily a question of *who I was*.

Changing

Change begins with knowing and acknowledging the truth about our self-centered nature. Out of need, we open our hearts and turn toward God. Our turning toward God is called *repentance*. Repentance is not to be confused with feeling remorseful (although we may), it is a change, an *about face*... a 180° turn from the direction we are going, toward God. This turning sets us on a journey of discovery.

An integral part of this journey must include a study of Scripture, for who God is, is revealed in part in Scripture. Scripture reveals God's nature, character, and plan for our life. It is also a manual on human behavior which explains how to "tune up" our lives, so that they run smoothly. Before the development of all other religions, philosophies, or psychologies... before analytical, psychodynamic, rational, transactional, behavioral, existential, multimodal, or any other therapy, was God's Word. Every *working* principle of all therapeutic processes, no matter how glossed over with contemporary terminology, is already mentioned in Scripture. When we *apply it* to our lives, it brings about healing and change.

Change come from a progressive *experience* of what God says to be true. God's method for healing and change is different from man's. Man's way to overcome sin is to suppress it, or deny that it exists. God's way is to get sin out in the open. God then releases us from the burden of sin by forgiveness. He frees us from the nature of sin by putting our old sinful nature to death. He then *replaces* our old nature with His. Many believers mourn their weaknesses thinking, "If I were only strong I would do better." Yet God says, "*My* strength is made perfect in weakness." Paul writes, "Therefore, I will rather boast about my weakness, that the power of Christ may dwell in me."[7] When we are preoccupied with the power of sin, focusing on our inability, it is only natural to conclude that we need more power. Yet, if we know Christ and focus on Him, and accept that we already have the power of the Holy Spirit within us, we will soon realize that God has already given us everything we need to live a full, satisfying, godly, transformed life.[8]

Change does not come by us getting stronger, but by discovering our weakness and therefore our need for Him. When our weaknesses are exposed, we become dependent on Him. Apart from Him, we never experience the grace, love, mercy, patience, kindness, compassion, healing, strength, or power we need. We fruitlessly try to exercise control over our old nature, because we do not recognize that we are powerless to change our inner man. Yet if we trust and depend on God, and reckon ourselves to have "died in Christ, being placed in Christ,"[9] God will bring forth His purpose. Then, and only then, will our human striving and self-effort end. If we present ourselves to God, and truthfully acknowledge what we are and who He is, then we will discover what He has already done for us, and is doing still. If can trust God to complete His work, we can rest gratefully in His ability... and in *His* time table. Coming to this place of rest is not without labor, but the labor is in holding on to our belief about God's faithfulness, not in our own abilities. The labor is to let go of self-effort in order to trust God.

A Process

To grow from babes in faith to mature believers is a progressive journey. It is a process which requires belief, dependency, yieldedness, obedience, trust, and patience. The journey is difficult, full of pitfalls and hindrances. Our old nature is deeply rooted in unbelief and self-reliance. Dependency on God is difficult, because trust is difficult. Trust is an issue of the heart, and our hearts, hardened by the deceitfulness of sin, are full of unforgiveness, resentment, and bitterness.[10] Our will is set on self-protection, self-preservation, self-gratification, and our heart is often filled with pain, fear, and anger. Our mind too, has an elaborate, complex, highly refined defensive system of its own. And our will, stubbornly set by habit and constrained by vows we have made, has firmly fixed our behaviors in unbroken, unyielding patterns.

Once we allow God to penetrate our human spirit, we must allow Him to minister to us wholly, body and soul. Otherwise, our woundedness and mistrust will keep us from growing spiritually. We cannot practice trusting God while insulting Him. Yet each time we are unwilling to take Him at His word, we in essence say, "I don't believe you are who you say you are. I don't believe you when you say you loved me enough to forgive me, accept me as I am, heal me, restore me, provide for me, or protect me." The difficulty is that we have not experienced any such love before, and can scarcely believe it exists.

Our old nature is deeply rooted in unbelief and self-reliance. Dependency on God is difficult, because trust is difficult.

We must ask ourselves, "Is God trustworthy? Will He do for me what He has done for others?" We will never know the answer until we take Him at His word. This takes some measure of risk. God must penetrate our perimeter and break down our defenses. We must be willing to examine those areas which separate us from Him. Yet if we remain unshaken in the assurance of God's stated truth, we will find that "He is faithful to watch over His word to perform it."[11]

One Step at a Time

The first step on this journey is to have our dead spirit made alive, our broken spirit made whole, or our slumbering spirit awakened. This is done through *regeneration*. Jesus said, "That which is born of the Spirit is spirit... unless one is born again, he cannot see the kingdom of God."[12] Paul describes those who have had such an experience as, "the church, or general assembly of the first-born... the spirits of righteous men made perfect."[13] If we want our life to be changed, we must turn it over to Christ. We must acknowledge our inability to heal ourselves, and trust Him to do it for us. We must die to our own confidence, wisdom, effort, or ability to comprehend or carry out this work. This is *the core* of all that I will say from this point on. All healing, transformation, and everything we need has been provided for us in Christ.

Once our spirit has been regenerated, our soul must be transformed. This is done through *sanctification*. In Jeremiah's words, "we are made like before."[14] God wants us to become the person He originally intended us to be before we got side-tracked. Bob Mumford puts it this way: By creation, we were *gened*. By sin, we were *degened*. By Christ, we are *regened*. And with this new set of "genes" (God's Spirit in us) we are now capable of doing all that God asks. Sanctification (made holy, whole or complete, set apart, separated from sin) is completed the second we receive Christ, but what God sees as already finished (knowing both the beginning and the end of a thing), we only experience progressively. Our experience of the new life in us comes through an ongoing process of exchanging our old way of living for a new way, our old nature for the new. This process takes time. It also takes knowing what, and when, God would have us yield to Him. Since our identity is now in Him, we must find out who *He* is. We must also discover what He has done for us, and what He promises to continue to do in the Way.

Last, we must step in God's direction one foot at a time, present ourselves to Him, and align ourselves with His will. As we do this, our experiences will progressively line up with what He says is true in His word. However, we can expect opposition in the Way. Where we are set in our old ways, we have a nasty habit of stubbornly resisting the Spirit. In addition, others may not want us to change. Certainly Satan doesn't. Yet if we stand firm through difficulties, God will progressively impart more of His Spirit to us. When this happens, we will bear witness to the truth that God is indeed real, and faithfully performs His word. Therefore, let us "present ourselves... and our members" to God in such a way that we are open to receive His healing.

Summary

Post-traumatic stress disorder, like all disorders, requires treatment in order for healing to take place. If what you have done or are now doing is not working, look elsewhere for a solution. God offers us effective, lasting solutions. If you perceived God as having turned away from you while you were in Vietnam, I ask you to reconsider your position. Satan is always trying to get us to turn away from God, to keep us out of His presence, or to convince us there is no way back in. Through temptation, failures, suffering, and trials, he tries to make us *feel* outside of Christ. If we stand steadfast on the word of God, we will find that *all* He says is true. What He says *about* us will eventually begin to take shape *in* us. If our confidence is in ourselves we will eventually fail and remain unchanged. So, whether you are just beginning or already on the journey toward healing, I encourage you not to become overanxious. The way out of any pit is not by focusing on the mud in which we are trapped, nor by concentrating on self effort to escape. If we focus our attention on Jesus, he will do for us what we cannot do for ourselves.

> I waited patiently for the Lord and He inclined to me, and heard my cry. He also brought me up out of a horrible pit, out of the miry clay, and set my feet upon a rock, and established my steps. `   –Psalms 40:1

-Questions-

1. What problems or complications have developed in your life as a result of post-traumatic stress disorder?

2. How is what you are presently doing working to free you from PTSD?

3. What keeps you stuck in the bondage of PTSD? (limiting beliefs, fear, stubbornness, unforgiveness, hopelessness, etc.?)

4. What gets in the way of your asking, believing, or trusting God to heal and deliver you from symptoms associated with PTSD?

5. Make a list of those areas you believe God would have you to change.

-12-

The Blame Game
[ACCOUNTABILITY]

"Glorious wars produce heroic veterans. Inglorious wars produce antiheroes, even villains and deviants. The Vietnam War was long and inconclusively fought in such a fire storm of political and moral controversy that it produced as much tension and ambiguity upon its conclusion as throughout its duration. One result of this tension and ambiguity was American society's *shifting the blame* for the war from its own structure to the young men who fought it. In so doing, America estranged its youngest patriots, the very men who went against their peers and entered the military, and were sent to risk their lives in a dubious struggle in Southeast Asia."

–Strangers at Home[1]

"One way to explain why we don't have satisfactory relationships is to blame other people. That's just part of the human tendency to find a scapegoat. If we become terribly narcissistic, we don't have good relationships with others because we are selfish. If we blame ourselves, that would be too much of an attack on our narcissism, but if we blame other people then we can remain a victim."

–Paul Vitz[2]

Figley and Levantman[3] suggest that perhaps the most difficult problem for vets to overcome, and certainly the cruelest irony of the war's aftermath, was their being blamed for the war itself. They contend that the men who were victimized by fighting the war, were also victimized by society when it blamed and labeled them. They imply that veterans had no control over their fate, but were instead victims of American society gone amuck. Are these suggestions true? Can we rightfully assume that we were totally innocent? Did we have any responsibility in the matter? Has *being* blamed been as damaging as blaming others? Are we true victims? If so, what has been the result of assuming a *victim* mentality? These questions are examined in this chapter.

Blame
Clearly Vietnam veterans have been feared, even hated, both as individuals and as symbols of America's embarrassment in Southeast Asia. They have been seen as a potential menace to society, and they have been portrayed as drug crazed, mentally unstable, baby-killers who

are walking time bombs. WW II and Korean War veterans often saw Vietnam vets as inferior, not measuring up to the heroic exploits of veterans who *won* their wars. Vietnam vets have been rejected, spit upon, treated like outcasts, and ignorantly held responsible for the way the war was fought in Vietnam. No doubt! Vets have been blamed! But I doubt if *being blamed* for the choices we made or didn't make has been nearly as damaging as our *blaming others*. Those who blamed us *are* accountable for their behavior, but so are we. Regardless of what was done to "us" by "them," *we* are still responsible for *our* response.

Victimization

One of the most self-defeating mindsets is *victimization*. The *Thorndike-Barnhart Dictionary* defines a victim as: "a person or animal injured, destroyed, or sacrificed to a god; victims of war; a dupe: the victim of a swindler." The *Readers Guide Great Encyclopedic Dictionary* includes: "those subjected to suffering; one who is tricked; a living creature sacrificed to some deity as in a religious rite." In our society being a victim has come to mean:

- I am not responsible for what has happened to me.
- I am powerless to do anything about it.
- Others are to blame for the way that I am.
- What happened *to* me is the reason for all my ills, failures, my lack of faith, and my lack of character.
- I'm not responsible for my actions because they're not my fault.

There are times when we are truly victims. We have very little say about the kind of family we were born into, our race, the economic conditions in which we were born and raised, our sex, or our age. We do not always ask for, desire, or seek out the treatment we receive. Children are true victims. Because of their size, their lack of strength, and their immature emotional, intellectual, or social skill development, they are often physically, emotionally, and sexually abused. In war, civilians are often victims. Some suffer for merely being citizens. Others suffer because they fail to carry out their responsibilities as citizens. We all have suffered, or still suffer, because of circumstances out of our control. Are these things blessings or curses... opportunities or hindrances?

When we settle for pity, and let our tragedies become lifelong disabilities, we are abdicating our freedom and power to continue to make choices.

The pain of being duped or sacrificed by leaders who worship power, money, or prestige is very real to many Vietnam veterans. However, what is more tragic is when we allow what has happened to us in the past to dominate our behavior for the rest of our lives. When we carry pain and anger, and become critical, bitter, guarded, passive, hopeless, or even consumed with self-pity, it is easy to develop a *sour grapes* attitude. We can then carry a defeated self-image, while no longer assuming responsibility for our actions. We can then blame others for our own unwillingness to move beyond tragedy, and never seek solutions. In other words, we can cop out! When we settle for pity, and let our tragedies become lifelong disabilities, we are abdicating our freedom and power to continue to make choices. This is simply a form of moral cowardice!

Victimization and Society

When a victim mentality affects our self image, it affects our relationships with others and ultimately with all of society. Jay Adams wrote, "One achievement with which Freudianism ought to be credited is the leading part it has played in the present collapse of responsibility in modern American society."[4] Adams points to our present society's therapeutic view of mental health and mental illness as one which allows for deviant or antisocial behavior. Because a person is seen as *sick* and can't help his sickness, then what he needs is sympathy and understanding rather than to be held accountable for his behavior. The extent to which this belief has permeated contemporary thinking may be seen in our belief that alcoholism can be blamed on genetics, that tobacco companies should be held responsible for people who choose to smoke and then get cancer, that society is to blame for criminal behavior rather than criminals, that Dallas, rather than Lee Harvey Oswald (or whomever) was responsible for JFK's shooting, or that murderers, rapists, burglars, and addicts "just can't help it."

The idea that *sickness* is the cause of personal problems obliterates all notions of human responsibility. Yet this belief forms the core of the victim mentality. We no longer consider ourselves responsible for what we do wrong. Society is easy to blame since what is everybody's responsibility is really no one's. Today, even society gets off the hook. After all, we live in a "sick" society. So, either "no one's to blame" or "*everybody is to blame*." If all our problems are caused by things outside our self then the natural result is a sense of powerlessness, helplessness, hopelessness, and personal irresponsibility. This victim script is illustrated in the following song by Anna Russell:[5]

> I went to my psychiatrist to be psychoanalyzed. To find
> out why I killed the cat and blackened my husband's eye.
> And here is what he dredged up from my subconscious mind:
> When I was one, my mommie hid my dolly in a trunk,
> and so it follows naturally that I am always drunk.
> When I was two, I saw my father kiss the maid one day,
> And that is why I suffer now from kleptomania.
> At three, I had the feeling of ambivalence toward my brothers,
> so it follows naturally I poison all my lovers.
> But I am happy; now I've learned the lesson this has taught;
> That everything I do that's wrong is someone else's fault.

The Effects of Victimization

Believing that we are nothing more than irresponsible pawns leads to the general degrading of the human personality. It robs us of our self-respect. If we believe our present undesirable behaviors are *solely* determined by the past, and that our experiences thus *excuse* rather than influence our present behavior, it robs us of all power, freedom of choice, and the possibility of change. Perhaps this explains why our present political leadership believes we can't take care of ourselves and therefore need more governmental assistance and control; that really, we are incapable of thinking for ourselves or arriving at *right* decisions, and therefore we need them to do our thinking and deciding for us!

Even when we have little or no control over what happens to us, we do have control over our response. If someone speaks unkindly, and we are injured by their criticism, we can either forgive them or have a critical, condemning response. Getting back might feel good, but it will affect us negatively as well. We can't always change how others treat us. We could try to force or manipulate others to be what we want, but this would never change who *we* are. We are best served by examining *our own* attitudes, rather than pointing the finger at others.

> Let no man when he is tempted, say I am being tempted from God, for every man is tempted when he is carried away and enticed by what *he* wants. Then when his desires have conceived, they give birth to sin; and when sin is accomplished, it brings forth death. Do not be deceived my beloved brethren.[6]

Perhaps this philosophy of personal accountability is one of the reasons why *authentic* Christianity is so unpopular in today's culture.

Victimizing Others

Research shows that invariably both those who have been victimized, and those who become victimizers, seek out and are attracted to partners with similar backgrounds. They are drawn to one another out of a sense of familiarity, need, and expectation about how others will treat them. The *predator*, feeling powerless and fearing rejection, seeks out and preys on those who are weak, unthreatening, and easily controlled. The *parasite*, feeling powerless and fearing rejection, seeks out people who are stronger than themselves, people they can vicariously live their life through. Parasites draw their life and strength from others, afraid to stand on their own. Whether predator or parasite, both behaviors are grounded in a victim mentality.

People with similar/familiar spirits attract one another. Street gangs are good examples. They are formed by kids with similar backgrounds who often share the familiar pain of rejection, isolation, anger, and alienation. They also share the same need to be cared for and to belong.

Unfortunately, the very characteristics which by their familiarity attract us to one another, later repel us. Subconsciously, we hate these characteristics in our lives, and therefore we hate them in others. When we marry someone who has the same deep emotional needs and then discover that we cannot fix or change them, we end up frustrated, intolerant, critical, and condemning. These attitudes eventually drive us apart and we end up looking elsewhere to meet our needs.

Deep emotional wounds cause us to flee vulnerability. To protect our emotions, we build an inner shell. Then, we try to control our exterior environment as well. When we try to extend control over our environment and the lives of others in it, either by force or manipulation, we victimize those around us. Eventually our self-centeredness, guardedness, and tyrannical behavior push those closest away. Then, *our* inner man ends up starving for lack of affirmation. We lose the nurturing love we need to be healthy. Intending to save our life, we instead lose it.[7]

We reproduce in our children
what goes unresolved in our life.

The families of Vietnam vets report suffering the most. Wives and children often:
- feel battered... emotionally, verbally, and physically by veterans' uncontrolled anger and need to "keep them in line,"
- feel over-regulated, controlled, over-protected, alienated, and uncared for, and
- see husbands or fathers as demanding and critical.[8]

Some vets have difficulty allowing their children to be children, fearing it leaves them vulnerable and unprotected. The children of vets often end up carrying their parents fears, mistrust, and hypervigilance. Sometimes they end up feeling responsible to care for or protect parents they see as unstable. When this happens, children step into a role of "parental inversion" that is not only unhealthy, but not meant to be.

The *need* to be in control, coupled with a general *distrust* of people in authority, can also make it difficult to sustain employment. It's not necessary to work for people who are abusive, but an inability to maintain employment undermines stability and security for families, and this is one of the ways vets end up victimizing themselves and loved ones.

Victims who become victimizers often end up becoming like the people who victimized them, and who they *vowed* never to be like. This pattern can continue for generations. If one generation does not take the responsibility to change, they reproduce in their children what goes unresolved in their own life.

My Experience

After Vietnam, my own political and social zeal to "save the world" was strongly intermingled with a desire to control others' behavior. First, to prevent them from hurting me. Second, to prevent them from hurting others. You couldn't have convinced me that my behavior was anything less than unselfish, altruistic concern for people, yet I vigilantly tried to control my environment and those around me through subtle manipulation and criticism. I surrounded myself with people who were either like-minded, easily influenced, or needy. Their needs met my need to expunge myself of guilt by being their savior. At the same time, their dependency made them non-threatening and easily controlled, and I could continue to live a guarded life. Periodically, I would isolate myself and withdraw as a means of *control by avoidance.*

At the same time I sought God, trying to touch Him in an attempt to eradicate my guilt and change my life. I devoted myself to philosophies and religions which exalted self-discipline, self-control, and denial as a means of overcoming feelings, desires, and reality. You name it, I tried it. Yoga, Hinduism, Buddhism, Zen, mysticism, metaphysics, the parapsychologies, numerology, astrology, the occult... I tried them all. Marijuana became an integral part of my lifestyle. I fell in love with it because it gave me a sense of peace and joy that constantly eluded my grasp. It also helped to suppress the pain. In the end I became only half a man, alive to my intellect and the flesh, but dead to my emotions. Yet no matter what I did, the pain and mistrust didn't go away. No matter how hard I tried to avoid, suppress, deny, or obliterate it, the pain and mistrust always surfaced in some way.

Taking Accountability

When we assign blame (you make me), and say that someone else is responsible for our emotions or behaviors, we are simply saying that we, in some way, are dependent on them. That is, we are tied to them in a way that if they behave correctly then we can behave correctly. *If* they do right *then* we can do right. *They* pull the strings... *we* only react. *We* are only marionettes. In reality we are saying that we don't have the power to choose how we will react... we are powerless. But, is this really the truth? Are we puppets, unable to control our emotions or our responses? Are we powerless... unable to make choices, without a will of our own?

I am not saying that people who wound us are not accountable for their behavior. They are! But the issue is not their accountability, it is *ours.* We can only take responsibility for changing our lives, not others. In the end God will set every injustice right. He is righteous and true. We must stop being judge and jury, and put our desire for justice in God's hand, if we want to move beyond our injuries. We must be merciful! If not, bitterness, fault-finding, and criticism will keep us bound to anger and tied to the past.

I have some personal accountability for my tour in Vietnam. I volunteered for the draft. It was my choice. I could have gone to Canada or filed for conscientious-objector status... others did. I could have hid out in America and evaded the draft. I did that nicely for nearly a year. I could have burned my draft card and gone to jail. My brother and some of my friends did. Did I want to do any of those things? No! But I still had the choice. I could have brown-nosed some officer or politician and acquired a nice quiet tour in Germany. Did I? No. Yet those options, as distasteful as they were to me, were available. I simply made different choices. While in Vietnam I could also have gone AWOL. I could have hid out in Saigon Alley. I could have gone over to the other side... it is said some did. I could have stayed in Hong Kong while on R&R or I could have gone to Sweden... I was offered the opportunity. At any time I could have refused to participate in the war, even though threatened with imprisonment.

What I'm saying is, I always had choices. As detestable as they might have been, they were choices just the same. I made mine... did you make yours? Can we then blame others? How many of us chose against our own conscience? How many didn't want to go, but went anyway because it was the easy way out? A study by psychologists in Grand Rapids, Michigan, on post-abortion trauma, concluded that the one predisposing factor among those who suffered the most from post-abortion syndrome was whether they *thought it was wrong* before they did it. Some of the most troubled vets I have known are not only guilt-ridden about what they did; they suffer tremendously from a sense of failure to defend what they believed to be morally right, either before or during Vietnam.

Summary

We are all accountable in some measure for what happens in our lives. Accountability is not self-blame, it is simply taking ownership for the part we play in our experiences. We are not accountable for what is done *to* us, but we are accountable for our response and the part we play in allowing victimization to continue once we can prevent it.

The unwillingness of Americans in every aspect of society, including vets, to bear their fair share of accountability for the war in Vietnam, has been extremely detrimental. It has been especially wounding for Vietnam vets, who have been blamed for everything from the way it was fought to the way it was lost.

Even though we may have been victimized, we don't have to remain victims, or become victimizers. We are rational human beings with a free will. We are responsible for, and in control of, our choices and actions. Watchman Nee says, "God has created man with a free will and He has determined not to accomplish His purpose without the free cooperation of man's will."[9] *We have the power to make a way for, or to obstruct, the power of God to bring healing and liberty into our life.* For our sake, and for the sake of those around us, let's stop playing the blame game and get on with our healing.

-Questions-

1. What is your accountability (the part you played) for ending up in Vietnam?

2. How do you continue to victimize yourself and others by carrying the effects of your experience in Vietnam?

3. Whom do you continue to blame for the wounds you received in Vietnam?

4. What, if anything, do you want to do about these things?

-13-

Fruit and Root

[RESOLVING BITTERNESS]

"For heroism and gallantry in ground combat in the Republic of Vietnam, 13 to 25 August 1970, Lt. Col. Dinky Dau Green Man distinguished himself while serving as commanding officer of a bunch of dumb-ass troops during operations near Firebase Barnett. During the entire operation the Green Man repeatedly supervised ground and air forces which got fucked up looking for a meaningless bunker complex. The Green Man directed artillery and tactical air support against enemy hills, trees, and grass. He listened on the radio repeatedly as his units were ambushed and attacked. After the enemy forces were routed, he, without regard for his personal safety, tabulated the reported dead. During the operation the Green Man also managed to take twelve hot showers in the rear, eat thirty hot meals, and read twenty-seven Fantastic Four Comic books. The Green Man's personal bravery and devotion to duty are in keeping with the highest traditions of the military service and reflect great credit upon himself, his unit, and the United States Army."

–a Vietnam veteran[1]

"We are holding onto much unexpressed resentment for things we did during the war and for sins others have accused us of doing. If anyone is wrongly blamed for a long enough period, he will begin to believe he is legitimately guilty. The resulting depression can immobilize him."

–Chuck Dean[2]

"Let all bitterness [mean-spirited], wrath [bad-tempered and rage], anger, clamor [quarreling, ranting and raving] and evil speaking [harsh and critical words, put downs] be put away from you, with all malice [dislike of others, intent to do harm]. And be kind to one another, tender hearted [vulnerable, sensitive to others' feelings, able to be touched], forgiving one another, just as God in Christ also forgave you."

–Paul, in a letter to the Ephesians[3]

Bitterness is a major stronghold which keeps us from moving beyond the past. It links present experience with unresolved issues and tends to cloud our ability to perceive events in our life with any degree of objectivity or accuracy. It prevents us from growing up. It robs us of joy and peace. It keeps us in bondage. To be truly free we must be free from bitterness in every area of our life. This chapter examines the roots of bitterness, the effects of bitterness, the effects of unforgiveness, the freedom forgiveness brings, the call to be imitators of Christ, and practical steps to rid one's life of the bondage bitterness creates.

Planting Seeds

When we are offended, there is always some degree of emotional pain. When others hurt us, we get angry. For many, anger is an immediate, habitual, learned response used to gloss over pain. Anger is natural, but what we do with our anger is *crucial;* for if we do not deal with anger in a way that resolves it, we end up carrying it. Anger doesn't just disappear or dissolve into thin air. When we carry and bury our anger, we plant it. When planted, even on a subconscious level, it grows into resentment. Resentment turns to bitterness, which hardens the heart. A hardened heart is one protected by walls of unforgiveness and mistrust.

OFFENSE > PAIN > ANGER > RESENTMENT > BITTERNESS > HARD HEART

Remember, Jesus said offenses are unavoidable. It is unrealistic to believe we can escape pain or suffering. Therefore, there must be a way to handle injuries that frees us from their *influence.*

Seed Taking Root

The writer of Hebrews says, "Pursue after peace with all men and after the sanctification without which no man will see the Lord. See to it that no one comes short of the grace of God; that no *root of bitterness* springing up causes trouble and by it many be defiled."[4] Peace is broken between men by conflict and unresolved differences. Often, conflict is created by offenses. Harmony and unity are not sustained through imposed order, or even justice, but by our having grace for one another. Grace goes beyond justice. It doesn't try to balance the scales. It gives mercy to those who don't deserve it. In place of retribution it gives forgiveness. This is God's heart toward us. This is His gift to us. It is also what He wants us to display toward others.

When we are not for giving people a second or third chance, the benefit of the doubt, mercy, or whatever God requires of us, then we fall short of the grace of God. When we fall short of grace, we fail to exhibit God's nature and character, which comes through a life set apart to God. The world sees God through us. When we are not merciful, we fail to reveal God to the world.

When we do not forgive those who have offended us, each time we are reminded of their offense, we water the seed of anger, keeping it alive. When watered, it becomes rooted in our heart. This "root of bitterness" eventually produces a plant. The longer roots are nursed, the deeper they go. The deeper the roots, the stronger the plant. The trunk of every life is made up of fixed perspectives. The trunk nurtures and sprouts branches, which in turn, produce fruit (attitudes and behaviors). Scripture describes the fruit of the flesh (nature's order), as:

"unrighteousness, a depraved mind, wickedness, greed, envy, murder, strife, deceit, malice, gossip, slander, hatred of God, insolence, arrogance, boasting, evil disobedience, lack of understanding, untrustworthiness, lack of love and mercy, bitterness, wrath, anger, clamor, etc."[5] It is easy to see how the "fruit" of bitterness can "trouble" us, and how it "defiles" those around us.

Root Producing Fruit

All bad fruit is rooted in unforgiveness. Scripture says, "If you forgive the sins of any, their sins have been forgiven them; if you retain the sins of any, they have been retained." It also says, "whatever we bind, is bound" and "whatever we loose, is loosed."[6] When we forgive people their offenses, we not only release them, we release ourselves... from the necessity of revenge, and from anger. When we retain people's sins, *we bind their sins to us*. In doing so, we carry both the impact and influence of their sin. They don't suffer. *We do!*

When we retain people's offenses, their sinful behavior also becomes the focus of our attention. What we focus our attention on fills our mind. What fills our mind generates emotions and behaviors. We are molded by our focus. Eventually we become like the thing we focus on. If an artist focuses his attention on another artist's work, eventually that artist's work begins to influence his own. He will soon find expressions of the other's work in his own. Most of us learn by observing and copying the behavior of those we focus our attention on. When we focus on the pain people have caused us, anger grates on our soul and like a cancer, spreads. This affects our attitude, perspective, and emotional well-being. Eventually it transforms our character. In the end, we become just like the ones we vowed never to be like. It doesn't seem fair that we would punish *ourselves* by carrying the burden of someone else's offense, but we do. This seems foolish now, yet when I was carrying offenses it seemed right. I felt justified! How deceptive sin is!

The Effects of Unforgiveness
• A lack of intimacy with God

Jesus said, "If you forgive men their transgressions, your heavenly Father will also forgive you. If you do not forgive men, then your Father will not forgive your transgressions."[7] The word *transgression*, "to go beyond a limit," is sometimes translated *trespass*, a "stepping over another person's boundaries." When people violate our space, do not respect our opinions, feelings, or desires, and force their will on us, they are trespassing. When we don't forgive them it creates a barrier between us and God, robbing us of His presence. We then become insecure in our relationship with God. Jesus said:

> Love your enemies, do good to those who hate you, bless those who curse you, pray for those who mistreat you... do not withhold... just as you want men to treat you, treat them in the same way. And if you love those who love you, what credit is

that to you? For even sinners love those who love them. And if you do good to those who do good to you, what credit is that to you? For even sinners do the same thing... But love your enemies, and do good... for He Himself is kind to ungrateful and evil men. Be merciful, just as your Father is merciful. Do not pass judgment and you will not be judged; and do not condemn and you shall not be condemned; pardon and you shall be pardoned... For whatever measure [standard] you deal out to others, it will be dealt to you.[8]

The more we forgive and accept people's shortcomings, the more we experience God's forgiveness and acceptance. We reap what we sow. The more acceptable we feel, the more secure and assured. Security and assurance produce courage and confidence, which enable us to take risks. Risk taking frees us from fear. Freedom from fear enables us to expose other hidden areas in our life. When what is hidden is brought to the light, it loses its power over us. We become even more free.

We may complain about God's fleeting presence, but His presence is often tied to the condition of our heart.[9] I am not saying that born-again believers can lose God's Spirit. The Spirit is a gift and "the gifts of God are irrevocable." What we can lose is the sense of His presence and intimacy. I have found that the same people who bemoan God's absence also tend to harbor unforgiveness. They carry a sack of debts that people owe them, along with hidden resentment. This weighs them down and dulls their spirit. Dullness of spirit causes us to lose the ability to sense God's presence, because God meets us Spirit to spirit.

• Spiritual torment

Unforgiveness produces torment. Paul says "it causes us troubles." This is illustrated in the eighteenth chapter of Matthew. When Peter asked, "How often shall my brother sin against me and I forgive him?" Jesus did not answer him directly, but shared a parable about a man who was forgiven a debt but would not forgive others. Jesus said this man was "*handed over to the torturers* until he should repay all that was owed him," and added, "So shall My heavenly Father also do to you if you do not *forgive* your brother *from your heart*."[10] Torment is produced by spiritual forces.

Paul wrote to the believers at Ephesus saying essentially, "Look, stop lying to one another. Be truthful because we are all brothers. Be angry when you are. Don't hide it, yet do not sin. Resolve your anger on a daily basis and *don't give the devil a place* [foothold] in your lives."[11] The literal meaning of the word "place" is *pality*. It refers to a physical place or territory, as used in the word "municipality." It is the same term used in Ephesians (6:12) which refers to demonic forces as "principalities" (prince/ruler over a specific territory). This means we can give demonic powers a legal "foothold" in our life through unresolved anger. Perhaps this is why Paul refers to bitterness as a root; it grows in our life wherever we provide fertile ground. Unforgiveness provides a valid opening through which Satan can torment us, much like the unforgiving servant was tormented. Is holding on to anger worth it?

• The removal of God's protection

The God of the New Testament is the same God of the Old! Listen to what Hosea prophesied, "I [God] will go away and return to My place until they acknowledge their guilt [or bear their punishment] and seek My face. In their afflictions they will earnestly seek Me." God is not a tyrant. He can, however, remove His protective covering. He lets us go our own way. We, however, invariably suffer consequences designed to turn us from our path and return us to Him. Whom God loves, He corrects. His correction only confirms that we are His sons or daughters. It is designed to refine and transform our lives. God is more interested in our character than in our comfort.

• Corrective discipline

Fine gold is refined and purified by fire. Flames heat the metal until it changes character/composition and melts. Then, the dross/impurities come to the surface where they are visible. They are then skimmed off. Our lives are like that. When faced with immovable circumstances or intense pressure, we drop our social mask. Our character changes. What is in our heart (impurities/shortcomings) surfaces. Trials, often the consequence of our own choices, cause us to see what needs to be changed in our lives. If we humble ourselves, and make the exchange God is after, He will deliver us from the "wretched men" that we are. If we hold on to pride and self-sufficiency, God will resist us. A flexible sapling yields to the high winds of a storm and is not broken. A hardened tree may stand firm for awhile, but under extreme winds it breaks or is totally uprooted.

Forgiveness Brings Freedom

God's remedy for bitterness is forgiveness. "Hatred stirs up trouble but love forgives all wrongs."12 We can go through life removing the fruit bitterness produces, or we can ask God to put the axe to its root.13 Once the root is severed, the trunk eventually dries up, the branches die, and the fruit withers. Can God do this? Mark's Gospel records this:

> When they [the disciples] had departed from Bethany, he [Jesus] became hungry. And seeing at a distance a fig tree in leaf, he went to see if perhaps He would find anything on it; and when He came to it, He found nothing but leaves, for it was not the season for figs. And He answered and said to it, 'May no one ever eat fruit from you again!' His disciples were listening... And as they were passing by in the morning [the following day], they saw the fig tree withered *from the roots up*. And being reminded, Peter said to Him, 'Rabbi behold, the fig tree which you *cursed* has withered.'14

With a word, Jesus can bring death to the fruit of bitterness by dealing with its roots. Like the disciples, we may not see the results immediately, but none the less, once the roots have been severed the tree begins to die. Roots in *our* lives are the judgments and beliefs we have sown. The fruit is our attitudes, choices, and behaviors.

Bitterness is a curse! In the Hebrew culture, dust often represents bitterness. In towns where they were rejected, the disciples were encouraged to "shake the dust from their shoes." They were not to carry anger from the way they were treated. Jesus spit into the dust, made a salve, and put it on the eyes of a blind man. In our culture, just as in the Hebrew culture, spitting on someone means we disdain them. It is like cursing them. Is it possible that by spitting in the dust, Jesus cursed a spirit of bitterness in this man's life, thus breaking its influence on the man's ability to receive healing. We know bitterness blinds us, both spiritually and intellectually. And although this man's blindness wasn't caused by sin, could he have been bitter because of it? I don't know. What I do know is that forgiveness frees us from spiritual blindness, faulty perceptions, hateful attitudes, and angry behaviors.

If we apply God's forgiveness to those wounds rooted in our Vietnam experience, God will begin to set us free from the fruit of PTSD. Must we forgive? The answer is simple... no. It is not something we *must* do. It is not God's nature to force us to do anything. We are free to choose. We will, however, reap the consequences of our choices.

Be Imitators of Christ

Scripture says, "A brother offended is harder to win than a strong city, and contentions are like the bars of a castle."15 Deep wounds create self-protective inner walls similar to the walls which protected cities. Mistrust and guardedness cause us to contend with God, and anyone else who tries to penetrate our defenses. We use contention and abrasiveness to keep people at a distance, like bars on a castle window.

In the end, our solitary existence accounts for nothing. It takes a real soldier to not let adversity be his master, but to master adversity. Only a real warrior can walk in Christ's footsteps. Paul says, "Be imitators of Christ, as beloved children, and walk in love, just as Christ loved you and gave Himself up for us."16

Jesus was no stranger to affliction. He was a Pointman. He walked down a path he knew would be ours. He was **rejected** by his own nation. He was **used, abandoned, ridiculed**, and **beaten.** He was **whipped** and **spit upon** by his own countrymen and foreigners. He was **falsely accused, unjustly punished, suffered alienation** from men, and was treated as an **outcast.** He was **separated** from both God and man. He was **criticized, slandered**, and treated with **contempt** and **unbelief.** He was seen as a **trust-breaker, hope-crusher**, and **promise-breaker**. He felt **grief, pain,** and the **loss** and **betrayal** of those closest to him. He was **misunderstood, unrecognized**, and **given neither thanks nor honor** for the sacrifices he made. He was **nailed to a cross** and had a **sword thrust into his side**. Yet his physical and emotional **injury** and **suffering** could have been prevented by his own countrymen.

While hanging on a cross... naked, exposed, and in excruciating pain, he said, "Father, forgive them for they do not understand what it is they are doing."[17] Surely no man has loved like this before! Can we be like this? It's easy to see why one may not believe this is possible, because it must have taken supernatural strength. But, Jesus says *his* life and power is ours through God's indwelling Spirit.

If you are a believer, a *true* follower of Christ, you already have the Spirit. For you, forgiveness is not an option. It is an issue of obedience, not ability. It puts the issue of discipleship and Christ's Lordship on the line. We may have had a *right* to our bitterness at one time, but we don't anymore. Our life is no longer ours; it has been purchased by Jesus Christ. And we, in turn, have given it freely. We have entered his service voluntarily. We are now subject to *His* will, not ours. Paul wrote, "Nevertheless we have not used *this right,* but endure all things lest we hinder the gospel of Christ, for if I do this willingly, I have a reward; but if against my will, I have been entrusted with stewardship."[18] We have been entrusted with the responsibility to reveal Christ's life and character to the world. That is our challenge. "Moreover, it is required in stewards that they be found faithful."[19] We must ask ourselves, are we going to live to please ourselves or are we going to be faithful followers? To follow means to walk in His footsteps; to no longer live to please ourselves. "For even Christ did not please himself."[20]

We are God's children, destined and encouraged to *be like Him*. Our behavior must differ from others in the world. We are to love our enemies and pray for those who persecute us. This is how we show that we are sons and daughters of God. If we love only those who love us, what credit is that to us? God is merciful. He is kind to ungrateful and evil men. Our love must be like His. God loves both good and evil men. His love is impartial. If our love is only a reciprocal love, it is a mere expression of humanity. (If you do what I want, I will love you. If you scratch my back, I'll scratch yours, etc.) God's love goes beyond reciprocity. It is unconditional. How many can say that we love Jane Fonda? Or those in government who betrayed our trust? Yet this is where our walk is challenged to be more than just talk. Is this the place where your walk is challenged?

Clarifying Forgiveness

If you want to know who to forgive for the pain and anger defiling your heart, you can. You may not know how it got rooted, but the Holy Spirit does. "Search me, O God, and know my heart," cried David, "Try me, and know my *anxieties*; and see if there is any wicked way in me and lead me in the way everlasting."[21] Hopefully, the following will help eliminate confusion over what forgiveness is, or isn't.

• *Forgiveness does not mean forgetting.* God doesn't want us to forget our experiences, nor the lessons we have learned from them. God has designed our experiences with a purpose. We are to be wiser, stronger, and perhaps more compassionate because of them. God doesn't want us to suppress our memories, but he does want us to be free from the pain that accompanies them. We know we are healed when we remember our experiences without pain.

• *Forgiveness does not mean rationalizing, justifying, or excusing* what others have done. Walking in truth means calling a spade a spade. It is important to acknowledge what has really happened to us.

• *Forgiveness is not the same thing as trusting.* Should we trust those who repeatedly harm us? No. Forgiveness is not an open invitation to be repeatedly abused. God calls us to love our enemies, but He has not called us to be doormats. He wants us to have secure boundaries, and to value our life as He does. Although we are encouraged to "guard our heart with all diligence," this does not mean hypervigilance or putting up walls. We are to guard our hearts from allowing anything to take up residence which would defile it, like anger, resentment, lust, greed, etc. We are to use wisdom in where, when, and to whom we open our hearts. Setting healthy boundaries shows people we respect ourselves, and that teaches them to respect us as well.

• *Forgiveness does not take away the offender's accountability.* God still holds those who defile us accountable for their actions, but their sin is now between them and God. Nobody gets away with anything. I've read the story. In the end, *everyone* answers to God.

• *Forgiveness is not justice.* Rather than balancing things out, forgiveness tips the scales leaving justice to God. If you don't want to forgive, be honest. God will honor your honesty. He is at work in our life both to will and to work for His good pleasure. He will give us both the desire and the power to forgive... if we ask.

• *Forgiveness is not avoidance.* It is not sticking our head in the sand, pretending that we are OK, or that what others do doesn't matter.

• *Forgiveness does not depend on feelings.* It is a choice. God's Spirit will make it alive in our heart if we are willing to choose His way.

Uprooting Bitterness

If you know there is unforgiveness in your heart, take this opportunity to go through these steps and get free!

• Acknowledge your condition, whatever it may be. Remember, a root of bitterness springs up when *we* fall short of the grace of God. It is *our response* to the offense, not the offense itself, that keeps us in bondage. Take responsibility for *your* attitudes and stop blaming others. "You are without excuse, every one of you who passes judgment, for in the same way you judge another, *you condemn yourself*, for you who judge practice the same things."[22]

• Give forgiveness to those who have offended you. Be specific about their offenses. When Peter asked, "Should I forgive a man seven times?" Jesus replied, "I tell you, you must forgive him more than seven times. You must forgive him even if he does wrong to you four hundred and seventy seven times."[23] Surrender your right to judge. "God resists the proud, but gives grace to the humble. Draw near to God and He will draw near to you."[24]

• Ask for *and receive* forgiveness for carrying anger, resentment, and bitterness. And, for condemning those who have wounded you. If we confess our sins, "God is faithful and righteous to forgive us our sins and to cleanse us from all unrighteousness."25 God abhors pride, yet He exalts the humble. Don't be stubborn, rebellious, or hard hearted. Repent, and return to God that your sins may be wiped away, *in order that times of refreshing may come* from His presence.26 Unbelief on our part discredits God's gift of pardon.27

• Ask the Lord to apply the cross, both his death and burial to any habitual responses (anger, withdrawal, criticism, etc.) that have developed in your life. Our old nature was crucified with Christ.28 If we are in Him by virtue of what God has done for us, our old nature was included in His death and burial. This includes *all* we have been before coming to Christ. Ask God to cause what He says is true, to become your experience in life.

• Forgiveness does not heal emotions, comfort does. Ask God to release His comfort and healing, and replace your "heart of stone" with a "heart of flesh."29 Jesus came to "bind up the broken hearted." He heals emotional, as well as physical, wounds. He will restore compassion and tenderness where there has been anger and hardness.30

Tearing Down Strongholds

It's one thing to forgive, be forgiven, and have judgments we were meant to reap stopped at the cross. However, forgiveness doesn't necessarily free us from the defiling influence of a life-time of repeating choices. Where our will has been set, it must be broken and converted. Where self-interest has ruled our lives, this too must be dethroned. The lawlessness rooted in our old nature must also be pulled out. Apart from self-denial, the fruit of the Spirit in us will not surface or remain. There is a war to be waged, but we are often our worst enemy. Paul said, "For though we walk in the flesh, we do not war according to the flesh, for the weapons of our warfare are not of the flesh, but divinely powerful for the destruction of strongholds [fortresses]." The word *strongholds* literally means "fixed firm." Beliefs, emotions, behaviors, and demonic oppression can become fixed in our lives, and must be addressed.

Mental Strongholds

Mental strongholds are fixed mindsets or ways of perceiving life such as: beliefs, philosophies, thinking patterns, fantasies, assumptions and speculations. We are to "destroy speculations and every lofty thing [ideas] raised up against the knowledge of God, and take every thought captive to the obedience of Christ."31 It is not the truth that needs to be cast aside, but conclusions we have reached based on faulty reasoning, limited understanding, imagination, arrogant assumptions, judgments, and pride. Our behaviors are transformed by the renewing of our mind. Our minds are made new by exchanging untrue beliefs, for the truth. Once we know the truth, we are to practice a disciplined thought life. We adhere to the truth whether we feel it or see it. This does not mean, however, that we deny feelings or reality. We acknowledge *the facts*, but we hold to the belief that there is an even greater truth working behind the scenes that will eventually supersede our present limited perspective.

Paul says, those who don't follow Christ get off on the wrong foot by "suppressing the truth," relying on their own "speculations," and "exchanging the truth for cultural philosophies or traditions contrary to scripture." This results in the development of a progressively "depraved mind." This, in turn, motivates us "to do things which are not proper."[32] To undo this learning experience our mind must be renewed and "conformed to the word of God." Jesus said, "I have given them [the disciples] thy word... sanctify them in the truth; *Thy word is truth*. For their sakes I sanctify Myself that they themselves also may be sanctified in truth." The truth sets us free by progressively separating us from what is false. The truth is not just a knowing, it is a person. Jesus said, "I am the Way, *the Truth*, and the Life." His life and mind in us, transforms us. His Spirit writes God's guidelines on our mind and in our heart. The written word confirms the Spirit, even as the Spirit confirms the written word. Both help us to identify, and separate from, our old mannerisms. As we develop a new way of looking at things, our beliefs change. We must learn to hear God's Spirit. We must study the written word. We must *put it into practice* if we are to *experience* truth. A mind set on the things of the flesh eventually produces death. A mind set on God's Spirit produces life and peace.[33]

Sometimes it may feel as if our thoughts have a life of their own. It takes a concerted effort to control them. There *is* a battle in taking every thought captive. When we become Christians we become soldiers in His service. As soldiers we have a responsibility to govern our lives. Authority is first developed by self-government. "He who is slow to anger is better than the mighty, and he who rules his own spirit, mightier than he who takes a city." We must allow God's Spirit to rule our mind. We must learn how to use the weapons He has given us for our protection and liberty. Otherwise, how can we protect or fight on the behalf of others. To hear the word of the Lord, and to see Him as He is, we must recognize and repent of mental strongholds.

Emotional, Willful, and Behavioral Strongholds

Fixed emotions like fear, mistrust, guilt, shame, loneliness, self-pity, or grief, can rule our behaviors. Breaking emotional strongholds will be covered in the next chapter.

Willful strongholds are constructed by vows, or by choices we habitually repeat. These are generally subject to emotional and mental strongholds. While some habitual choices are good, others are destructive. Willful vows might include:
- *I will* never stand in line again as long as I live!
- *I will* never allow myself to be used by anyone again!
- *I will* never trust anyone in authority!
- *I will* never let another man/woman hurt me like this!
- *I will* never allow anyone to get close to me again!

Inner vows make us rigid, preventing us from living flexible, yielded lives. They limit our responsiveness to God because they form barriers that we refuse to cross. Vows about authority figures can also stand in the way of our trusting or having intimacy with God. We must recognize their influence on our present life, acknowledge their limiting nature, and renounce them. We break their power using the authority inherent in the name of Jesus, and we ask Him to free us by applying the cross to any habitual behavior which has a vow as its foundation.

Behavioral strongholds are obsessive, compulsive habits such as: alcoholism, workaholism, drug addiction, sexual obsessions, and eating disorders. They are also fixed patterns of social isolation, emotional withdrawal, or silence. Behaviors *are subject to* faulty beliefs and unre-solved wounds. Once the foundation (ruling stronghold) is torn down, structural behaviors generally follow. Since habitual behaviors are formed by habitual choices, we can end them by *choosing* to behave dif-ferently. A set will is broken by repetitious denial, yielding to God's will. Freedom, therefore, requires brokenness, humility, and a con-certed effort to die to old behaviors. This, in turn, requires trust, dependency, and enduring faith. God can, but does not always, remove habitual strongholds from our life miraculously (without effort on our part), but whatever the manner of deliverance, God designs it for our ultimate good.

Spiritual Strongholds

Spiritual strongholds are demonic forces. The Bible refers to them as "principalities, rulers, and powers of darkness." We are to "stand firm against the schemes of the devil. For our struggle is not against flesh and blood, but against *principalities*, against powers, against the rulers of the darkness of this world, and against spiritual wickedness in high places." Spiritual beings, whether demonic or angelic, are real. They are neither figments of our imagination nor old century supersti-tion. All demonic forces, however, have been vanquished by Christ; we simply stand in agreement with Him about what he has done. We resist demonic forces by the strength of *Christ's* indwelling Spirit, the power of *His* name, and the authority given to every believer.

In Vietnam, a country dominated by Buddhism, Hinduism, and Spiritism, pagan spiritual powers and sorcerers ruled villages, directed battles, and were called upon to destroy opponents.[34] According to an ex-Buddhist priest, an entire sect of Vietnamese Buddhist monks spent years diligently praying and invoking the following curses upon all Americans that came into their country:[35]
- that American soldiers would become wandering men for the rest of their lives,
- that they would never find peace, and
- that they would be angry people for the rest of their lives.

Has this come true? Does this mean we should be fearful? No! The good news is that Jesus brought us out from under the authority of darkness and placed us under his authority and protection. Demonic forces have no power over the life of a *submitted* believer except by

God's design, Satan's deception, or our rebellion. "The Son of God appeared for this purpose, that He might destroy the works of the devil."36 God allowed Satan to oppress Job, sift Peter, and kill Christ, but in each case the ultimate end accomplished God's purpose.

We get involved in our own deliverance by giving up those things which give Satan jurisdiction in our soul. To remove the foothold anger gives, we must forgive those who have wounded us. Only then can we take authority over oppressive demonic forces with any assurance of victory. Other footholds are: immorality, pride, covetousness (greed), idolatry, lust, fear, and rebellion. Freedom from demonic influence is first and foremost an issue of the heart. If we do not truly forsake the sin which gives tormentors their place, no methodology will bring lasting freedom. In fact, things often get worse.37

This book is not a primer on deliverance, but as believers we should *know our authority*. Once we turn from our sin we can renounce ungodly spiritual influences by identifying the enemy, binding him, verbally and behaviorally taking back any ground we have given, and refusing to yield.38 Jesus said, "The kingdom of heaven is forcibly entered and forcible men [warriors] seize it for themselves."39 Like the land God promised Israel, God's kingdom is inherited by what we believe in our heart about God, what we confess with our lips, and by actions consistent with our beliefs.40 Our authority is based on who we are in Christ, not in ourselves. The foundation for *our* authority is that we are first *under* authority. Every good soldier knows this principle.41

Jesus was given authority over all dominion. Every knee will eventually bow to him, whether in heaven, on earth, or under the earth. Jesus commanded unclean spirits and they obeyed Him. "Calling the twelve together, He gave them power and authority over all demons." Christ's authority is in His *name*. Jesus said, "Holy Father, keep them in Thy name, the name which Thou has given Me. While I was with them, *I was keeping them in Thy name* which You gave me; and *I guarded them*." There is no other name under heaven that has been given by which men might be saved. On the basis of faith in His name, we are protected, strengthened, and given perfect health.42

Stand To!

In Vietnam, my Battery often went through an early morning ritual designed to prevent us from being surprised by enemy forces. At five a.m. somebody would shake us awake with the command to, "Stand to!" We had to put on our helmet and flak jacket, and with M-16 in hand, stand fully prepared to meet a "suspected" enemy assault. We consistently lived with sleep deprivation and this meant one hour less. I hated it! So did everyone else. However, when "Top" was in the field he came around to make sure we were up and awake! Those who didn't get up were given a swift kick in the pants. Uncomfortable as it was, it was required. The same diligence is required in every believer's walk.

"Finally, be strong," Paul says, "that you may be able to stand firm… against principalities… against powers… against forces… resist, and having done everything, *stand firm.*"[43] Edwin Cole says, "It is always easier to *obtain* something than it is to *maintain* it." We have a responsibility to resist the enemy, and to stand firm in the freedom God gives us. True disciples are separated from those merely practicing religion in the same manner that wheat is separated from chaff, by being tossed around and beaten up. Warfare is what sets true soldiers apart!

The full armor of God, by which we are equipped to battle enemy forces, is discussed in Ephesians 6:14-18. Study it! Apply it! Team up! Join other soldiers to protect yourself and others. The true battle for freedom did not take place in Vietnam. That was merely basic training, preparation for the real battle which is still being fought. Did you go to Vietnam to deliver the oppressed? Well, the oppressed are everywhere. Do you ever think of going back to Vietnam to save the POWs and MIAs? There are thousands who are still Prisoners Of that War, who are Missing In America. What about them? Let's get back to the basics of training in the Word and in Godly discipline. We need to be filled and empowered by the Holy Spirit in the same manner the disciples were. If we first equip ourselves and learn how to stand in the world, we can then battle for others.

Cancel all debts! Give up the "you owe me" attitude. Let go of the offenses of others. No matter what anyone has done, forgive them. Then go to the cross of Christ, and the altar of God, and get all *your* debts canceled. We can't afford the luxury of rehearsing what Vietnam did to us. Take a look around. Read the signs of the times. The hour is getting late! Let us lay aside every weight of sin which so easily entangles us, and get on with it.

Summary

Bitterness is a major stronghold which, when rooted in our life, causes us trouble and defiles others. Forgiveness is the key which frees us from the torment and troubles bitterness produces. Giving mercy, even to the undeserving, frees God to pour His mercy upon us. Whether we are separated from God, man, or from peace of mind, forgiveness brings reconciliation. It opens the door to restoration.

Whether we are yoked to burdensome pain, woundedness, anger, insecurity, guilt, or blame, forgiveness lightens our load. Whatever the seed, whatever the root, whatever the tree, whatever the fruit... forgiveness allows God the freedom to apply the axe to it. "Whom the Son makes free, shall be free indeed."[44]

-Questions-

1. What are you still angry and bitter about?

2. Whom do you hold responsible for these things?

3. What beliefs, choices, and behaviors are you holding on to that virtually guarantee future dissatisfaction and unhappiness?

4. Will you forgive the people who have offended or betrayed you? When?

-14-

Mending Broken Hearts
[RESOLVING EMOTIONAL PAIN]

"I was a medic. I spent my time putting pieces of human flesh and body parts back together. Out of the unit that I was assigned, only thirty men remained at the end of my tour. I learned that you didn't get close... that the only thing that happened to friends was that they died."
                                                    –Bob Chester, Vietnam vet

"Golf Company was a family. That was two hundred and twenty kids that had a job to do. They were twenty years old. They were eighteen, nineteen. They were kids. I had to protect them. Somebody had to protect you guys. When somebody died in that platoon, a piece of you died with them. After a while, there were no more pieces left. You couldn't give another piece, because the moment you gave another piece you were going to die with them. Then you began to come apart."
                                                    –Frank Ciappio[1]

"The post-Vietnam syndrome confronts us with the unconsummated grief of soldiers, in which an unending, encapsulated past robs the present of meaning. Their sorrow is unspent, the grief of their wounds is untold, their guilt is unexpiated."
                                                    –Dr. Shatan[2]

Emotional pain is inescapable. We have all been hurt or offended in some way. Throughout life we have all suffered losses. Pain does not go away by avoiding it; it is unrealistic to expect it will. The truth is, it's healthy to express pain and to learn from it. However, trying to alleviate pain without first identifying what creates or sustains it, can leave us further victimized. Pain shows us where there is a problem. Leaving a painful problem unresolved can cripple us. This chapter examines pain and God's plan for healing emotions and pain-based behaviors.

Feelings
We use the terms feelings and emotions interchangeably. Feelings are *physical* sensations created by touch. They are automatic reactions created by the autonomic nervous system, and for the most part, are not designed to be controlled. We describe these sensations as cold, hot, soft, smooth, painful, pleasurable, etc. Feelings enrich our life. They are a way we communicate with our environment. We may see feelings

as being good or bad, but they are simply communication tools and a sign that we are fully alive. Pain, in itself, is a good messenger. It communicates that something needs to be attended to or repaired. We sometimes try to control feelings and emotions, when it is more appropriate to control behaviors and attitudes.

Emotions

Emotions are a *psychological* response created by a mixture of feelings, attitudes, and beliefs. They are also normal and a part of being fully human. Although emotions in and of themselves are not destructive, attitudes, beliefs, and behaviors in response to them can be. Emotions have an indisputable, even mysterious, collective power that often appears stronger than we are. Emotions can weigh us down or free us up, and there is an undeniable consequence for disregarding them. If our life is *controlled* by emotions, they can exact a heavy toll. Emotions can make us feel weak rather than strong, disdain for our self rather than respect, or pitiful rather than loved. We have a right to emotions, including pain and anger. Emotions change. They rarely last for long unless we work to keep them alive. Our *reactions to* emotions, however, often have life-long consequences.

Emotions do not function independent of intellect or will. We use our imagination to evoke emotions, and we can sustain them by obsessively replaying events. We can carry emotions, disregard them, act on them, or give them expression. If we do not attend to them, some emotions slowly erode our mental and physical health. We either rule our emotions, or are ruled by them. We may try to avoid unsettling emotions through painstaking denial, but if we present them to God He can heal them.

There is a natural progression of emotions and activity following loss that is unavoidable. The same is true when we are wounded. Yet self-preserving beliefs, attitudes, and behaviors, including denial, distrust, guardedness, isolation, resentment, and revenge, *can* be avoided. Peace, joy, and the ability to behave rightly in all our relationships is possible. These things are rightfully ours as new creations in Christ. It is Satan, the destroyer, who would have us believe otherwise.

Pain-Based Responses

Unresolved pain almost always results in a series of negative thinking patterns, critical attitudes, and destructive behaviors. These *harmful* patterns develop as a means of coping with injury. When unchanged, these patterns create *additional* pain for us and often injure others. Scripture refers to pain-based behaviors as "iniquities." *Iniquity* has broad meaning, being translated throughout the Bible as: wickedness, malice, perversity, depravity, lawlessness, vanity, criminal acts, injustice, sin, and unrighteousness. Iniquity comes from the Hebrew word *avah*, which means, "to make crooked; to pervert that which at one time was straight." Tom Deuschle describes iniquity as: a) the propensity to, or leaning toward a particular sin, b) a behavior or predisposition passed down from generation to generation, and c) a malpractice; something done to you which was not your own fault.[3] Today, iniquity is called "dysfunctional behavior," which is merely a psychological term for *sin.* Psychological terms may help us to clarify what sin is, but if we make sinful behaviors amoral, we remove personal accountability for them. We also substitute human jurisdiction where God has ultimate authority.

Trauma only creates an *opportunity* for our lives to become dysfunctional; it doesn't dictate that we do. Tragedy can make it hard for us to walk the narrow path, but we ultimately choose whether we stay on course or get off. It is *our response* to tragedy that makes the difference. What happens *to* us *influences* us, pushing our lives in a specific direction, but it doesn't have to destroy us.

A futile, dysfunctional lifestyle can also be passed on from generation to generation. Peter wrote, "You should know that you were not redeemed [ransomed] with perishable things like silver and gold from *your futile way of life inherited from your forefathers.*"[4] Behaviors we observe and mimic are a part of our inheritance. So are attitudes, beliefs, and emotions. There are also spiritual principles, that when violated, cause us to duplicate the same behavior we judge in others. Although we aren't responsible for what others do to us, or for things we cannot control, we *are* responsible for not getting over it. We are also responsible for breaking dysfunctional patterns, and for behaviors that injure others as a result of our not getting healed or changing.

The Healing Process

Forgiveness and healing are not synonymous. We can forgive others and still carry the defilement of their sins, especially that of a wounded heart. Emotions need to be healed. Deep emotional wounds often take time to heal. Healing can come in bits and pieces or take place in cycles. Each time the wound is revisited, healing comes on a deeper level. Emotional health, like physical health, can also require changes in our behavior. Consider the link between cancer and smoking or being overweight and eating.

We must first acknowledge our pain to do anything about it. Treatment requires an accurate diagnosis of cause. This means a careful, thorough examination of our history, as well as present behaviors, attitudes, and beliefs. If we cannot find the cause, we must be willing to go to others for help. We must also *apply* appropriate solutions. Once healed, we may need to change in order to stay healthy. All change comes by way of exchange, and *we* must decide whether *we* are willing to pay the price for healing.

Leaving Familiar Territory

All recovery groups emphasize that the road to healing involves first accepting the pains of the past. Only then can we resolve them. Many of us have been told to put the past behind and forget it. However, to lay aside *behaviors* and *attitudes*, we must deal with the pain that creates and sustains them. Paul said, "In order that I may obtain *a new and powerful* resurrected life, I press on that I may lay hold of that for which I was apprehended. Brothers, I do not regard myself as having obtained it all yet, but one thing I do: forgetting what lies behind I reach forward to what lies ahead."[5] This should not be construed as an excuse to deny past pain. Jeremiah tells us that "you cannot heal a wound by saying it is not there."[6] Paul is referring to his old habit of trusting in his own ability to achieve God's righteousness, not denying the past.

Exodus is a good illustration of leaving the past behind. It shows how what once worked to *save*, can in the end, *enslave*. God's provision for Israel's *survival* during a time of extreme *stress* ended up years later as a source of bondage. It was not God's intent for Israel to stay in Egypt, even though it had once been their salvation, comfort, and safety. When God asked them to leave their old habitat, they resisted. God promised them a new place of provision, still Israel hesitated. They had become familiar with Egypt. Even though Egypt had become a place of bondage, hardship, and misery, they wanted to stay. What had once been profitable began creating their ruin, and circumstances had to become unbearable before they were willing to leave their former lifestyle behind. As it was for Israel, so it is for us. We must leave behind old patterns of anger, denial, avoidance, isolation, guardedness, self-protection, and chemical dependency, even though they are familiar and once helped us survive. To move forward, Israel had to risk leaving the familiar. If we want God's provision for healing, so must we.

Jim Lakewind, a seasoned Vet Center counselor, says that the biggest precipitator of PTSD is cognitive dissonance (mental discord), the sense that the myth and reality do not jive. When vets begin to admit that the war in Vietnam was not about life, but about gold, they begin to penetrate a strong, well-defended *denial* system. And, when vets examine the bottom line, they are subject to some psychic and spiritual *pain* that seems downright unbearable. He, like most mental health professionals, believes that growth and integration require *pain*.

Refusing to acknowledge or experience the pain that resolution often requires keeps us bound to the past. To leave pain behind we must grieve our losses. To not act fully human, by shutting down emotions, is to become *inhumane*. The more we remove ourselves from emotions, the harder they are to identify. When we become experts at hiding our emotions, we become experts at covering up the truth. This keeps us from acknowledging painful realities about ourselves.

Truth as Reality

The road to emotional healing begins and ends with truth. Jesus said, "*If* you abide [lay hold of] in me *then* you shall know the truth and the truth shall set you free." Freedom is provisional. *If* we abide, *then* we shall know. The key word is "if." Seeking truth requires diligent, fearless examination. We are challenged to live as a people of authenticity, to be genuine and real. To do so we must set aside our masks.

Truth means "actual, unconcealed, or true to fact." When we are truthful, we deal faithfully with ourselves and others. Truth is not just an ethical matter, it is a *correct rendering*. Although reality exists whether we acknowledge it or not, without truth we create little reality for ourselves. Without truth, trust cannot be built. Relationships flounder. Integrity falls by the wayside. Without integrity we send mixed messages which create confusion. We lose self-respect and a sense of our true identity.

God wants us to see that in spite of the fallen
character of mankind, He remains unchanged.
His mercy and love still cover us.

Emotional Honesty

Many men see grieving as a weakness, a character defect. Yet consider how amazingly open God is about the character defects in His family. Scripture is full of examples of men who were less than perfect, but were still accepted and loved by God. In the very first family, one brother murdered another, yet God did not hide that from us. Noah's feet had barely walked on solid ground when he got drunk. Abraham, the father of all people of faith, was so fearful he told his wife to lie about their relationship and say she was his sister. Samson carried on with a whore and lost his hair, his sight, and his life because of it. David slept with another man's wife and arranged to have her husband killed. Peter openly lied, denying that he even knew Christ. Yet God did not keep any of these things hidden. God wants us to see that in spite of the fallen character of mankind, He remains unchanged. His mercy and love still cover us. What then should we fear?

What God requires of us, He first reveals in Himself. When Christ openly wept, he set an example for transparency and honesty.[7] He did not hide his emotions. The nature of the world, on the other hand, is to lie, hide, and deceive. We were created with emotions, does it make sense to keep them hidden? Are we to hide only the "negative" ones? We are to live openly and honestly, committed to the truth about ourselves and others. This means being real about our emotions.[8]

Knowing Ourselves

The first step toward emotional healing is to recognize and identify emotional garbage. This requires examination. David says, "Surely you [God] desire truth in my inner parts, you teach me wisdom in the inner place."[9] We do not take the journey of self-examination alone, but with the Holy Spirit. We must *seek* to heal and purify our heart, diligently and courageously appraising our life. Once we identify areas of blindness, we can take the next step to change.

Acknowledging Truth

Acknowledging truth means: 1) to know or recognize fully or thoroughly, and 2) to recognize a thing to be what it really is. If we are unwilling to take ownership for our emotions, we have no hope of changing. If we acknowledge the truth about our emotions and let them surface, they will soon lose the hold they have over us.[10]

Paul wrote, "If a man cleanses or purges himself he will become a vessel for honor... so, with gentleness, correct those who oppose themselves... perhaps God will turn them around and lead them to a *knowledge of the truth* so they can come to their senses and recover from the snare of the devil, since they have been held captive by him to do whatever he wants, whenever he wants."[11] If we want to be used to bring honor to God we must cleanse our hearts, for out of the heart comes every behavior which defiles a man's life. To cleanse our hearts we must discover those areas where we "oppose ourselves;" that is, where our behaviors contradict our words or where heartfelt beliefs contradict head beliefs, thus creating emotional and mental discord. The fear of pain and suffering can keep us torn between serving our own desire for self-protection, and God's desires. We end up with opposing allegiances. We may *say* one thing, but *do* another. Or, we may think we *should* do one thing, but do what we want. The danger of keeping our inner struggles hidden is that we end up being snared by deception. Hidden sins eventually become compulsions. Compulsions captivate our will.

God wants to prune the pain from our heart because it defiles us. A good gardener knows that pruning causes a tree to bear more fruit. Pruning, however, can be painful. And, while we know that self-examination may uncover past hurts, it is the only path to real healing because it makes us more fruitful. Honesty with ourselves and others creates humility. Humility releases God to act on our behalf. Humility is simply truthfully acknowledging who we are and our need for Christ.

Confession

Confession is publicly acknowledging the truth. "Is anyone among you *suffering*? Let him pray. Confess your offenses to one another and pray for one another so that you may be healed."[12] We may acknowledge our pain silently before the Lord, but confession is interpersonal, not private. We are told to "cast all our cares on Christ" and "confess our sins to one another," yet many of us confess our sins to Christ and cast all our cares on one another.

Confession is difficult for the proud and self-sufficient. It is easier to ask God to minister to us privately, so that we can keep our sins hidden. God does meet us individually, but He has designed our healing to also take place in relationships. We are wounded in relationships and that is what creates separation and isolation. God uses relationships to bring healing because it restores trust, unity, and a sense of belonging.

Confession is God's way of bringing iniquity into the light. Iniquity operates in the darkness of deception; so it will not be exposed and rooted out. Just as the confession of our mouth is necessary to salvation, the confession of our mouth helps create healing. Just as "besetting sin" (addictive habits) cannot be conquered by denial, suppression, or rationalization, so it is with grief.[13] We break the bondage of pain through disclosure. If we keep our wounds hidden, our heart remains guarded. "The heart knows its own bitterness, and a stranger does not share its joy."[14] We may not be aware of our guardedness, but it is often painfully obvious to those around us. It is difficult to experience emotional healing without being comforted, and others cannot comfort what we deny is there. We must *also* decide if we really want to be healed. This is vital, for many times sick people ask to be made well when deep down inside they want nothing of the sort. Illness is often used as a life strategy to gain attention and attendance from others, or simply as a means to avoid responsibility.

Change is an Exchange

Healing does not come by identification, acknowledgment, or confession alone. The VA Medical Centers and PTSD clinics use a number of techniques to uncover pain, but tragically, too many vets leave treatment in touch with their pain but without healing or resolution. It is futile to expose pain if there is no hope for healing. This does not mean that we are healed by getting in touch with our pain or by expressing it. Emotions are a *sign* of what needs to be addressed, but they are not necessary for our healing. We must allow ourselves to be comforted by God's Spirit if we want to be healed.

All growth, from beginning to end, is acquired by exchange. It may be our pain for God's comfort, our anxiety for His peace, or our guilt for His righteousness. God can also take a heart of stone and exchange it for a heart of flesh. He can take a heart full of pain and give it lasting comfort. We need only to present ourselves to Him and invite His Spirit to work. Healing is a partnership... it takes God and us working together. We must say, "God, search my heart. Uncover and deliver me from any unclean thing." Jesus said, "Blessed are the poor in spirit, for theirs is the kingdom of heaven."[15] If we are willing to acknowledge our spiritual poverty; that is, our inability to heal ourselves, we will see our need for Him and cry out.

Christ's Mission

Jesus came into the world to restore broken hearts. He said:

> The Spirit of the Lord is upon me, because the Lord has anointed me to bring good news to those who are depressed, beaten down, and afflicted. He has sent me to *bind up those whose hearts have been broken* and whose wills have been crushed. To proclaim liberty to those who are now held captive, and freedom and an opening to those who are now bound up as prisoners. To proclaim the favorable year of the Lord when all debts are canceled.[16]

Jesus knows our pain. Isaiah says of him, "He was despised and forsaken of men, a man of pain and sorrows and acquainted with grief."[17] Paul wrote, "We do not have a high priest who cannot sympathize with our weaknesses, but one who has been tempted in all things as we are, yet without sin."[18] David said, "The Lord is near the brokenhearted and saves those who are crushed in spirit."[19] In the book of Jeremiah, we hear these words from God:

> I [God] will restore you to health and will heal you of your wounds. Call to me and I will answer you... I will bring to you health and healing, and I will heal you; and I will bring to you an abundance of peace and truth... and I will rebuild you as you were at first, and I will cleanse you from all your iniquities... and I will pardon all your iniquities. I will certainly rescue you... because you have trusted in Me.[20]

God's Comfort

Emotional healing is not as simple as merely saying the right words. Pain cannot be absolved intellectually, it can only be resolved on an emotional level. An injured heart needs understanding. It needs to be comforted. Paul describes God as "the Father of all comfort, who comforts us in all our tribulation, that we are able to comfort them which are in any trouble, by the comfort we ourselves experience."[21] Comfort comes from God's manifest presence and requires *experiencing* God's love. An analytical mind will block emotions, but we must release them to the mercies of God. The heart needs time for sorrow. That is why we need the strength and nurturing of the Spirit, for God's Spirit bypasses the mind and ministers directly to the wounded heart, bringing peace and an end to sorrow.[22]

Paul says, "God comforts the depressed, those who are cast down."[23] The word depressed is also translated, *humble*. Humility and depression are similar, for both result from a state of helplessness. We are helpless to heal our hearts, and time, contrary to popular opinion, does not heal all. Jesus said, "Blessed are those that mourn, for they shall be comforted."[24] We must allow ourselves to mourn if we desire healing. Holding on to pain, anger, and a desire for revenge will keep us from being comforted. God wants to heal those wounds that have not yet felt His healing presence. This is one way He enlarges His life in us. The heart cannot contain both pain and love in the same area; one must go to make room for the other. Exchanging one for the other requires a choice on our part. Ultimately, allowing ourselves to be healed is an issue of trust and Lordship.

The Nature of God

Our God is an approachable God! As our Father, He did not remain aloof or disengaged from our life so that He would not have to feel our pain, as our earthly fathers might have. He didn't withdraw to a place which was safe or comfortable for Him. Neither did He remove Himself emotionally or physically, as many of our earthly fathers may have. Instead, He came to us in the midst of our pain and suffering, in the person of Jesus. He was physically present with us. He gave up His position of power in the heavenlies to become vulnerable, dependent, and powerless... all for our sake. He came to assure us that He cares.

God saw us as orphans: abandoned, disenfranchised, abused, rejected, and alone. Yet He made a way for us to be adopted into His family. He not only adopted us, He *regened* us through the Holy Spirit, giving us the genetic capability to become sons and daughters. He did this so we could know the love of a true father. He wanted to nurture us in a way we could become healthy, fully functional adults. When we discover that we are loved perfectly, we are able to love others perfectly. This makes us better fathers, mothers, and spouses. God reparents us to free us from the influence of abuse and neglect, and from the generational influence resulting from the fall of man.

The Application of Comfort

For years, I resisted trusting God with my pain. I relied on temporary, quick fixes to bring immediate relief from my suffering. I didn't want to acknowledge my pain, much less expose it. I was only interested in escaping it. I believed God cared for me on some level, yet in my innermost heart I didn't trust Him with my emotions. God was too slow to act. I had difficulty admitting I didn't trust Him because I equated intellectual agreement with faith. However, I was even unwilling to act on my belief, so my faith was dead. This was one of those areas where I was "opposed to myself." My head said one thing while my heart said another. It wasn't that I didn't believe God was able, it was, "will God do it for *me*?"

When I finally began to face my mistrust and pain, I discovered God was there. I began to know with certainty God's mercy and willingness to comfort me in *all* my affliction. The pain in my life was slowly replaced by God's peace, comfort, and joy. I now see that apart from the pain I have suffered and the comfort I have received, I have very little to offer a hurting world.

The Holy Spirit is our Comforter. He is the "Medic" who comes when we call. We also need the comfort of others, the Spirit with skin on it. God has not designed us to be emotional islands. He has given us a family which includes the body of Christ, our spiritual community.

The Holy Spirit is our Comforter.
He is the "Medic" who comes when we call.

Healing must also be apprehended! God calls us to press in... even as Jacob took hold of the Lord and would not let go of him until his life had been changed, so we must dedicate ourselves to opening our heart to God and pursuing Him until our heart is completely whole.[25] We must be committed to making *progress* until the *process* is completed.

God, in His wisdom and mercy, has designed our healing to come by way of dependency on Him. This means death to self-reliance. The good news is that death in Christ is always followed by a resurrection.

Relying on God

Although there are practical steps you can take to be healed, there is no sure-fire formula. Biblical principles, when followed, produce specific results, but the Christian life is not a regimen of formulas, rules, or methods. *Life* does not result from following laws. Emotional healing isn't accomplished by introspection or the application of methods. Healing does not come by self effort in and of itself. The number of suicides following treatment in VA PTSD programs is evidence enough of this. God is sovereign and works within His *relationship* with us. He has His own timing, and His own way.

I am not asking you to go on a personal witch hunt to exorcise yourself from past hurts. God surfaces *all* unresolved issues of the heart *according to His timetable.* It is detrimental to the church, and all other relationships, when we feel compelled to fix one another. Our attempt to fix others, to fit them into our mold, or into our definition of what it means to be a good Christian or a good spouse, is terribly wounding. Conviction is the work of the Holy Spirit. It is *our* job to love one another unconditionally, to bear one another's burdens and so fulfill the law of Christ. It is God who is at work in us, both to give us the desire and the power to accomplish *His* purpose.[26] It is our responsibility to be yielded and unresistant. A true warrior wades through all resistance to come to the truth, either about himself or his circumstances, in order to obtain lasting healing.

Summary

Feelings and emotions are natural to us all. They are God's gifts. They help us to identify personal problems and areas in relationships that need to be addressed. Denying feelings or emotions, and the messages they send us, only creates additional problems. Carrying the sorrow of unhealed emotional wounds can produce life-long patterns of anger, mistrust, guardedness, denial, avoidance, and depression. Emotional healing is not easy. Walls, like scar tissue, have to be removed. Tender wounds must often be exposed to a painful cleaning process. Washing with the water of the word of God, when applied correctly, works like an antibiotic. It brings hope and healing.

Allowing our hearts to be purified of pain and anger requires an examined life, a diligent pursuit of the truth, a willingness to acknowledge pain, and the desire to exchange it for the comfort God and others have to give. Jesus alone is ultimately our healer, but He often chooses to bring emotional healing through others. To those who choose God, He says, "I will restore you to health, and I will heal you of all your wounds, because they have called you an outcast, saying, it is Zion, no one cares for her."[27]

-Questions-

1. What experiences created emotional wounds for you in Vietnam?

2. What emotions are you still carrying from your tour of duty?

3. How do you victimize yourself by carrying pain and pain-based behaviors?

4. In what ways might your life be different if you humbly submitted to God and trusted Him to heal your emotional wounds?

5. What gets in the way of you either asking for or receiving God's healing for your heart?

-15-

Laying the Foundation

[RESOLVING GUILT]

"I can't disentangle it yet... I saw three young children detonate a booby-trapped mine. I was also with their father (maybe three or four years older than me) when we tried to get help back at the aid station. He was beautiful... pitiful... tortured, frantic. They were dying, the young girl and one boy died while at the aid station. The medic told me they were going to die... they did. The father's eyes were imploring, pleading, praying. I felt guilty, how can I say I'm not with these people. I just wanted to see what it's like... And I don't like it. He can see the tears in my eyes reflected in the tears in his. Talk about guilt."

–Erik, suicide victim

"A case was presented at psychiatric grand rounds with excellent detail and formulation, but with no material at all about the patient's tour of duty in Viet Nam. The diagnosis presented was borderline personality disorder, not withstanding excellent functioning for three years in the military. A visiting consultant asked about the missing Viet Nam military history, to which the senior psychiatrist on the patient's unit responded by asserting that the individual had not been in combat, but rather in the 'rear' support forces, and that his job had been 'merely' to direct artillery strikes. Therefore, concluded the psychiatrist, there was no war trauma present and no need to pursue the details of the year in Viet Nam. Indeed, the military history was not further pursued. Sometime later the patient killed himself."

–Arthur S. Blank, Jr.

Many vets have lost their way in life because of unhealed pain. They couldn't shake the dust of bitterness off their boots or find a safe point of reentry. Yet no loss is so tragic as the many who took their lives after safely returning home, because they could not shake the burden of guilt. Sadly, there are still far too many casualties produced by guilt induced self hatred and isolation. The following exchange portrays the kind of response many soldiers had to their experiences in Vietnam. Perhaps it also shows some insight into why guilt is still carried:

When correspondent Jonathan Schell was touring Quang Ngai Province in late summer of 1967... a GI who was driving him around in a jeep suddenly turned and said, "You wouldn't believe the things that go on in this war."

"What things?" Schell asked.

"You wouldn't believe it."

"What kind of things, then?"

"You wouldn't believe it, so I'm not going to tell you," the GI said, shaking his head no. "No one's ever going to find out about some things, and after this war is over, and we've all gone home, no one is ever going to know."[2]

Guilt: A Legacy of War

Guilt has been a residual effect of every war. Vietnam was no different. However, the reaction of both society and the medical profession to Vietnam veterans served to reinforce guilt. Social rejection, criticism, unbelief and condemnation, all created significant human tragedy. Not all Vietnam veterans feel guilty about their involvement in Vietnam, nor should they. Yet veterans who do feel as if they have done something wrong, often keep it hidden. Personal shame, coupled with social condemnation, has created a confusing legacy of guilt-induced behavior.

Legitimate Guilt

Guilt, remember, is the result of an *inner* conviction that we have done something wrong; that we have violated our *own* standards or boundaries in some way. This conviction springs from our conscience,. as a result of God's Spirit impressing our spirit with His personal standards. This gives us an *intuitive* understanding of God's desire. Without God's expressed expectations there are only those imposed by society. True guilt comes when we violate God's personal intent for our lives, and although uncomfortable, it is always accompanied by a quiet call to behave differently, and a clear sense of what that difference is.

False Guilt

False guilt is unreasonable and undeserved. It *has no legitimate foundation*. It is merely condemnation, accusation, blame, or shame from which there seems no escape. It is created by a distorted picture of our acts, or by assuming responsibility for things we have no responsibility for. These distortions (lies) are created by ourselves, others, and Satan. Distorted perceptions create unrealistic expectations, which when unfulfilled leave us feeling condemned or worthless. Condemnation then compels us to try harder or work faster to make up for the perception that we are failing. This produces *striving* behaviors. False guilt results more from a sense of inadequacy than from actual wrongdoing.

We all have a *social* and a *spiritual* conscience. Our social conscience is formed by our upbringing. It is a mix of memorized messages, emotional memories, and social training. It guides and directs our behavior and is reinforced by family and society. If our primary caregivers were excessively strict and critical, we may develop an strict, critical conscience. This then drives us, through condemnation and *a sense of guilt* which is really shame and blame. We sometimes comply with a harsh conscience even though it makes us feel condemned, criticized, or inadequate *because not to comply would cause us even more guilt.*[3] This type of guilt is not a result of spiritual conviction, but a result of social disapproval and the fear of rejection. It leaves us feeling damned for things God Himself doesn't condemn.

Social standards are often carelessly mixed with God's standards. Sometimes it is done purposefully by people who are manipulative and controlling. God's standards are also confused with social and religious tradition. Condemnation is one of the most powerful tools in Satan's arsenal. By trying to counterfeit the voice of the Holy Spirit, he uses the conscience to accuse and denounce his victims with ceaseless torment. What better way to discourage the human spirit than to create a feeling of guilt which cannot be forgiven.

Survival Guilt

Survival guilt results more from a sense of inadequacy or power-lessness than from actual wrongdoing. It's the nagging doubt that we didn't do all that we could, or in the accusation that we deserved to die rather than someone else. Survival guilt is sometimes a sense of misgiving, or an uneasy sense that in some way we were responsible for another's death. This is often mixed with conflicting loyalties to those left behind, to whom we felt a debt of gratitude.

Survival guilt can stem from unresolved inner conflict, a result of incompatibility between the way we believe things *should* have been, and what *actually* happened. The human tendency is to think that if we just look long and hard enough, we will understand all our experiences through some reasonable, logical thought process. We like to insist that everything conform to a justifiable list of explanations. If we can figure everything out, we can be self-reliant. We won't have to depend on God. Sometimes it's easier to accept guilt than it is to accept that some things are out of our control. Admitting our powerlessness means having to accept limitations. So we keep asking ourselves, "Why them?" "Why me?" We ask but don't really want an explanation. The *why* is more of a puzzling whine; an admission of our lack of understanding and of our own inadequacy.

The fact that people suffer tragedy does not necessarily impugn their character or ours.[4] People who die in war are not any more or less sinful than those who survive. John Sandford says, "Mens sins pile up like rocks on a ledge. Eventually that pile will break the ledge and cause a landslide. The man who happens to be walking by that moment and is crushed is not more or less sinful than those who do not. Thus the relation of sin to tragedy is more likely corporate than personal."[5] The tragedy of Vietnam, and the loss of individual lives, is more likely due to the sins of mankind in general than to the sins of those who fought.

Resolving Guilt

Guilt, whether real or false, always results in self-blame, self-reproach, and self-condemnation. Self-accusing beliefs create a sense of worthlessness and shame. Shame and a low self-image produce *hiding* behaviors motivated by fear. Hiding creates isolation and loneliness, which often lead to depression and despair.

Medical research links prolonged guilt to both internal and external destructive changes. So, regardless of their source, *feelings* of guilt must be faced. Many mental health practitioners classify all guilt as *pathological*. They see it as a symptom of mental illness. Yet they report that guilt is difficult to deal with because occasionally there is some *reality* to it. They also say there is no satisfactory answer to the question of survival guilt, and no realistic answer to the question, "Why not me?" As a result, humanistic methods for treating guilt among veterans are primarily geared to assist soldiers to recognize:

• the abnormal, psychotic nature of their experiences,
• that it's not shameful to do what one can to survive, and
• that it is not their behavior that killed fellow soldiers.

However, if we truly believe that our actions were wrong, providing a rational *reason* for them won't change how we *feel*. If our behavior *was* contrary to self, and at odds with our values, denying it, justifying it, or excusing it will not bring an end to the conflict we *feel*.

Edwin Cole writes, "In our modern era we have done away with sin, thinking to do away with guilt. We are taught that it is outdated thinking, coming out of our Judeo-Christian background, and that the concept of guilt only hinders our psychological development."[6] We no longer have sins, we have problems. We no longer have lust, we have biological necessities. Instead of humans being morally depraved, we are merely environmentally deprived. We are coddled into believing we have no other choices or that circumstances excuse our behavior. We are taught to believe that situations define our ethics, not the other way around. We don't talk about sins today, we talk about disorders. Disorders are more convenient to deal with. They solicit sympathy, understanding, and professional help. Sins, on the other hand, have to be repented of, confessed, and forsaken. They are *our* responsibility.

It is popular today to think that we can solve our problems by simply surrounding ourselves with individuals who will love and understand us…that their sympathy and support will eventually rid us of our hatred and anger. It is true that love and understanding are necessary for our healing and restoration, but it will not rid us of guilt. True guilt can only be alleviated by God.

God's Remedy For Guilt

To be free from anger and bitterness, we must *give* forgiveness. To be free from guilt, we must *receive* forgiveness. Many of us have tried to deal with guilt by denial. We have unsuccessfully justified, rationalized, or blamed others for our behaviors. God's remedy, however, is Jesus Christ. When we believe and receive what Jesus accomplished for us, God cleanses us…no matter what we've done.

God's remedy for guilt is confrontation, confession, and cleansing. Confrontation comes when the Holy Spirit convicts us of the sinfulness of our deeds. Confession comes when we personally and publicly acknowledge what we have done. Cleansing comes when we accept Christ's death in place of our own. Jesus said about his life's blood, "This is the blood of the covenant [promise, contract] which is to be shed on behalf of many *for forgiveness of sins*."[7] Christ's blood, and therefore his life, was poured out on our behalf. His death was necessary for God's contract with us to be fulfilled. The exchange of blood as a sign of covenant can be seen in both European and Native American cultures. It has always been the sign of a solemn, sacred vow.

Confrontation and Confession

We are all guilty of something. Yet we do not escape guilt by running from it. When we confront, confess, and forsake sin, Jesus provides merciful pardon and relief. Instead of running, we need only accept forgiveness.

Peter was a follower of Jesus. He was also a close, trusted friend. Yet when Jesus was arrested, Peter abandoned him. Three times he publicly denied knowing Jesus; such was his fear and desire for self-preservation. Even though Jesus had told Peter that he would deny him, Peter vigorously denied that he would. He was cocky, arrogant, and self-confident. He *felt* sure of his loyalty. Jesus, of course, was right. The third time Peter denied knowing him, Jesus turned and looked him in the eye. That was all it took. Peter remembered Jesus' words and was instantly *confronted* with his behavior. *Convicted*, he "went out and wept bitterly."[8]

Following his resurrection, Jesus visited Peter at the Sea of Galilee, and here we see the progressive working out of Peter's redemption.

> Jesus said, "Simon [Peter], son of John, do you love me more than these [referring to the other disciples]?"
> He answered, "Yes, Lord, you know that I love you."
> Jesus said, "Take care of my lambs."
> Again Jesus said, "Simon, son of John, do you love me?"
> He answered, "Yes, Lord, you know that I love you."
> Jesus said, "Take care of my sheep."
> A third time he said, "Simon, son of John, do you love me?"
> Peter *was grieved* because Jesus asked him the third time, "Do you love me?" Peter said, "Lord, *you know everything*. You know that I love you!"
> Jesus said unto him, "Feed my sheep."[9]

Jesus cared enough about Peter to confront him face-to-face. He wanted to address Peter's past behavior so he could deal with it, and put it to rest. He did not want Peter carrying guilt. Peter could hardly mistake what Jesus was after. He had denied Jesus three times, and now Jesus was reminding him of his failure by asking him three times if Peter loved him. Peter must have been squirming in his shoes, but Jesus did not let Peter's discomfort keep him from pressing in. He persisted until Peter took personal accountability for his behavior.

When Jesus asked, "Do you *love* me?" he used a term meaning "reverence which is *given by choice*." Peter replied with a term for love which meant, "the inclination to be friendly which is *prompted by senses or emotion*." Jesus chose his words carefully, knowing that love based on senses and emotions could not be commanded, but was simply a response to sensual, visual stimulation. Peter's love was subject to whim and preference; that was not what Jesus wanted. Jesus wanted a love *governed by will*. He knew too well the fallacy of human love. It was human emotion that moved Peter to say he would never deny him.

It was human emotion that caused Peter, in the heat of the moment, to cut an ear off the servant of the High Priest. Jesus knew that human emotions change, and that human love fluctuates depending on whether we are getting anything out of it. This kind of love quickly dies in the face of sacrifice. Because Peter was led by emotions, when over-whelmed by fear, he abandoned his convictions, denying Christ to save his own skin. Peter had to see the folly of trusting in human emotion to understand the kind of love required to follow Jesus; and to lead others. When Peter finally realized the grave ineffectiveness of self-reliance, his personal pride and self-confidence were shattered. In the light of his failure, his boastful and presumptuous attitude could no longer bolster his pride and insecurity.

Like Peter, we all go through times of sifting when we are con-fronted with our humanity and convicted of our pride. These times *should* produce greater meekness and transparency, for we are all blind in some way to our shortcomings. God is faithful to expose our weak-nesses because they leave us open to assault from the powers of dark-ness. If we run from times of proving and resist God, we will never see what is wrong in us or face our need to change.

As painful as it was for Peter to acknowledge the truth about him-self, Jesus did not abandon or condemn him. Instead, He affirmed Pet-er's acceptance and said that God still had a plan for his life. It is kind-ness in the midst of our sin that breaks our stony heart and brings repentance. God's mercy is like rain upon hardened ground. It makes it soft and pliable... able to receive and sustain seeds which are planted. It makes clay soft and workable, able to be shaped into usable vessels. The fact that Peter received Christ's love and forgiveness and was rec-onciled enabled him to go on and live a productive, courageous life as God's instrument. Not so with Judas. Although both men struggled with betrayal, remorse, and guilt, *it was their response that determined their destiny*. Peter received forgiveness *and* forgave himself. Judas remained stuck in self-pity and guilt, and eventually took his own life.

Christ may not personally appear to us like He did to Peter, but he does deal with our sins directly. He confronts and convicts us to recon-cile us to himself. Just as there was no condemnation of Peter, there is no condemnation for us. "The Lord redeems the soul of His servants, and none of those who take refuge in Him will be condemned."[10]

Cleansing

We all fall short of God's standard to love perfectly. What fellowship can perfection have with imperfection? God's nature is light. Ours is darkness. It is impossible for light (purity), and darkness (impurity), to inhabit the same space. The result is separation, and no amount of self-effort or good deeds can cross the gulf between us. It was necessary for Jesus to come to bridge that gap. In the apostle Paul's letter to the Romans, he says:

> When we were utterly helpless with no way of escape, Christ came at just the right time and died for us sinners who had no use for him. Even if we were good, we really wouldn't expect anyone to die for us, though of course that might be barely possible. But God showed His own love for us by sending Christ to die for us while we were still sinners. And since by his blood he treats us as if we had never sinned, and declares us 'not guilty,' he will surely save us from the wrath to come.[11]

> Yes, all have sinned... yet now God declares us 'not guilty' of offending him if we trust in Jesus Christ, who in his kindness freely takes away our sins. For God sent Christ Jesus to take the punishment for our sins and to end all God's anger against us. He used Christ's blood and our faith as the means of saving us from his wrath... But isn't this unfair for God to let criminals go free, and say that they are innocent? No, for he does it on the basis of their trust in Jesus to take away their sins.[12]

If we interpret these scriptures to portray God as an angry Father whom Jesus must appease, we miss the truth of God's nature. God is a God of Justice. He cannot be something apart from Himself. Justice requires a balancing of the scales. God's justice is not only revealed in ethical or moral standards, it is expressed in those principles which undergird the very fabric of the universe. The world is held together by laws which balance. In physics, for every action there is an equal and opposite reaction. In math, every formula must balance. In nature, what you sow into the ground you reap. In law, the punishment must fit the crime... an eye for an eye, a tooth for a tooth, a life for a life. In a moral, ethical, just universe, our sins must also balance out. There is a price to be paid for every sin. In God's economy, sin results in death. By one man's sinful life (Adam's), death entered the world. By one man's perfect life (Jesus's), life was redeemed. Christ's death balanced the scales for us. In Vietnam, one person's heroic death often saved another's life, or even the life of a whole platoon. In the same way, Christ's life, death, and blood operate as an effective sacrifice for all of mankind and frees us from guilt. It affects three specific relationships: our relationship to God, to man, and to Satan.[13]

Our Relationship to God

Christ's blood is for atonement. We might think of atonement as "at-one-ment," for it restores our *unity* with God. To *atone* means to make up for, pay back, or make restitution for crimes committed. The God of the Old Testament, who required "an eye for an eye" to balance the scales of justice, has not changed. A life is still required for a life. God's holiness and sense of justice demand it. A *sinless* life must be given for *sinful* man. Christ satisfied the law of justice by balancing the scales on our behalf... He gave his life for ours. Our sins are not forgiven because God chooses to overlook them, but because when He looks at us He sees the perfect life of Jesus and is satisfied. Christ's perfect life provides us with a "robe of righteousness" which covers our shortcomings. This "robe" is not primarily for us, but satisfies God. Someone had to satisfy the law for our lawless acts or there would be no justice. Therefore, apart from Christ there is only rightful accusation, guilt, and judgment.

If we want to understand the value of Christ's life, we must accept God's valuation of it. The value of the shedding of blood was first described in Genesis. When the first man Adam sinned, he sought to *cover it up* by deceit. He hid from God, believing he could also hide his sin. God saw it anyway. *It was He who killed* the first animal, *shedding blood* in the Garden *on Adam's behalf*, providing a covering for him. God set the standard... not man, a life for a life.

God's intervention is seen throughout history, revealing both His *intent* and *plan*, to redeem mankind. When God chose Abraham and his offspring (Israel), He chose a people through whom He would reveal His plan of salvation. The book of Exodus records the rites God established for Israel. These rites reveal His provision for grace and mercy, which were but a shadow of Christ to come. Before delivering Israel from bondage to Egypt, God had the Israelites sprinkle the blood of a Lamb on the lintel and doorposts of their dwellings. When God's judgment came, it fell on all, Egyptians and Israelites alike, who had not believed in or accepted God's plan. The spirit of Death, however, passed over every household which had followed God's direction.

God's provision for Israel, now free but still in sinful rebellion, continued to be a blood sacrifice. On the Day of Atonement the life's blood of an *unblemished* lamb was brought before the Lord. The blood was an "offering for sin," presented to God in private, away from the eyes of those who were to benefit. No one could bring this offering to God but one man, the High Priest. God accepted the life of a lamb for the life of a people. Then, in the fullness of time, God sent Jesus.

> Christ, appeared as a high priest...through His own blood He entered the holy place *once for all*, having obtained eternal redemption...how much more then will the blood of Christ, who through the eternal Spirit offered Himself without blemish to God, cleanse your conscience from dead works to serve the living God.[14]

Following God's pattern, Jesus became both High Priest and "the lamb of God who takes away the sin of the world."[15] He delivered his life's blood to God on our behalf to free us from guilt and sin. As unbelievers, we may be totally unaware of this and wholly untroubled by our conscience... at least until the Spirit of God begins to arouse and awaken us. Then, when our conscience is awakened, our sense of sin and guilt is intensified. Sometimes this awakening occurs in the midst of our sin, sometimes later. *Awakening* is designed to draw us to God. When we resist God, or deny His provision for our relief, our guilt starts to weigh us down and may trouble us to the point of despair.

Our deliverance comes by believing and accepting God's provision. The blood cleanses us because God says it does, *not because we feel it does.* "Know that you were not redeemed with corruptible things like silver or gold from your aimless conduct...but with the precious blood of Christ, as of a lamb without blemish and without spot."[16] Some deeds cling to us like glue. Attempts to erase old memories fail...miserably. Yet the wonderful nature of forgiveness is that God promises to forget our sins and remember them no more. And, what God forgets, we can put behind. Forgetting then, becomes natural and unconscious. Denial, on the other hand, is a strained and artificial means of avoiding guilt which only haunts us later. It is easy for us to believe there are some sins worse than others, maybe even unforgivable. God, however, does not see it that way. All sin, no matter how little, is still darkness, and light has no fellowship with darkness. Big sins, small sins, black sins, gray sins, they are *all* cleansed by the blood of Jesus.

Our Relationship to Man

If the blood of Christ satisfies God, it *must* satisfy us also. If God accepts us on the basis of Christ's performance, rather than on our own, so should we. *If we truly accept* God's provision it will change our attitude toward self and others. Many people say, "I know that God forgives me, the hard part is forgiving myself." That person has not fully accepted God's forgiveness. If we say we receive God's forgiveness, yet do not forgive ourselves, we set ourselves up as having higher standards than God. We are saying we are better judges than He, that we can better evaluate the sinfulness of our deeds, and therefore the punishment we deserve. In doing so we set ourselves on the throne, having final authority. This is self-exaltation. We are saying that God's plan is good enough for everyone else, but *my* sin requires some other sacrifice, some additional attention. When we refuse to forgive ourselves we reject the gift God has given and the sacrifice Christ made. We then cling to self-pity. Hebrews says, "Let us draw near [to God] with a true heart in *full assurance* of faith, having our hearts sprinkled from an evil conscience." To walk in self-condemnation is to walk in unbelief, not faith, and "without faith it is impossible to please God."[17]

If we live under the mistaken belief that we must continue to punish ourselves, it is because we believe it is *our* performance that determines our goodness and acceptance, not Christ's. If we have never known acceptance or approval apart from performance, then it is hard to accept that God's acceptance is unconditional. If we *choose* to accept Christ's performance in our place, we will see that this "sprinkling" of blood cleanses us from a conscience which condemns us. When we cease from trying to save ourselves and receive what God has already done for us, we experience rest and peace.

A conscience clear of accusation is essential to a life of faith. As soon as our conscience becomes uneasy our faith begins to dwindle. So when we first recognize our sin, we should confess it immediately. Then we need only come to God on the basis of the finished work of Jesus. If we understand that God responds to us on the basis of what is in our heart (our intentions), rather than on our performance (which invariably is lacking), and on the basis of the blood (Christ's perfect performance, not ours), we can stand securely.

If God is willing to show us mercy and forgive our failings, we ought to have the same response toward others. If we are reconciled to God by virtue of His giving, we can also be reconciled to others by virtue of what *we* give. If God forgives, so should we. If God neither judges nor condemns, neither should we. If God loves us while we are still in a state of imperfection, then we should love ourselves, and others, the same way.

Our Relationship to Satan

Our sin gives Satan the grounds to accuse and condemn us. When we believe in and receive God's forgiveness, we can face the Accuser with security and assurance, free from guilt and false accusation.

> Now salvation and strength, and the kingdom of our God [peace, righteousness, and joy in the Holy Spirit: Rom.14:1], and the power of His Christ have come, for *the accuser* of our brethren, who *accused* them before our God day and night, has been cast down.[18]

Satan's strategy is to prevent us from coming into God's presence. He wants to hinder us from experiencing God's love, power, knowledge, wisdom, counsel, peace, and strength. Nothing is more harmful to our fellowship with God than a guilty conscience. Whether it is our own heart or Satan's voice, guilt makes us feel condemned and unacceptable. We then tend to avoid fellowship with God.

When the Accuser tries to oppress us, attacking our minds with condemning thoughts, we must do battle. Jesus withstood every attack from Satan by using scripture. Scripture is God's viewpoint. God's viewpoint is truth. The most beneficial strategy I have used in dealing with condemnation has been to agree with my conscience and with Satan.[19] Scripture clearly says, "If we say that we have no sin, we deceive ourselves and the truth is not in us."[20] I say, "Satan, you're right. I am guilty. I am not sinless. However, the word of God says that when I confess my sin He is faithful and just to forgive me, and to cleanse me from all unrighteousness. I have done that, so I am free. I refuse your accusation." Watchman Nee says:

> Our temptation is to look within and in self-defense try to find in ourselves, in our feelings or our behavior, some ground for believing that Satan is wrong. Alternately, we are tempted to admit our helplessness and going to the other extreme, yield to depression and despair... if we accept his accusations.[21]

As long as I defend myself I am involved in a battle. When I agree with Satan, and let the word of God be my defense, the accusations soon end. Because of God's mercy I am no longer bothered by accusations about my past. Nor do I care about the accusations of others.

Ultimately, every sin is against God. Therefore, true and lasting forgiveness can only come from Him. God has made a way out from under condemnation. His peace comes without works, but not necessarily without labor. It is a struggle to hold onto the truth, especially in the face of doubt and accusing lies. We must labor to stand on the word of God and not be moved. Rest and peace come from an abiding belief and trust in Him, and from abandoned dependence on His love and mercy.

Building a Foundation

The most important part of any structure is the foundation. There is a fixed relationship between the strength of a foundation and the quality of the building upon which it stands. A building without a firm foundation tilts and develops cracks. If the foundation does not remain stable, neither does the building. Our spiritual life is like a structure, if it fails it is generally because the foundation was not properly laid. We must set our life on a firm foundation to endure the storms of life.[22]

A life free from guilt is built on the work of Jesus Christ, "For no other foundation can anyone lay than that which is laid, which is Jesus Christ."[23] When we make Christ's work the foundation upon which we stand, we are always on solid footing. "Come now and let us reason together, says the Lord, though your sins are like scarlet, they shall be as white as snow; though red as crimson, they shall be as wool."[24] God will blot out our sins with a thick cloud if only we will let Him. Why live a life of guilt, inner turmoil, and depression? God will forgive anything we have done, or failed to do. We need only acknowledge our sin, confess our wrongs, ask for forgiveness, and receive it. Then we can dismiss whatever troubles us, change our behavior, and not sin again.

Summary

Legitimate guilt, false guilt, and survivor guilt have always been by-products of war. Guilt is created by what we do, as well as by what we fail to do. Our mind and conscience, operating through self-perception and introspection, can seek out our failures and produce false guilt as well as the real. An unchecked mind can be driven and tossed by both accusing and excusing thoughts until finally, filled with remorse, we choose to escape into drink, drugs, or even suicide to relieve our torment.   Guilt cannot be alleviated by denial, rationalization, justification, or by excusing our behaviors. If we are unable to arrest the cutting work of our conscience, we can easily become depressed, dissociative, or even suicidal. Guilt either produces an unescapable burden or turns us to God. If we turn to God we can find relief through forgiveness and acceptance. The blood of Jesus frees us from guilt. His blood is sufficient to cover every deed. If we trust in Him, we can withstand the strongest condemnation. However, it is of little help to be forgiven by God if we are unwilling to forgive ourselves. We can lay our guilt at the foot of the Cross, unburden ourselves, and find the peace for which we seek.

-Questions-

1. For what experiences are you still blaming yourself?

2. What experiences have left you feeling ashamed, worthless, guilty, or unacceptable to God?

3. What keeps you from accepting God's forgiveness?
   (Needing other's acceptance and approval? The belief that you are not loved because of your failures, or that you deserve blame and condemnation?)

4. How does carrying the burden of guilt and pain, and not accepting God's forgiveness affect your relationship with God and others?

-16-

Repairing the Breech
[RESTORING TRUST]

" In the South Bronx where I live, nobody trusts anybody else. I'm used to that and I feel safe. If you trust someone, you might get a knife in your back."

–a Vietnam vet[1]

"He was a nasty, mean, one-percenter and sergeant-at-arms for the Bandida Motorcycle Club. Violence pumped his blood and still does. The world owes him everything and he owes nothing. Things are done his way with no compromise. He'll damn you to hell with one breath and with the next he'll ask for sex. He expects everyone to treat him with respect, yet he gives none in return. He will hold you firmly to your word but he will not keep his.

"Anger walks and breathes with him. You never know what will set it off. His emotions are anger, and anger. The few times I have seen him even act like he was happy, or enjoying something, were when John Wayne or Clint Eastwood get the bad guy. Aside from his weekend of westerns, everything is a burden he has to deal with. The glass is always half empty, unless it's full.

"I have been married to this man for five years. I know that it is by God's grace and will that I am still here because to me he is not human, he is a machine, and I don't really know anything about him.

"God has blessed us with 40 acres in Texas, and He has given me a wonderful vision of finally coming home, a place for roots. However, my home is not complete without my husband. He is here physically but nothing else. I want him to come home."

–wife of a Vietnam veteran

Mistrust, a common characteristic among combat vets with PTSD, is an "equal opportunity employer." It affects all people who have been deeply wounded... regardless of sex, race, or religion. Yet trust must first exist in order for it to be broken. It is broken only when we have been betrayed by those we first trust. The closer and more trusted the relationship, the deeper the wounding.

Edwin Cole says, "We live in a world of betrayal caused by the breakdown of ethics and morality. This breakdown occurs largely because men no longer reverence the Word of God, and therefore do not reverence their own."[2] Mistrust develops when our expectations, spoken, understood, or intuitively felt, are crushed. Once broken, trust is difficult to rebuild. To restore trust, we must first understand what destroys, what builds, and what inhibits the development of trust.

Truth and Trust.

Trust plays an important role in our ability to live a healthy life. Although we all approach relationships with varying degrees of trust and expectations, we generally trust only to the extent that we believe people are being truthful. Truth and reality are synonymous. The absence of truth results in lies, deception, and illusion. When we are deceived, we feel betrayed. Repeated betrayal leads to disillusionment. When men no longer walk in truth, the innocent become easy prey. Once preyed upon, it is difficult to extend trust, even to those who are trustworthy. Due to both the perception and reality of betrayal, deep abiding trust is difficult for Vietnam veterans. Because of the breakdown of integrity in our society, mistrust is difficult to heal. It is only natural that alienation, withdrawal, and isolation follow... not just for veterans, but for society as a whole.

Developing trusting relationships takes risk... risk that many Vietnam veterans are unwilling to take. Fear of vulnerability keeps them distant. It makes them resist receiving help, advice, or even love. Yet in order for their growth and healing to occur, for marriages to work, for families to become loving, caring, interdependent units, and for relationships in society to function with any degree of success, there must be trust. Need may be the basis for all relationships, but *trust is the basis for all intimacy* within them.

We generally trust only to the extent that we believe people are being truthful.

Building Trust

Transparency, honesty, and a commitment to the truth are necessary to build and restore trust. Trust also develops within an environment of confidentiality, consistent integrity, and unconditional regard. To me, *unconditional regard* means acceptance and love without condemnation, or the requirement to change. This does not mean we *condone* what a person does, it only means we do not *condemn* them for it. If we are honest about our own shortcomings and sinful nature, it is hard to stand in judgment of others.

Forgiveness doesn't automatically restore trust, nor does emotional healing. Forgiveness and trust are not the same. If someone steps on our feet every time they come near us, we may forgive them and the pain may go away. That doesn't mean we trust them not to step on our feet the next time. When that person learns to avoid stepping on our feet, they prove themselves to be trustworthy. Their behavior influences our willingness to rebuild trust.

Trust must be restored on a two-fold level, horizontally and vertically... between both man and God. God's faithfulness to perform His word enables us to trust Him, and our unfailing commitment to perform our word builds trust with others.

Trust is developed as people prove themselves to be trustworthy.

Restoring Trust with God

In order to trust God, we must first discover that He exists. Then we must *know* His nature and character. God's character exemplifies the qualities it takes to build trust: faithfulness, a commitment to truth, consistency, unconditional acceptance, transparency, openness, and honesty. The following are examples:

• Truth and faithfulness

The Gospel of John says simply, "God is truthful." David says, "I will worship toward your holy temple, and praise your name for your loving kindness and your truth [lit. faithfulness]; for you have magnified your word above [or together with] your name."[3] God elevates His word above His name because *His name is only as good as His word.* This is true for us as well. Our faithfulness to perform our word establishes our reputation. God can be trusted to do as He says. Can we?

The word *truth* is often translated *faithfulness.* Every word spoken by God is a promise. That is the measure of His faithfulness. Scripture says, "I [God] am watching over my word to perform it," and "I will perform that which I spoke."[4] God's word is His bond; it is a covenant He has made with Himself to do what He says. God makes Himself accountable to Himself because there is no higher power! God does not say one thing and do another. What He has said, He will do. What He has spoken, He will make good.[5] God is not only consistent in word, but unchanging in character!

What God desires in us, He first reveals in Himself. He teaches by example. This is the mark of a good leader. Jesus said of himself, "I am the way, *the truth,* and the life," and "I and the Father are one." Jesus was the *Word* of God made visible, and just as Jesus was an expression of God's character, so our word is an expression of our character.[6] Jesus often started his messages saying, "I tell you the truth." Truth is the lifestyle of God. It enables us to trust Him. The reward of the trustworthy is trust, there is no better measure. The closer we draw to the word of God, the closer we draw to the truth. The closer we are to the truth, the closer we are to reality. Jesus said we were to be sanctified by the truth. God's word is truth. True freedom comes from knowing and abiding in the truth, and this results from following Him.[7]

• Consistency

God remains constant. "In Him there is no variation nor shadow of turning." God is unchanging. He is "the same yesterday, today and tomorrow." It is God's unchanging character which provides the world *stability*. Only someone or something that is constant and unchanging can create *security*. All that is unchanging in the world and in our lives is built on a foundation upheld by God's word.[8]

• Acceptance

Although we have examined God's heart of love toward us in previous chapters, it will do no harm to affirm it here. Paul says, "God demonstrates His own love toward us in that while we were still sinners, Christ died for us." Remember, it was *while we were yet sinners*. He didn't wait for us to make ourselves clean and holy. Scripture says:

> God so loved the world [us] that He gave His only begotten Son, that whoever believes in Him should not perish but have everlasting life. For God did not send His Son into the world to condemn the world, but that the world through Him might be saved. He who believes in Him is not condemned...Who shall bring a charge against God's elect. It is God who justifies. Who is he who condemns? It is Christ who died and furthermore is also risen, who is even at the right hand of God, who also makes intercession for us. Who shall separate us from the love of Christ? For I am persuaded that neither death nor life, nor angels nor principalities nor powers, nor things present nor things to come, nor height nor depth, nor any other created thing, shall be able to separate us from the love of God which is in Christ Jesus our Lord.[9]

• Transparency, openness, and honesty

Jesus said, "When you see me, you see the Father." God did not keep His nature or character hidden. Jesus came to reveal both. He was referred to as "the Light of the world." The very character of light is that it enables us to see things as they are. Another characteristic of light is that we can see through it. This is called *transparency*. John wrote, "Light has come into the world, but men loved darkness instead of light... and will not come into the light for fear that their deeds will be exposed. But whoever lives by the truth comes into the light so that it [their behavior] may be seen plainly."[10] God has recorded His dealings with mankind, and in this record we see life as it is, openly and honestly. We also see that His acceptance of us does not depend on our being perfect, but on *His* perfect love for us.

Restoring Trust with Man

Restoring trust in man is not as easy as restoring trust in God. We are not like God. We have a fallen nature. We all do things that prevent us from trusting one another, and trust cannot be restored until we are willing to acknowledge and accept one another's failings. In order to have grace for others, we must first know that God has grace for us and that He loves and accepts us in spite of ourselves. Once we truly *accept* God's mercy and forgiveness, we can extend it to others. Yet grace and mercy is just the beginning. God wants us to move toward holiness by abandoning character defects which destroy trust and replacing them with traits which build trust.

Knowing Our True Nature

Does God trust us? I think not. He knows our fallen nature only too well. Scripture says:

> What is man that he should be pure, or who is he born of a woman that he should be righteous. Behold he [God] puts no trust in his saints, neither are the heavens pure in his sight. How much less one who is detestable and corrupt, man who drinks iniquity like water.[11]

God trusts neither His saints (those chosen, called, and set apart by the new birth) nor the angels in heaven, a third of whom rebelled against the boundaries and limitations God set for them and were consequently banned from heaven. God knows our frail, self-serving nature. Jesus, did not go about blindly entrusting himself to any man. He knew all men and did not need any one to tell him about man's degenerate condition, or what was in man's heart.[12] Jesus was selective in his trust. As his disciples proved themselves to be faithful, he began revealing more of the Father's heart to them. He also seemed to selectively entrust himself to the disciples, revealing more to Peter, James, and John than to the others. Yet his knowledge did not prevent him from being disappointed with their lack of commitment. His exasperation is seen clearly in his response to those who would not wait and watch with him during the excruciating distress he felt in the Garden of Gethsemane.

On some level we have all experienced disappointment from trusting others. The Bible says that man's heart is deceptively wicked, and that we can be blind to our hard, divided, prideful, envious, bitter condition. How many of us discovered to our own surprise the dark side of our own nature while in Vietnam? How many, like Solomon, discovered that "madness dwells in our hearts?"[13] We are fallen creatures, no doubt. If this were not true we would have no need for a Savior.

We may have ended up disillusioned in Vietnam, but it simply meant that our "illusions" had been broken. Our misconceptions, false impressions, and false judgments about life came to an end. It meant for many of us, freedom from the deceptions we carried about our self and about others. The truth is, much of what we suffer in live we inflict on ourselves because we refuse to lay aside our illusions. We live with a *veil* over our mind and over our heart. We do not see ourselves or others as we really are, and cling to our misconceived ideas. Even though the greatest thing God could have done for us was to allow us to become disillusioned, freeing us from being deceived, it actually left many vets cynical and overly critical in our judgment of others. Much of life's pain, injury, or grief come from the fact that we suffer and hide behind illusions, and refusing to be disillusioned causes even more suffering. Once stripped of our illusions we can better see and face truth.

After all, it is God who tells us to put our trust *in Him alone.* David wrote, "It is better to take refuge in the Lord, than to trust in man." Jeremiah wrote, "Cursed is the man who trusts in mankind and makes flesh his strength." "Blessed is the man who trusts in God." "Do not trust in your neighbor." Micah wrote, "Do not trust in a friend."[14] Why is this? Does God want to spare us the pain of having our expectations shattered? Perhaps God wants something more than trust. But, if so, what is it? Are we supposed to trust others or not?

Personal Hindrances to Trust

The reality of *man's* own untrustworthy nature is a major roadblock to trust. If we acknowledge this about others, we must also acknowledge it about ourselves. Things that get in the way of trust are:
- a critical, condemning, judgmental attitude
- an unwillingness to let go of a desire for revenge
- behaviors controlled and dominated by fear
- an unwillingness to suffer or let go of control
- selfishness, self-preservation, and a hardened heart

We are generally most intolerant and critical of people who are most like us. Although we may be blind to our weaknesses or skilled at hiding them, we are at the same time intolerant of weakness in others. *Behaviorally* we may appear to have our weaknesses under control while inner thoughts, feelings, and attitudes remain unchecked. Fearing we will be found out, we focus on the faults of others to take the focus off ourselves. We mistakenly believe that controlling behaviors, whether in our life or in the lives of others, will make us all right. Man judges by outward appearance, but *God judges by the inner heart.*[15] Jesus repeatedly taught that righteousness is an issue of the heart, not appearance. Right behavior flows from a right heart. Jesus said:

> Judge not, that you be not judged. For with the judgment you use, you shall be judged. And with the same standard you measure it shall be measured to you. Why do you see the *speck* that is in your brother's eye, but don't consider the *beam* that is in yours. Or why tell your brother, "Hey, you need to get your life straight," and behold your life is even more crooked. You hypocrite, first take the beam out of your eye and then you will see clearly to take the speck out of your brothers.[16]

Objects at a distance appear small. The closer they are to you the bigger they appear. That is the principle behind the "speck" and the "beam." The closer the sin we judge in others is to our own life, the larger it appears to us. One sure way of knowing what is hidden in our hearts is to look at what makes us angry and critical of others.

Some scriptures say we are to judge, while others condemn us for it. Not all Bible translations convey the subtle distinctions for words used in early Greek manuscripts. The Greeks used six different terms for to *judge*. These terms have two separate meanings, and three distinct applications. They are:

- *krino*: to distinguish or decide (mentally or judicially), and by implication to try, condemn, punish, or avenge
- *anakrino*: to investigate, scrutinize, question, interrogate, determine, examine, or search. The root implies we should do these things repetitiously, as a lawyer or reporter might.
- *dikastes*: a Judge (job description or position)
- *krites*: a Judge
- *kriterion*: a rule of judging by a tribunal, to judge righteously from a judgment seat
- *diakrino*: to separate thoroughly, to withdraw from, to oppose or hesitate, or to discriminate. The root implies that some kind of action is taken once correct discernment is made.

To "judge" implies the intellectual pursuit of the correct perspective. It means to distinguish right from wrong, true from false, or bad from good. It also implies a response to what we discover. We are to seek and find what is true, and having done so, to act appropriately. Yet we are not to condemn or sentence people *unless it is our job*. Judges and juries have this responsibility because of their position. Few of us are judges or jurors, but many of us live as if we were. We are critical, condemning, back-biters who rarely have anything to say about others unless it exposes their weaknesses. Unwilling to "commit ourselves to Him who judges righteously," we seek personal retribution, not mercy. Jesus said, "You people judge according to the flesh; I am not judging anyone."[17]

Archbishop Raymond E. Hunthausen was quoted in the Elijah House News (1996) as saying, "People would rather part with a precious possession than give up a grudge. Sentiments of bitterness and hatred and rancor, poison our system and cause us suffering. This is the principal reason why the prayer of so many people is lacking in power." A wounded heart hardened through unforgiveness, fearful and guarded, does not easily trust. We fear injury, so we avoid vulnerability. We fear suffering, so we are unwilling to risk pain. Instead, we withdraw, isolate, develop defensive, guarded behaviors, and avoid intimacy. This causes others not to trust us.

A wounded heart, hardened through unforgiveness, fearful and guarded, does not easily trust.

Self-preservation keeps us from yielding our lives to God. It keeps us from reproducing His life in us. Unless a grain of wheat falls into the earth and in a sense dies, it does not bear fruit. Jesus said, if we seek to preserve our life we only end up losing what real life is. If we love our own life more than we love God, we cannot be obedient. Yet if we give up a lifestyle of guardedness and self-preservation for Him, we will reap all that we feared we would lose.[18]

God's Provision

In spite of who we are, God has chosen to entrust us with the indwelling life of His son. It is Christ's life that enables us to trust God, in spite of the fact that our old fallen nature resists. Our old beliefs will argue against trust and try to justify resistance. Yet we are free to choose to yield to Christ, or resist him. It all boils down to an act of our will. Our *unwillingness* to trust God will hinder us from growing. We will discover the depths of God's faithfulness, to the extent that we are *willing* to resist our old way of living and embrace the new, . We can be confident in God's ability to complete the changes He has started in our life, since Jesus is both the author and finisher of our faith. God remains faithful even when we are faithless.[19]

God's heart toward us is one of mercy, forbearance, understanding, and forgiveness, regardless of our fallen state. With Christ in us, we are no longer alienated from the life of God. Because we are in Christ, we are holy, blameless, and without reproach. Christ's work, not ours, allows us to live grounded in hope. However, we must believe this and be steadfast. Christ exerts His power on our behalf. He transforms our life.[20] Once we understand and *accept* this, we will begin to trust God anew.

Restoring Trust

We all approach trust differently. We may put our trust in everyone until they fail us. We may put our trust only in those who prove themselves trustworthy, or we may trust no one. We also have varying degrees of trust. If we entrust our lives to God, we can be as open as He wants us to be. Our ability to trust won't depend on how others live their lives. Bob Mumford says, "The only absolute truth is that there is nothing absolute about men." This should help us to set healthy boundaries, and keep us from having unrealistic expectations. If we expect people to fail us, it won't come unexpectedly. If we put our trust in God alone, looking to Him for every need, we won't be shaken when others fail us. People are then free to fail us and still know acceptance. Paul says:

> And so, as those who have been chosen of God, holy and beloved, put on a heart of compassion, kindness, humility, gentleness, and patience; *bearing* with one another, and *forgiving* each other *whoever has a complaint against anyone.* Just as the Lord forgave you, so also should you.[21]

Forgiveness is the glue that holds *any* relationship together. Without it we can never experience true reconciliation. Truly righteous men are not perfect, but they are willing to admit to their wrongdoing, make restitution in order to restore broken relationships, and change their hurtful behaviors. With such men it is easy to have grace. This one thing we should trust, *men will fail us and we will fail them.* Yet real love covers a multitude of sins.[22]

Although it is forgiveness that restores relationships, it is trust that develops intimacy. We cannot be naive, but neither can we withhold our hearts. We must recognize those whom God has entrusted to our care and commit ourselves wholeheartedly to them. In all other relationships we must have wisdom. With those entrusted to our care, we cannot have a *wait and see* attitude fostered by mistrust. Like the father who embraced his prodigal son, we must cast aside criticism and unforgiveness, and hold our arms open. Without forgiveness and a commitment to work at trust and intimacy, relationships will not thrive. Perhaps they will not even survive! Let's be gracious and accepting of one another's weaknesses.

Practical Steps to Restore Trust

Once deeply wounded, trust develops slowly. It must be built, and like a building it must have a strong foundation. Christ provides an unshakable foundation which sustains our relationship with the Father, and with mankind. As our knowledge and experience of the Father's love grows, so does our trust. Trust in God provides security. Security enables us to risk building relationships with others. At the same time, God's presence changes us, and we learn to do the following:

Honor Our Word

We build trust when we do what we say, regardless of personal cost. Trust is destroyed by our *failure* to do what we say. This is especially true in our relationships with our spouse and children. Our word *is* our honor. It reflects our character, integrity, and manhood!

> When we make a vow to the Lord our God we shall not delay to pay it, for it would be sin in us, and the Lord our God will surely require it of us…we shall be careful to perform what goes out from our lips…just as we have promised.[23]

Be Accountable

Accountability means having to answer to someone for something. Genuine accountability cannot be forced. It has to be given freely. Once given, accountability provides support, encouragement, and counsel. It helps keep us on a path of moral purity and ethical maturity. When we are accountable we remain teachable and correctable. Accountability also provides us a safeguard. Safeguards provide security. Scripture says, "submit yourselves one to another." Rebellion, independence, and an unhealthy self-sufficiency create mistrust in relationships.

Show Moral Courage

We need moral courage to live in an immoral world. If we don't encourage and hold one another accountable to our professed convictions, we may waiver. Without firm convictions we ultimately end up ruled by reason or controlled by feelings, desires, and circumstances.

It takes courage to examine *our* accountability in every situation and to acknowledge the role we play in letting what happens to us rob us of our present and future goals. It takes courage to face pain and fear and to stand alone when everyone else is fleeing. Courage allows us to be vulnerable, transparent, and open. It takes us down a narrow, untraveled road when we face a risky uncertain future.

Be Honest And Truthful

Authenticity involves the full and free expression of our true self, with all of its uniqueness, strengths, and weaknesses. When we are not real, we are known only for the social or religious masks we wear. We can intuitively sense when people are being real or not, so there is no reason to believe that others do not see through us as well. If we are hypocrites, then people learn not to trust us. We are all better off just being real. We wear masks because we fear rejection, yet what do we gain if only our mask gets accepted? What about *our real self?* Acceptance and intimacy are only forged through honesty.

Frances Hesselbein, a Drucker Foundation executive, says this in *Fortune* magazine of leadership: "Leadership is not a basket of tricks and skills. It is the quality and character and courage of the person who is the leader. It's a matter of ethics and moral compass, the willingness to remain highly vulnerable." Honesty and transparency require vulnerability, yet disclosure builds trust. Both are necessary for true friendship.[24] Honesty helps us discover our strengths and weaknesses. Honesty builds trust, and trust generates safety and security. This makes it possible to risk being vulnerable. Our vulnerability, in turn, makes it safe for others to be open and honest.

The Challenge

Because of the transcendent bond most vets have, they are able to open themselves to one another without a lot of trust building. With this already in place the challenge then becomes to walk together committed to the bond of unity, giving one another the same kind of support and encouragement we gave one another in Vietnam. Solomon said:

> Two are better than one because they have a good return for their labor. For if either of them falls, the one will lift up his companion. But woe to the one who falls when there is not another to lift him up...And if one can overpower him who is alone, two can resist him. A cord of three strands is not quickly torn apart.[25]

This passage was written for people like us, who wonder, "How can I make it in this hostile, dog-eat-dog world?" It was written for those 150,000-plus men who, during their despair and loneliness after Vietnam, gave in to hopelessness and suicide. Who was there to catch them when they fell? Every time our unit came under attack in Vietnam, I was grateful to have other men alongside. Their encouragement, protection, support, and assistance were there when I was most vulnerable. I was grateful for every gunship, every grunt, and every artillery round fired in my support. Knowing there was always another unit covering my back was comforting. Knowing there was another soldier down the bunker line I could rely on was assuring. Their support helped me to persevere and survive even the toughest times.

Most of us fight a continuing battle today. We live in a hostile world, and few burdens in life are more difficult to bear than alienation and loneliness. We need people with whom we feel safe, with whom we don't have to weigh each thought or mince our every word... people to whom we can pour our hearts out, just as they are... chaff, husk, and grain together. We need friends who will help us sift through our thoughts and feelings, with kindness... who remember that we are but dust because they are all too familiar with their own dirt.

I do not readily admit that I need others. My wife can attest to this. I do not lean easily on others. Intimacy and trust are areas where I am continually challenged. Yet God has remarkably broken down many of my walls, especially the wall between myself and all other Americans. I have a select group of men who know me, because I have chosen to be transparent with them. These men have proven themselves trustworthy, and I look to them for encouragement and godly counsel. They provide both accountability and safety for me. Most of these men are Vietnam veterans. All are true believers. My regular contact with and accountability to these men has provided me with support, stability, and insight through many rough times. Exposing myself to others has been challenging, yet it has also been instrumental in the restoration of trust in my life. What God has done, and is doing for me, He can do for you.

Summary

Trust is broken by betrayal. Trust is difficult, but not impossible, to restore. We extend trust to those we believe are truthful and faithful to perform their word. If we allow trust to be restored vertically in our relationship with God, His faithfulness will enable us to begin trusting others. The more we receive God's unconditional acceptance, grace, and mercy, the more we will be able to extend these same gifts to others. If we are willing to give up our judgmental attitudes, guardedness, and bitterness, we can learn to trust and be trusted. The biggest challenge for each of us is to set the example by living an exemplary, trustworthy life.

-Questions-

1. In what ways have you felt betrayed? Write them down.

2. Who was the person or persons you held responsible for wounding you?

3. How have the above experiences affected your ability to trust? How do they continue to affect your present behaviors?

4. How do you continue to victimize yourself and others by carrying mistrust?

5. Would you be willing to forgive that person/those persons today?

6. Would you be willing to ask God to forgive you for carrying resentment, bitterness, or a judgmental attitude toward others?

-17-

Rebuilding the Walls
[RESOLVING STRESS]

"Beginning eight years ago, up to last year, I had seven years of insomnia. Seven years! Outside of cancer I don't know anything that can be as bad as that. It was all of a sudden, I could not sleep... Then there was my nightmare, a recurrent nightmare... a feeling of exasperation. I would dream I am on a hill and all these faceless people are charging up at me. I am holding an M-1 Garland rifle, the kind of rifle I used to take apart blindfolded. And in the dream, every time I shoot one of these people a piece of the rifle flies off until all I have left is the trigger guard. The trigger guard! Then I would wake up. So that's why I began sleeping in the garage with the lights on all night so that when I woke up from the dream, I'd know where I was.

"So, there was another thing too, it was the noise. Noise! In combat, you see, your hearing gets so acute you can interpret any noise. But now, there were all kinds of noises that I couldn't interpret. Strange noises. I couldn't sleep without a weapon by my bed. A pistol. Because the least little noise bothered me. That's why I had the garage made into a bedroom, to be away from the noise. The least little noise, there was a time when a cannon wouldn't wake me. And now I could barely survive in the garage. It was as if I wanted to destroy everything I had built up. I got irritable. I hated everything and everybody. The last two or three years of it, I was just sleepwalking. There are only two of us left from the old outfit, and we're both half dead."
–Audie Murphy, famed WW II hero at his death, age 45[1]

Researchers conclude that repeated, prolonged, intense stress produces *irreversible* physiological and psychological damage. This also seems to be the prevailing conclusion of most mental health workers at VA facilities. I have often heard that "post-traumatic stress disorder is incurable. It is something you have to learn to live with." Thank God that His prognosis is not so bleak, for He makes healing available to all those who seek Him. What is impossible for man *is* possible for God, and He promises to restore our lives regardless of the potency of influence stressors have had on us.[2]

Recovering from deeply ingrained responses to stressors is not easy, but it can be done. Once recognized, we can turn from destructive patterns and learn how to replace them with positive ones. We can access both the essential perspective and the resources necessary to overcome physiological and psychological stress reactions. Perspective and perception play a major role in both creating and intervening in stress, as does the availability of resources.

The Pressures of Life

Anxiety and stress (interchangeable terms) are intensified by beliefs, physical and emotional responses, and fixed coping patterns in our behavior. They are also intensified by prevailing social values, religious, social, and personal performance expectations, negative thinking, and preoccupation with self. Conflicting values and beliefs, as well as our own personal needs, compete for our attention every day and pull us in different directions. Sorting through life's conflicting demands contributes to stress. Therefore, what we know and believe about God's nature and character profoundly influences our ability to cope. It also affects our ability to combat life-long negative habits. All this influences our quality of life.

Can Stress Be Avoided?

Freedom from stress cannot be achieved by denying it exists. Nor is it possible to totally avoid it. Leserman, in his study of mental and behavioral efforts to manage internal and external stress, discovered that people who practice *denial* experience more anger, depression, helplessness, chronic feelings of illness, discontent, and poor self-esteem.[3] He also discovered that *the healthiest* people shared the following characteristics. They:
- adopted a fighting spirit,
- reframed stress to maximize personal growth,
- planned a course of action, and
- sought social support.

People who have the most difficulty coping with stress ignore their experiences or distort and deny them. Accepting and assimilating difficult experiences is hard, but since all stress cannot be avoided it must be worked through. Trials often challenge rigid beliefs and surface insecurities. They force us to abandon what is familiar and safe. However, recognizing, acknowledging, and openly communicating our struggles helps us to overcome them.

Because our environment affects us, sometimes environmental changes *are* necessary. It is important, however, to remain engaged with people rather than become recluses. Christians are called to be "*in* the world, yet not *of* it."[4] Avoiding environmental pressures may bring temporary relief, but that may also cause us to miss God's call on our life to develop godly character. This would only hinder our healing. Most of us would be better served by changing our way of thinking and our lifestyle, not our environment. Dr. Dean Ornish says:

> There are a lot of misconceptions about stress. The ability to respond to stress, and the ability to relax, are equally important in being able to function effectively while remaining healthy.

The ideal response is to respond to challenges or difficult situations fast and efficiently, and then to relax.5

Do we respond to life's challenges or do we avoid them? When we respond, is it on our own or do we rely on God? Do we seek help from others? Once we have done all we can, do we enter the rest that comes from trusting God or do we continue to worry and struggle for control? Our answers determine how successful we are in overcoming stress.

The Psychology of Change

Psychotherapeutic methods of treating stress syndrome, in and of themselves, have limited success. So do religious methods which advocate denying reality or promise quick and easy deliverance. Even when we are relying on God, His supernatural outworking is not always miraculous. When it is, and healing and restoration are instantaneous, our newfound freedom is always challenged and we must struggle in some way to *establish* our healing. There is struggle in all growth and change. Growth has many dimensions, of which healing is only one. Deeply ingrained patterns rarely give way without some effort on our part, and even when they do something new must take their place. Old patterns are eradicated when they are displaced by new behaviors. Unhealthy attitudes are erased when replaced by virtuous ones.

Cognitive and behavioral strategies for change *are* valid when they line up with Scripture; however, simply controlling behavior or manipulating mind set does not bring lasting freedom. Any technique, religious or psychological, which relies solely on self-effort is ultimately doomed to failure. In a classic experiment, Pavlov trained dogs to salivate (a natural autonomic response to food) upon hearing certain sounds (an unnatural stimulus) by repeatedly pairing the ringing of bells with the giving of food. Once trained, Pavlov's dogs would salivate when they heard bells, whether there was food present or not. What Pavlov created was a *conditioned reflex*. This was only a learned behavior, not an alteration of the dog's true nature. In Vietnam, we also developed conditioned reflexes. We learned to pair certain sounds and activities with danger, creating an automatic nervous system reaction. Instead of salivating, our bodies released adrenaline. This was advantageous, as split second reactions often saved our lives. The problem is, some of us are still living like finely trained dogs, activating adrenaline whenever we hear loud noises, and reacting to sound and other stimuli whether there is real danger present or not.

Over time, learned behaviors degenerate *if they are not periodically reinforced.* Unlike dogs, we do not need external experiences to reinforce learned behavior. We can reinforce behavior simply by mentally rehearsing past experiences. Replaying memories reinforces conditioned behaviors and the emotional reflexes associated with them.

The pattern of *stimulus and response* can be broken. We can learn new behaviors. But, is that *all* we want? A little boy was standing on his chair at the dinner table. When his father told him to sit down, he did not respond. His father told him again but he replied defiantly, "No!" His father then got up from the table and headed toward him. Knowing he was in trouble, the boy quickly sat down. When the father returned to his seat the child said angrily, "I'm sitting down, but I'm still standing up inside." We can be like that little boy. We can learn to control *external* responses while stubbornly remaining the same *inside*.

Change from the Inside Out

If we do not change our inner life, sooner or later we find ways, overtly or covertly, to act out our feelings and desires. If we control behavior but remain unchanged inside, the incongruence between our behavior and inner desires pulls us in two different directions. This inner conflict creates inner turmoil, which we experience as anxiety. Thus stress always exists when there is incompatibility between:

- a person's beliefs and events inconsistent with those beliefs;
- a person's ideal self and how they actually live;
- a person's beliefs or values, and their behavior;
- a person's experience and what they think *should* have happened;
- a person's conscious beliefs (what they think they *should*
  believe) and heartfelt beliefs existing on a subconscious level.

Harmony with God, ourselves, and others helps to alleviate stress. That is why scripture says to live in peace with all men, as much as possible.

We all face life with a finely tuned *system* of balanced and counterbalanced conditioned reflexes. In fact, maintaining a coherent, unified system of beliefs and behaviors is thought by some to be the single most important motive in human behavior. It is this elaborate system of ethical codes/beliefs which control our behaviors. When our system becomes too elaborate or confusing to manage, we can break down. We find ourselves without answers, unable to figure life out, and unable to manage or control our circumstances. Then, there is no escaping our limitations or our need for others. God often allows our system to become overloaded to bring us to Himself.

Sometimes we think that adhering to codes will also control circumstances. That is what *religion* is, adherence to an elaborate code through determined self-effort. Christians young and old have elaborate sets of Biblical codes to govern their behavior, believing that is what God wants. But the Christian life is more than substituting social codes for religious ones. If our inner drives are merely suppressed, but never changed, we are simply practicing a form of religious self-righteousness based on self-discipline and personal performance. That is not *authentic* Christianity. We may as well be practicing Hinduism. True freedom, rest, and change, come when we see that *our* performance, *our* righteousness, and *our* efforts account for nothing. We must recognize that our inner drives are humanly untransformable and *invite* God to transform them for us.

Controlling behavior doesn't necessarily reflect true change. A man may bite his tongue to control his anger, but that anger still resides somewhere. Eventually it surfaces, although we may not recognize it as anger when it does. When *God* changes behaviors, it is from the inside out. He begins by renewing our spirit and then transforms our heart, mind, and will. Inner changes alter our behavior. We need to make good choices and cognitive changes, but neither positive thinking nor self-talk will change our nature. We also need to restrain behaviors which harm self and others, but restraint based on willpower always comes to an end. Internal desires constantly vie for expression, and eventually our will breaks down. When that happens we fall back into the same old behaviors or substitute new ones. Self-reliance is not the same as a life controlled by God's Spirit within us. If we understand this, then we know that freedom from PTSD means addressing the *core* issues of our stress, not just external, environmental issues.

We must examine our lives, discover where we do not line up with God's plumb line, and move our position closer to God's. Examination touches consciousness and conscience. *Consciousness* involves being fully awake... apprehending and engaging the world with all of our faculties and senses. Our mind, emotions, will, and physical senses must *all* be functioning. We cannot deny any of them. For our *conscience* to function, our spirit must also be fully alive, awake, and functional. Together, these faculties lead us to correct unhealthy, destructive patterns. When our facilities are actively assisted by the Holy Spirit, we will soon discover healthy alternatives to old stress patterns.[6]

Stress, Perception, and Resources.

It is normal to experience stress when we believe our life, comfort, or safety is being threatened. The perception of danger, the emotion of fear, and the body's physiological reaction are all natural mechanisms which help us to survive and adapt. Stress *disorders* result when a stress reaction occurs when it is not rationally necessary, or when chronic activation begins to produce damaging effects on the body, soul, and spirit. *Distress* is cured by eradicating its cause, not by addressing its symptoms. Because stress is rooted in our perception of events, our interpretation of the event must be altered. Because the availability of resources also alters our response to distressing events, we must access additional resources. A relationship with God puts us in touch with the King of the Universe, and as adopted children, we inherit His resources. Herein lies our hope!

One key to overcoming unwarranted stress is our ability to distinguish between *real* and *perceived* threats. An inaccurate perception of danger produces the same physiological reaction as an accurate one. Inaccurate perceptions then produce incorrect behaviors. If our perception of the availability of resources is incorrect, then our reactions to stressful life events will also be imbalanced. Holding on to limiting beliefs, or refusing resources that are available, limits our ability to experience joy, peace, and lasting freedom from fear and anxiety.

Perspective and Perception

Perspective is defined as the position or vantage point from which we view life. *Perception* is our interpretation of what we see. The way we perceive life often has to do with the vantage point from which we see it. Let me give two examples. Three blind men ran into an elephant. Not knowing what they were up against, they began to grope around and shout to one another. One grabbed the tail and said, "It is a thin creature, like a snake, with hair on the end of it." Another grabbed a leg and said, "No. It is a large, round creature with rough, baggy skin." Yet another grabbed the tusk and said, "You are both wrong. It is a hard, smooth creature with heavy breath and large, pointed teeth." None really knew because they all examined the elephant from a different vantage point. In addition, they were all blind, and therefore *couldn't* use all their senses. Again, a certain wise man, wanting to teach his sons a lesson, sent them one by one to view a fig tree and come back and describe it. But, he sent each of them in a different season. Because of this, they all saw the tree somewhat differently and therefore, described it differently.

The point I am making is that what we have touched by way of experience, and what we have seen, even when we believe we have seen it clearly, does not mean we have seen it in whole or even touched it in whole. *We are limited* in our perspective. God, on the other hand, sees everything. Moreover, He sees everything clearly. It seems wise therefore to trust Him, to seek His perspective, and to filter all our experiences and perceptions through Him.

The Development of Perspective.

There are two primary views on life... God's view and man's. Man's view is called humanism. The basis of humanistic philosophy is the belief that man's perception of reality is all there is. Humanism is the exultation and worship of man... man rules! God's view is that mankind has limits and boundaries established by God, and that He exists independent and apart from any notion mankind may have concerning Him. God is not only real, but all other reality is contingent upon Him.

Child development specialists say that our *primary* perspective on life... that is, our fundamental beliefs, values, sense of worth, identity, and interaction skills... are formed within our first six years. By age twelve or thirteen our developmental pattern is set. As we grow into adulthood we build on childhood perceptions until we have a set way of perceiving or interpreting life events. Ongoing experiences then tend to support or confirm early conclusions; as this happens, our beliefs become rigid and inflexible. It then takes a severe shaking of some kind to change our perceptions.

If the conclusions we reach early in our development are incorrect, then the perceptions and beliefs *we carry into adulthood* will be incorrect as well. Paul writes, "When I was a child I spoke as a child, I understood as a child, I reasoned as a child; but when I became a man, I put away childish things."[7] We need to use mature reasoning to be sure we are not still operating out of childish beliefs or an immature perspective. We need to examine our beliefs because they undergird our behaviors.

Paul says that even as adults "we see through a glass darkly"[8] and that our perceptions are distorted and clouded. How much more so if we are still seeing life through childish eyes. Can we always trust ourselves? There is a way which seems right to man, but the end of it is death.[9]

Our beliefs develop in our mind but are strongly influenced by our emotions and our desire to survive. We must understand that the human mind functions first and foremost to protect and secure our life. In doing so, it filters and blocks out data that is life-threatening. Apart from the presence of God's Spirit, and apart from our spirits being fully functional, *our mind rules.* Even those who are *seemingly* controlled by emotions are actually ruled by the beliefs that govern their emotions.

If our spirit is not nurtured through touch, appropriate affection, and affirmation, it is crippled in some manner. When this happens the spiritual faculties given us for the purpose of knowing and communing with God do not develop. Our spirit remains asleep, unregenerate, unused, and essentially dead. We then end up interpreting life events strictly through our soul, without the help of conscience, intuition, or guidance from God. We rely *only* on reason, feelings, and will-power. Our perspective then develops from conclusions based on faulty reasoning, half-truths, limited understanding, and immature childish reasoning. These beliefs are then filtered through a canopy of personal temperament, shortsightedness, and sometimes the faulty beliefs of others. Is it no wonder Paul can say, "we see through a glass darkly."

Perception

Because *perception* is the chief mediating factor that determines how we react and respond to stressors, it is important to perceive things correctly. Jesus said, "The eye is the lamp of the *whole body.* If your eye is clear, your whole *body* will be full of light, but if your eye is bad, your whole *body* will be full of darkness."[10] *Perception affects our whole body.* Scientific research clearly establishes this link. Health comes from having the same mind which was in Christ Jesus.[11]

Look at picture No. 1. Do you see a mouse or an old man with glasses balanced on his nose? Now look at picture No. 2. Do you see a young lady with a feather in her hat, her face turned slightly away, or do you see an old hag with her beak of a nose and toothless grin?

No. 1

No. 2

Depending on our perception we may see one face or the other. Although both views exist simultaneously we cannot focus on both of them at the same time. We must choose which we will focus on. We may interpret our experiences one way, while God and others see them quite differently. When this happens, we must choose whether our perception is true, or if God's is. If we allow God's word to define our perception, the truth will eventually change *how we feel* about our experiences. If we stubbornly cling to views which are contrary to God's, we will also be bound to the emotions which accompany them.

The Results of Limited Perspective

Imagine sitting on top of a mountain and watching a battle going on. You can see all movement between troops. You know where and when the enemy is assembling and the direction of his advance. You have time to prepare all of your moves. Now imagine being a soldier on the ground in the heat of battle. All you can see is your immediate surroundings. Your vision is obscured by sweat, dust, and smoke. You don't know if this is the last soldier charging or if two hundred follow. You recognize the beginning of a battle, but you might never know the end. Scripture says we are lifted up with Christ and seated in heavenly places. Because of this it is possible for us to have God's perspective. He always knows both the beginning and the end of everything!

Perception Limits Change

A poignant example of man relying on his own limited perception is recorded in the Book of Numbers. When the children of Israel were delivered from their captivity in Egypt they came to the border of Canaan, a land which God had promised to *give* them. Before crossing, Moses sent in twelve "point men" on a "recon" mission. When they returned, they gave a "situation report." Ten of the men perceived that the land was a hard place; a place which "eats up its inhabitants," with "walled cities" and "giants." *Because of their perception* they believed the land was unconquerable. They not only saw their objective as untakable, they saw themselves as inadequate, equating themselves with "grasshoppers." But two of the men said, "The people are strong that dwell there and the cities are walled; and it does have giants dwelling in the land. However, it is also a land flowing with milk and honey, and the fruit is in abundance. Let's go up and take it for we are well able." These men saw the same land but perceived it, and their abilities, differently. *Their perception affected their behavior.*

Like present day society, the Hebrew people were swayed by the perception and fear of the majority. Instead of going into the land and taking what God had promised to give them, they ran from the challenge. In fact, they wanted to get rid of Moses, select a new leader, and return to Egypt. Because of fear they were willing to give up their freedom and return into captivity. How many times are we like that? God delivers us from bondage, and within months we return to the same old familiar habitat. The Hebrews were in bondage so long to the Egyptian system they developed a *slave mentality*. The length of their imprisonment, the severity of their bondage, the depth of their poverty, their failure to overcome enslavement, and the deep grief they carried over the wounds they suffered, combined to create a *victim* mentality. They not only had a poor perception of themselves (we are powerless grasshoppers), they had an even poorer perception of God. As a result, they also had a false perception of the "giants" in Canaan. This hindered them from entering in and receiving the blessings God had in store for them. Rather than choose to fight, to put forth the necessary effort to struggle and obtain what God had promised, they preferred to play it safe. Their preference, based on faulty perception and fear, led to their spiritual, moral, and physical death.

A whole generation of Hebrews, refusing to trust God, wandered in a forty-square-mile wilderness for forty years. They went around in circles, stuck in the same old place, grumbling, complaining, and maintaining a constant cynical attitude even in the face of God's miraculous provision. They questioned God's love for them, mistrusted God's willingness and ability to provide for them, and challenged God's integrity and character. They were stubborn, disobedient, rebellious, critical unbelievers... stuck in the same old patterns and forever wanting to return to Egypt, to the security of being provided for by the Egyptian government even though it meant poverty, slavery, and hardship.

Does this sound familiar to 20th Century America? What about the welfare state? Benjamin Franklin said, "They that can give up essential liberty to obtain a little temporary safety, deserve neither liberty nor safety." What the Hebrews thought would be the easy way ended up being the hardest. What they thought was impossible was accomplished by the next generation. That generation was led by Joshua and Caleb, *the only two point men who survived.* These men understood their destiny. They knew they were brought out of Egypt to inherit a new kingdom. They survived and lead the next generation into God's promises. Were we brought out of Vietnam for a similar destiny?

Perception and Behavior

Our *perception* of an event, rather than the event *itself*, determines how we behave. We are not victims of our circumstances! The biological stress *reaction* may be automatic, but our *response* to it is chosen. Habitual choices can be changed! So can the way we interpret life events. Emotions follow perceptions. Behaviors follow emotions. We can alter how we feel and behave by altering our perception.

- Events lead to thoughts (interpretation/perception).
- Interpretation produces emotions (positive/negative).
- Emotions produce desires/wants (fight/flight).
- Desires lead to choices (will/won't).
- Choices determine behaviors (react/respond).

We interpret events by filtering them through our own personal histories. Long-standing beliefs, experiences, and past choices color our interpretation of events. We may see life through a set of rose-colored glasses or a set of green ones. Yet regardless of how we have seen life in the past, we can choose to align our perceptions with God's. God's word is the plumb line to which all our beliefs should be measured.

A random event (if there are such things) such as a car accident, has neutral moral value until we assign it meaning. We may see it as good or bad, depending on our perception. If we choose to believe that everything works together for our good, as God says it does for all Christians, then we can assign the accident a positive value. We can rejoice that God is in control, and await a positive outcome. The other alternative is to assign it a negative value. and then get angry, upset, or depressed, depending on how awful we view the circumstances.

Renewing Our Hearts and Minds

Growth requires change. Change requires learning. We learn by acquiring new information. Mere information, however, doesn't change us. We may, as scripture says, "be ever learning and never come to a knowledge of the truth." The prophet Isaiah said of God:

> My thoughts are not your thoughts, nor are your ways My ways, says the Lord. For as the heavens are higher than the earth, so are My ways higher than your ways, and My thoughts than your thoughts.[12]

If God's perspective differs from ours, then true wisdom comes from acquiring His perspective.[13] For our life to be transformed, we must renew our mind. Changing how we feel and how we behave requires changing our belief system.

Change also requires *applying* what we learn by exchanging incorrect ideas for correct ones, unhealthy behaviors for healthy ones. Good mental health requires exercising deliberate control over our thoughts. Much of what we think about results from what we see. That is why the Psalmist says, "I will set no wicked thing before my eyes."[14] This is PM, preventive maintenance. You can't fill your eyes with garbage and not expect to have problems. The gospel writer Paul says, "Whatsoever things are true, honest, just, pure, lovely, of good report; if there be any virtue, and if there be any praise, *think on these things*."

Controlling our thought life takes diligent effort. Martin Luther said, "You cannot help the birds flying over your head, but you can prevent them from building nests in your hair." When Paul says to cast down imaginations, doubt, and unbelief which war against a true knowledge of God, and bring into captivity every thought which is contrary to truth, he is saying *this is warfare*. The Christian life is not for fearlings, or those looking for the easy way out. There *is* a spiritual battle being fought. However, many believers mistakenly attribute to Satan what is in reality our own carnal mind. Our old views *are* at odds with God's, and wherever our old unregenerate mind has not been converted, it's still in darkness and resists truth.[15] Examining our beliefs, regulating our thoughts, and coming to a knowledge of truth is essential in order to reflect truth in our behavior. Repentance involves change in both our way of thinking and in our behaviors. "Gird up the loins of your mind," Paul says, "and be sober." Girding is an act of protection.16

A callous heart affects our intellectual and spiritual perception, so we must also find healing for our emotions. "No longer walk just as the Gentiles walk, in the futility [vanity] of your *mind*, being *darkened in your understanding*, alienated from the life of God because of the *ignorance* that is in you, *because of the hardness of your heart...*"17 Callousness leads to ignorance (the product of a closed mind), alienation from God (who needs God? I don't need anybody!), and to mental darkness (an inability to see things clearly). Life apart from God leads to reliance on self-reasoning to figure everything out. This is not only futile, it leads to the sin of pride. Futility causes us to fill our lives with diversion (the pursuit of sensual pleasure and materialism) to fill our emptiness.

Mind sets fixed by constant life-threatening experiences can cause us to see threat where there is none, to fear danger even in the safest places, to live guarded, isolated, hypervigilant lives of self-reliance even when people can be trusted. Past experiences can leave a devastating imprint on present perceptions. They can create unrealistic expectations and therefore, unhealthy behaviors. Are we willing to examine them? Socrates said, "The unexamined life is not worth living." Remember, perspective and perception influence daily decisions, and daily decisions determine our destiny.

Relationships Determine Resources

If the old adage is true that it's not *what* you know but *who* you know that makes a difference, then relationships are very important *resources*. Self-reliance limits relationships. Self-imposed isolation, along with the perception of being isolated from resources, are fundamental triggers of human stress, and both affect our ability to cope.

Elijah was a prophet of God who saw and performed many mighty miracles. Yet there was also a time when he ran and hid himself in the wilderness when threatened by ruling authorities. God sought him out and found him hiding under a tree. He asked, "What are you doing here, Elijah?" Elijah answered, "*I alone* am left, and they [the government] seek my life to take it away." Elijah's perception that his life was being threatened was true, but his perception of being alone wasn't. God revealed that there were 7,000 people in the area just like Elijah, who had not bowed their knees to fear, or to false gods. God called them His "reserves." It was Elijah's perception, not reality, that sent him scurrying to the woods.

As Jesus approached the fulfillment of God's call on his life, Mark the gospel writer says, "He began to be deeply *distressed* and troubled." In spite of his distress, he diligently pursued his goal. His mind was set on God, not circumstances. He believed God was going before him and trusted God fully. His focus on his relationship with God brought him security and stability. He was "not shaken" by fear... in fact, he had "hope" and "joy."18 His perception of events was not limited to what he saw in the natural. He trusted that God was working behind the scenes on his behalf. Do we have that same trust?

The Father, Son, and Holy Spirit

God the Father is the source of unlimited resources. God is not just someone or something out there. We can know and experience Him in a tangible way. The same is true of Jesus. Christ's life in us brings forth the same gifts, character, power, and ministry that he displayed while on earth. His life in us produces right thoughts, right feelings, right choices, right urges, right desires, and even right dreams. His life comes forth from our spirit as we are influenced by the Holy Spirit. God's indwelling nature and character comes forth without reason or cause, because it exists apart from our own nature. It cannot be conjured up by mental, emotional, or spiritual technique. Nor is the Spirit manufactured by fleshly senses. The Spirit of God, although living in and through us, operates apart from us. Watchman Nee says:

> Man's ordinary sensing is caused or brought out by people, things, or events. We rejoice when there is reason to rejoice, grieve if there is justification to grieve, and so forth. Each of the senses has its respective antecedent. The life of the spirit, on the other hand, does not require any outside cause but emerges directly from within.[19]

The *love* of Christ, the *joy* of the Lord, and the *peace* of God all surpass and exist apart from human knowledge and understanding.[20] These emotions do not depend on us. They are the fruit of the Spirit.[21] God's Spirit can give us peace even during circumstances that would ordinarily create distress. The "fruit of the Spirit" is not dependent on circumstances. That is why Paul says we can experience God's joy and peace even in the face of hardship and suffering. His life in us "keeps our heart and mind" from being controlled by circumstances. His life in us increases, growing and maturing in proportion to our yieldedness to His authority and rule. We can either resist or allow the expansion of God's Kingdom.[22] Although we do experience soulish emotions, we also experience spiritual life which can overshadow our natural life. The transcendent nature of the Spirit does not come by denying or suppressing natural emotions but by calling out to Him.

To fulfill his promise to "never leave nor forsake us," Jesus sent the Holy Spirit to assist us in the stresses and strains of daily life.[23] Paul writes:

> We have this treasure [Holy Spirit] in earthen vessels, that the power of the life that shines forth in us is seen as coming from God, not from ourselves. We are troubled on every side, yet we are not *distressed*; we are perplexed, but we do not despair; persecuted, but not forsaken; sometimes we fall, but are not destroyed.[24]

The literal meaning of the word "perplexed" is: at the end of our mental resources. God wants us to exercise our minds, but when we are unable to make sense of the events around us, we must *trust and rely on Him* to give us insight and understanding. We have the *mind* of Christ for this very purpose.[25] Our problem is that we have difficulty trusting and relying.

When we are led by our soul, our behaviors follow our natural thoughts, feelings, and desires. When we think we have good reason to do something, our emotions generally support us. Our will decides to act on our desire, and our body carries out our will. Yet sometimes in our inner-most being, we sense an unuttered, soundless voice which opposes what *we* want to do. This is the voice of our spirit touching God's. It may lead, urge, or quietly prompt us to do something we believe is highly unreasonable. It may also lead us to do something contrary to what we would normally do, or even like. When the leading of the Spirit goes against our natural inclination, we are forced to make a choice between God's will and our own. We need to learn how to listen to God's Spirit. If we do, it will prompt us through the still, quiet voice of conscience and intuition, and often give us a perspective beyond our natural ability to see. If we do not learn to recognize the Spirit we can miss God's leading. We may stumble into something God wanted to save us from. The result may be unnecessary hardship and pain.

When we obey the old man rather than yield to the Spirit, we remain stuck in the same old life. When we yield to the Spirit, the old ways die and Christ's life and character comes forth. All lasting change comes from an exchange. Ultimately, we determine whether we will grow or stagnate by our choices. God wants us to walk after the Spirit, for no other path possesses spiritual value nor has eternal results.

> All lasting change comes from an exchange.
> Ultimately, we determine whether
> we will grow or stagnate by our choices.

Joe Blow and Jon Doe

Joe and Jon are two fictional Vietnam vets who are friends. They met while in therapy at a Vet Center. Both men were diagnosed with PTSD, and given a 100% disability rating. When Joe received his disability compensation, he used his benefits to purchase land and a trailer house in the country. He was tired of the constant hassle and conflict at work, and felt powerless to do anything about it. So he quit working and isolated himself to control his life and environment.

Jon, too, was tired of the constant hassle and conflict. His life seemed to be going in circles and he was tired of it. He began to examine his life, to see if there were some personal changes he could make. He sought the counsel of a few trusted friends, used his benefits to get out of debt, and began retraining himself for a different occupation through the VA's rehabilitation program. He wanted to become self-employed so he could have more control over his life and environment.

Joe and Jon both receive counseling. Joe goes once a week or so. He knows he must continue therapy to prove that he is still having problems; his disability and income depend on it. Still, he remains closed to both his counselor and group. When they offer possible solutions to his problems, he rarely acts on them. When he does try, he rarely follows through. He takes the medication the VA prescribes for his depression and sleeping problems, but it doesn't always work as quickly as he likes, so he drinks and continues to smoke a little dope.

Jon, although guarded and somewhat skeptical, decides to open up to his group. He allows the frustration and pain he is going through to surface, and he receives both comfort and counsel from the group. Instead of assuming he has all the right answers, and that everyone else in the world is screwed up, he listens to what the group says and mulls it over. He's tired of relying solely on himself to figure things out, knowing the frustration and loneliness it brings

Once a month each man takes his family out to eat. When they enter a restaurant their natural response is to silently, almost automatically, find out where the exits are. Neither of them wants to be trapped if something happens. Both prefer to sit in a corner with their backs against the wall so they can see everything. Surrounding conversations and activity always distract them from their present company because they feel compelled to concentrate on what goes on around them, just in case. Both men recognize these patterns as learned behaviors associated with combat, and they have been taught that they are simply protective measures, but old habits die hard.

One night a waiter leads Jon to a table where there is a lot of incoming traffic. It requires him to sit with his back exposed. He feels apprehensive but he doesn't put up a fuss because he's determined to be free from fear. He feels himself becoming hypervigilant but he knows this reaction is irrational. Throughout the evening he struggles with a growing uneasiness. His normal pattern is to get up and leave, but he doesn't give in to the rising discomfort. Instead, he prays silently, confessing fear as coming from old perceptions. He believes that God has not given him a spirit of fear, but of a sound mind, so he asks God for peace. When his mind strays to old memories he takes his thoughts captive, silently confessing his faith in Christ's ability to free him from his emotional baggage. He's tired of his present being controlled by the past.

Joe faces a similar situation. He doesn't like the table he's given, so he heads for a table in the corner. He doesn't care what the waiter thinks. He wants what he wants, and has little regard for protocol. His wife is slightly embarrassed and looks away from the waiter, not wanting to see his reaction. She follows Joe silently, not wanting to make a scene. She feels helpless. "It's hopeless," she tells herself, and she resents Joe for her own fear and sense of inadequacy. Before Joe can get to the corner table, someone else is seated there. He silently curses, as he feels his anger rise. A slight sense of panic follows as he looks around to see if there are any other safe tables available. In anger he says, "the hell with it," and turns to leave. His wife makes a small fuss, but she knows better than to go against him. She fears becoming the source of his rage. She knows she is dependent on him, and fears he will leave her and the kids if she upsets him. "We're going," Joe says, and leaves.

Fear is Joe's dictator. Because he gives in to it, he becomes a dictator as well. His wife doesn't understand why they must leave when other tables are available. All she knows is that her expectations are crushed. To her this is just another example of his insensitivity and self-ishness, and why he can't be trusted. She and the children are confused and hurt. She sees the disappointment in her children's faces. Joe is still thinking only of himself... his security, his safety, his feelings. As they hurry to the parking lot the children are crying, and Joe and his wife are angry. As soon as they get in the car, an argument erupts.

You probably get the picture by now. Joe limits himself and his family by hanging on to old patterns. He has allowed his past to squeeze him and his family into a narrow, constraining lifestyle. He lives imprisoned while thinking he's free. Everyone suffers.

One day Joe and Jon walk out of a local store. As they enter the parking lot, a car behind them back-fires. Like a highly sophisticated computer, their minds do a split-second data search of past memories to identify the sound. It kicks out "Gunfire!" Before they are even conscious of it their bodies have set off an autonomic nervous system response. Their adrenaline is off and running, preparing them for fight or flight. All the muscles in their backs and necks tighten, and their stomachs knot. Joe dives to the ground in a knee jerk reaction, while Jon spins on his heels. Each draws a short, deep gasp and holds it, freezing in time and space. The pupils of their eyes open wide as they strain to locate the source. Their hearing is suddenly more acute. They must find and identify the danger!

Both are in the middle of an exaggerated startle response. They perceive themselves to be in a life-threatening experience and are responding appropriately. Unfortunately, their perception is wrong. Because this reaction was triggered so often in Vietnam it is second nature to them. However, mini-seconds after their initial response their minds have already processed new information, taking into account their surroundings. They are able to conclude the noise wasn't gunfire. Although they can now reason they have nothing to fear, the biological stress reaction has already kicked in and is still going strong. The tension is so thick you can almost taste it. It is *distressing*. The temptation now is for them to let their minds stray back to those memories intrinsically linked to their biological reactions. They are faced with a choice... either focus on the present or focus on the past... take their thoughts captive or yield to compulsive, intrusive memories.

"Startle response," Jon says to himself, taking a deep breath. "This is not Vietnam," he tells himself a couple of times. He takes a deep breath and lets it out slowly. He continues to breathe deeply as he walks toward his truck, consoling himself with the knowledge that it will soon pass... grateful to be walking on peaceful soil again. He focuses on the present, knowing that if he starts reminiscing he will stay in a prolonged state of hypervigilance and it will affect his behavior. As he nears his truck it's over. He is breathing normal again.

Joe responds differently. As soon as the stress reaction is triggered, so are past memories and unresolved emotions. Some are so strong he is overwhelmed by them. He immediately thinks about the past. His pattern is to blame somebody, which only makes him angry. Even though his anger eats him alive, he won't let go of it. He has a right to it! "Why forgive those who were responsible," he says, "they don't deserve it! Besides, I can't let them get away with it." So, he goes from one bad memory to the next, each painful scene playing out in his mind as real as when it happened. This triggers more blame and anger and keeps his adrenaline pumping. Finally, he is driven by feelings that are out of control. He'd like to talk to somebody, but he has isolated himself. Rather than talk to his wife, he stuffs everything.

Joe's wife and children see his agitation but know better than to ask him what's wrong. They avoid his angry glare and quietly withdraw from his presence. Finally, when he can take it no longer, he slams the door, jumps in his truck, and heads for the nearest liquor store. On the way he smokes a joint and although the memories remain, he begins to feel no pain. He wants to talk to somebody now because it's safe; he's emotionally numb! But, few people want to talk about Vietnam and nobody has the time or patience for a drunk who relives the same old war stories, dredges up the same old guilt, and repeats the same old angry accusations. If he persists, Joe might find someone to talk to, possibly another vet stuck in the past. But, talking about the same old stuff doesn't help much. Joe can vent his anger, blame others, and talk about his problems on an intellectual level, but all along he avoids the emotional pain and resentment that keep him trapped.

Summary

• Breathing patterns mirror emotional patterns. We hold our breath when frightened or when repressing our emotions. Rapid and shallow breathing often accompany strife and anxiety. These behaviors create shortness of breath which, in turn, create lightheadedness, dizziness, and a feeling of loss of control. These physical sensations can create additional feelings of fear, vulnerability, and panic. Simply learning to breathe more deeply and slowly can relieve tension and affect physical health. Blending meditative confessions based on God's truth with breathing techniques reinforce the body's natural parasympathetic nervous system response.

• Stress is personal. Although stressors are real they do not always *cause* stress. Our reactions stem mainly from our interpretation of events.

• Stress escalates in relationship to the number of stressors we experience. We often have some control over the number of stressors we allow in our life. Draw and enforce healthy boundaries.

• When under stress we tend to react in extremes. We blow things out of proportion. We take our anger out on others who have nothing to do with the real issues. Don't let unrestrained anger create additional problems in your life.

• Fear, and life's pressures, are compelling motivations to examine our beliefs and behaviors, and to rid ourselves of junk which keeps us from experiencing God's presence. They can also be loving reminders for us to arrange our priorities around our relationship with God.

• Stress can be good. It produces physical, mental, emotional, and spiritual growth, depending on how we respond to it. Scripture says to "count it all joy when we encounter various trials." The pressures of life give us an opportunity to observe our true character. Stress also activates inner resources of courage, boldness, and assertiveness.

• What distinguishes life from death is that things which are alive are flexible. Unless a steady state of growth is maintained, all life forms die. They become stiff and lifeless. Rigidity occurs. Without flexibility things break under pressure. Learn when to stand, and when to bend.

• Too much stress produces apathy, passivity, pessimism, helplessness, hopelessness, and despair. A good support system can make a difference in how we feel. Relationships help us to cope. God and people are resources that don't cost a penny.

• Stress is debilitating. Make time for rest, relaxation, meditation, and prayer. Jesus took time apart for all of these.

• It is difficult to engrave anything on a tense, overly active mind. Relaxation and safety are necessary to receptivity. Try taking a less defensive position.

• The impact of stress is modified by duration, intensity, repetition, our degree of control, personality, temperament, genetics, learned behavior, disabilities, drugs and alcohol, maturity, coping strategies, availability of resources, attitude, perspective, and choice. All things are possible but not all things are productive. Make healthy choices.

• Distinguish pressure from tension. Pressures come anytime we fulfill our God-given responsibilities. They are part of the ebb and flow of life. Pressure can produce untapped sources of creativity and energy if we draw upon God's grace and power. Tension results from adding our own plans to God-given responsibilities, or by striving to carry out God's plans in our own strength and in our own timing. Learn to distinguish God's plan from your own.

• What has been learned can be unlearned. We can exchange negative thoughts for positive ones... lies for the truth... His life for ours. When we know the Healer, nothing is impossible.

• We can have the mind of Christ. We can also study His behavior. Jesus was no stranger to pressure or suffering. He is an example of how to live with stress. Learning to sit at His feet and hear His voice should be a priority for all who desire healing.

Overcoming chronic stress is often a long-term project. Compulsive and habitual responses to stressors are generally deeply rooted. However, Jesus came to "set those who were in captivity free." The main thing is to get started, and once in the race, not to quit.

-Questions-

1. Write down specific examples of the kind of events that create internal stress/anxiety for you.

2. List the kinds of thoughts/beliefs that go through your mind when you are struggling with stress.

3. List the specific emotions that accompany the examples you gave.

4. What are the normal ways you behave when feeling the above?

5. Which of these behaviors create a strain on your relationship with God and others?

6. If God was all powerful, and nothing came into your life apart from His consent and purpose, how would this change the way you perceive and respond to life events?

-18-

Freeing the Captives
[OVERCOMING ADDICTIONS]

"My step-dad is an alcoholic. I hate it because I had to see my mom get beat up a lot. I think people with this problem definitely need a lot of help. He's better now, but he's still lazy. He and Mom also smoke pot. They have always argued and still do. When he is drunk, my step-dad sometimes hits me and my half-brother when he fights with mom."

–female, age 15[1]

"My dad grows pot and smokes it a lot with all his friends. When my parents were married, he'd come home really drunk and high and stuff and beat my mom up. So my mom, my brother, and I moved to California. I just recently moved up here to live with my dad. My mom and dad got a divorce because of his habit. He beats my step-mom up sometimes. When he comes home really high and stuff he's real edgy. But he's been laying off a lot lately because he's been going to school."

–male, age 17[2]

"One afternoon I was sitting outside, struggling with feelings of guilt, powerlessness, and unworthiness over having fallen back into using marijuana again. Why couldn't I let it go? What was wrong with me? All I could feel was shame and condemnation! I looked down at a tuft of grass that was growing up between the driveway and edging around the flower bed. I had tried to kill that clump of grass at least four or five times. Even though I had cut the blades of grass back as far as I could reach, the grass kept growing back. Man, I thought, I'm gonna have to take the trouble to get down to the roots if I ever want to get rid of that grass. As I heard myself say this, I heard the voice of the Holy Spirit. 'That's right!' He said. 'And if you ever want to get rid of your addiction you're going to have to do the same. You're going to have to stop running from your pain and get to the root of it. You're going to have to trust me to walk through it with you, and stop avoiding it.' As soon as I heard this I *knew* it was true. I had to make a decision."

–the Author

For many Vietnam vets, what started off as an effective form of self-medication turned into a vicious cycle of drug abuse and chemical dependency. Over time, consumption increased and tolerance decreased. Then, what once worked to suppress the symptoms of PTSD now caused them to surface. Reducing consumption only resulted in an increased arousal of symptoms. Not able to find their way out, vets found themselves trapped.

The deception of addiction is that what we believe will bring release and freedom, brings bondage and despair. This chapter reminds us that regardless of how difficult it seems, no one has to remain captive to addictions. Although the path to freedom is not always easy, there is a way out! What I believe is important to know about addictions, ourselves, and God, in order to be free, is covered here.

Addictions

Addictions are habits. Habits are formed by repeating behaviors; they are built like buildings, one brick at a time. If they are constructed by repeating choices and behaviors, they can be torn down the same way. Just as we have the ability to build habits, we have the ability to destroy them.

In order to combat addictions, intervention is necessary at the earliest stage possible. The longer we nurture fleshly desires and behaviors, the harder it is to combat them. Life-long habits are not easily dislodged apart from God's supernatural intervention. Almost all twelve-step programs successfully dealing with addictions admit that we must first become, and then stay, "spiritually fit." Paul wrote, "Who is adequate for these things... not that we are adequate in ourselves to consider anything as coming from ourselves, but our adequacy is from God.3" Where we are unable, God's Spirit will enable us.

We must acknowledge our addictions for what they are. Addictions are not harmless quirks (those which God "winks His eye at"). Addictions are relationships! We *trust* and *depend* upon them to:
- bolster our sense of inadequacy or our self-esteem,
- give us recognition, approval, acceptance or power,
- escape responsibilities, realities, or stress,
- avoid, evade, deny or mask negative emotions,
- substitute pleasurable physical feelings for emotional pain,
- bring us a sense of rest, happiness or pleasure, and
- create the ability to relate rightly through altering our mood.

Anything or anyone we trust or depend upon other than God is an idol. *God sees* addictions as "idolatries."4 They are *gods* we serve. We are often our own idols. We worship self-sufficiency, trust only in self, and rely on self to have all the answers. *We* sit on the throne of our life.

In addition, what we *give our affections to* then occupies the attention of our *heart*. When we turn to addictions to satisfy and meet emotional needs, they become *love affairs*. God sees these relationships as "adulterous."5 We are told to "*love* the Lord our God with *all* our heart, mind and strength," and to "have no other gods before Him." God wants our affections to be centered on Him. All else must be secondary, and originate out of His expressed will for us.

Addictions are also *iniquities*. They cause us to stray from God's original intended path for us. They deceive us by bolstering false beliefs and feelings that do not bring lasting satisfaction.6 They offer only temporary relief by substituting sensuality, feelings, or mental experiences for true spirituality and healing. Because addictions require a deceptive hidden life, they also create the oppressive burden of self-condemnation. They create neither safety nor refuge, and ultimately result in shame, humiliation, and reproach. When we trust and depend on our addictions we mimic the children of Israel. They also trusted in alliances with other things rather than in God, and this eventually led to their downfall.7

Knowing Ourselves

It is imperative that we discover our true motives for seeking freedom from addictions. Those who seek healing simply because they want someone's approval, or to get people off their backs, rarely remain free. Neither do people who are motivated by pride, a need to be perfect, or for want of personal gratification. Seeking help requires the ability to acknowledge personal limitations, and a *genuine* desire for freedom. God can give us desire if we don't have it, "For it is *God who works* in us both *to will* and *to do* His good pleasure."8 Both the desire and the power to be free are available in Christ, if we ask.

To become what we want to be, we must first humble ourselves and acknowledge what we really are. Humility is a prerequisite to healing. The simple admission of need opens up doors that are closed by self-reliance and pride. God gives grace to the humble but opposes the proud. Therefore, bringing our addictions into the open is the beginning of freedom.9 Remember, all change is an exchange. Giving up familiarity is difficult for the fearful and insecure, and receiving is difficult for the self-reliant and proud.

I can't tell you how many times I picked up and laid down marijuana. I believed I wanted to give it up when, in reality, I wanted nothing of the sort. It took many failed attempts for me to see that I was not being honest with myself. Christ in me wanted me to be free, but I wanted what was familiar. He wanted healing; I wanted safety. It was only after truthfully acknowledging what I really wanted that I could say, not my will God, but yours be done.

Acknowledging Our Need

Isaiah writes, "In repentance [turning toward God] and rest [reliance upon His ability, not our own] you shall be saved. In quietness and trust is your strength, but *you were not willing*."10 God calls us to Himself, but are we willing? Do we rely on Him or on our addictions? God offers comfort, but do we allow ourselves to be comforted?11 If we say we believe, yet we daily fail to appropriate God's healing and deliverance, then our faith is only theory. If we are not willing to live or die by our beliefs, then of what practical use are they?

Chronic unbelief and mistrust keep us from turning to God. After all, why turn to God if we don't need Him? And, if we have no limitations, then we certainly have no need for God. The Kingdom of God is promised to those who are "poor in spirit," and "pure in heart."[12] The *poor* acknowledge their lack and therefore, their need. They approach life with an open hand. They look for more and are filled. God gives the Kingdom to those who persevere in asking, seeking, and knocking. The self-righteous and self-reliant rarely ask or seek because they think they already have it all. The *pure* are not hiding anything; they are truthful and transparent about themselves. They guard their hearts, but it is to prevent pride, lust, envy, jealousy, pain, anger, or resentment from finding a home there. It is not that they don't experience these things, for they are common to all mankind; it is that they refuse to allow these things to lodge in their heart. Instead, they entreat God to fill their hearts with love, mercy, compassion, and forgiveness.

Knowing God

Addictive behaviors result from a lack of faith. Those who lack faith are often condemned by the "religious," creating additional feelings of inadequacy and hopelessness. But faith is like a seed, which when watered and nurtured, grows over time. Faith, like every tree, has a small beginning. *Faith-less-ness* is not necessarily a character default, a lack of will power, or a lack of righteousness. It results more from an immature *knowledge* of God, which causes us to resist trusting Him, and prevents us from relying on Him. God will, however, light the way out of our present darkness if only we will trust Him.[13] When we truly know God, we have no trouble trusting Him.[14] It is our preconceived ideas of God formed by limited understanding, painful relationships with our fathers, and what others have said about God, that limits our faith.

Eventually, all our behaviors can be traced to what we truly believe about the nature and character of God. A. W. Tozer, in *The Knowledge of the Holy*, states, "The gravest question before the Church is always God Himself, and the most pretentious fact about any man is not what he at a given time may say or do, but what he, deep in his heart conceives God to be like." How we *perceive* God not only dictates our behavior, but our identity, security, sense of belonging, and the kind of relationships we have with Him and others. The absurdity is, we tend to trust what *we* believe to be true about God, whether it is true or not. And we often trust what others say about Him rather than examining the Scriptures for our self.

To trust God, we must first know Him to be real. Then we must know Him to be faithful. As I have said, truth and faithfulness are interwoven. God is *truthful* because He is *faithful*.[15] As much as we know God to be faithful we will honestly rely on Him. This is not blind faith, but rather it is trust which is firmly grounded in knowledge. Faith, however, is not mere head knowledge. It is not just knowing facts, thinking positively, or vain repetition of the promises of Scripture. Neither is it mere mental assent in which we say we believe because it appears reasonable to do so. True faith is agreeing with God, and *believing enough to act* accordingly. When we act on what we believe, we soon discover it to be either truth or presumption. If we never act, we either live by assumption or presumption... neither of which is a true knowing. *It is either action or revelation that creates experiential knowledge.*

Faith comes from our innermost being. It is a response which comes out of our true belief system, after which our feelings and behaviors must honestly follow. Knowing *about* God is not the same as knowing Him. One is head knowledge, the other is relational experience. We not only need to know that God *is*, we need to discover *who* He is. Once we discover Him to be loving, forgiving, accepting, long suffering, forbearing, and full of grace, kindness, patience, and mercy, we will trust Him.

All who believe have been *given* some measure of faith, for God gives us the faith necessary to believe, and to please Him.16 Faith is a gift... not something we strive for or earn. Because faith *is* a gift, all we really have to do is desire and receive it. All who believe in God have experienced the reality of God's love and nature to some extent,

God plants the seed which gets us started, even if it is quickly stolen away.17 Faith which remains, then grows. It develops as we trust what little we do know about Him, to trust Him more. As our faith is exercised we develop a history with God, and then build upon our history. We grow from "faith to faith." When we trust God enough to obediently respond to Him in each successive situation, His life gradually emerges. His kingdom rule expands, and we go from "glory to glory."18 Our growth may be slower than what we want, but God is able to do in a day what may have taken a thousand years. As the end of the age approaches, things will happen faster than we can imagine, and our tangible *experience of God* will grow as we trust and obey.

The Battle to Change

Jesus is still in the business of miracles... he is unchanging. His deliverance is as real today as it was yesterday. I was miraculously freed from my own dependency on drugs. Still, like a dog returning to his vomit, I picked it up again a few years later during a time of spiritual drought and pain. When I picked it up, I did it freely. I made the *choice*. This time there was no miraculous intervention. I had to learn to walk in the liberty God gave me, one step at a time. It was a struggle! I had to battle to reverse my choices and stand firm in His grace.

Once free, always free? Not so with addictions. It is often a continual, daily, sometimes moment by moment, choice to die to old patterns and obey Christ. Unless we renew our minds and substitute new patterns for old ones, we tend to return to what is most familiar. There is no resurrection life apart from the cross, and because we are living sacrifices, we can get down off the cross anytime we want. Freedom then, becomes a daily choice... and struggle.

The Purpose of Struggle

As far back as Creation there has been opposition to God's purposes... first from Lucifer, then from man. And as far back as man's fall from a life of ease in the Garden, God has used struggle for His redemptive purposes.[19] Struggle results in growth, change, and the formation of character. It produces an intimate knowledge of self, and of God. In struggle we discover strengths and weaknesses, and are often learn what we would not have learned any other way.

Struggle indicates the presence of resistance or opposition. Resistance-type exercises strengthen muscles, causing them to grow the most. So it is with our spirit and soul, for when we struggle we exercise our intellect, emotions, and will. In Vietnam, we exercised our physical senses, intellect, and our intuition to detect danger, discern the enemy, and to protect ourselves and others. The longer we struggled through combat, the better we became at it. Spiritual strength and discernment are developed the same way.

A baby chick must struggle to free himself from the hard shell which encases his life. This shell is designed to protect the tender, immature life within. Yet if this hard shell is not eventually broken, it will suffocate the chick. What once provided protection will then produce death. If we try to help the chick by breaking the shell for it, the baby chick will die. The struggle the chick has to endure to break the shell is necessary for its health. The struggle exercises its beak and muscles, thus producing changes in him necessary for future survival.

Struggle, Growth and Change

When the human body grows, cells change shape. They stretch, separate, and divide. When God works to grow us up, He changes our character, behavior, and sometimes even our appearance. God is like a potter. When clay is shaped in a potter's hands, it is pulled, pushed, and stretched. When a pot is thrown, one hand squeezes while the other creates resistance, forming a vessel. Sometimes both hands squeeze together and the clay is confined and can only move in one direction. In doing so, it takes the shape the potter desires. Being stretched is painful. So is being separated and divided, yet it often produces growth.

Stretching into something new is a struggle. It is hard. Sometimes we see hardship as a curse, when in reality it is most often God's hand of blessing. We may resist being pushed into a particular direction because we don't see the end result, but God does. Trials are generally God's grace and mercy toward us, not His punishment. When He corrects our direction or the way we are living, it is because He knows that the end result is for our good... and for the good of others. Yet trials do more than correct our steps; they test our convictions, our resolve, and our character. They bring to light the inner man and provide opportunities for us to separate from former behaviors, beliefs, and emotions.[20]

Struggle reveals what is hidden in the heart. "I the Lord search the *heart*, I test the *mind*, even to give to each man according to his ways, according to the results of his deeds."[21] God responds to faith, and true faith is an inner condition which reflects the desires *God* has birthed in us, not our own. God does not want our faith to be frustrated. He knows that standing on Scripture, just because we desire God's promises for want of self-gratification, will do nothing if our heart is far from Him. That is why He reveals what is in our heart… to purify it.

Self-denial and discipline are always difficult, yet exercising our will strengthens our ability to consistently make good choices. Consistency is necessary to obtain goals. Goals, once obtained, give us a sense of confidence, mastery, and peace. This encourages us to engage in even greater struggles in the future where battles are won by lengthy intercession, patient waiting, and trust which never wavers. Each successive victory builds greater faith and hope.

The Struggle for Faith

If freedom from ungodly dependencies comes from exercising resistance and dependence on God, it does so for our benefit. Learning to rely on God for our acceptance causes us to depend on *His* righteousness, not our performance. In spite of repeated failure on our part, God never withdraws or withholds His love from us. His love is unchanging. He suffers long, is patient, and bears with us… proving His faithfulness. When we believe this, and act accordingly, God responds… because we are exercising faith. Jesus said, "According to your faith let it be done unto you."

Faith, if fought for, will free us from our addictions. Once a seed of faith is planted, it needs to grow and multiply. This parable, told by Jesus, provides a picture of the travails of faith:

> The sower went out to sow his seed and as he sowed, some fell beside the road; and it was trampled under foot and the birds of the heaven devoured it. And other seed fell on rocky soil, and as soon as it grew up it withered away because it had no moisture. And other seed fell among the thorns; and the thorns grew up with it and choked it out. And other seed fell into the good ground, and grew up and produced a crop a hundred times as great. He who has ears let him hear.[22]

Jesus is referring to people who really have no desire to hear what he has to say. As song writer Paul Simon said, a man hears what he wants to hear and disregards the rest. Jesus explains that the seed is the Word of God. God's word is truth. Some hear the truth without it ever penetrating their heart.

> Those on the rocky soil are those who, when they hear, receive the word with joy; but these have no firm root; they believe for a while and in time of temptation fall away…

This typifies my struggle with drugs. I would believe for a while, then return to the quick fix for comfort during times of stress rather then lean on God. I struggled with doubt, conflicting beliefs, and self-reliance. Would God be there or wouldn't He? My trust in God was not deeply rooted. Christlike character was lacking. Still, my repeated failures were not without lessons. I discovered painful, humbling insight about my own limitations, and discovered valuable insight about God.[23] And, I did not drop out of the race.

James wrote, "Blessed is the man who endures temptation; for when he has been proved, he will receive the crown of life." Studies of addictive behavior say that the period of temptation (the craving) that an alcoholic faces lasts only about three minutes. And, if alcoholics make it through the craving period, which comes and goes, they can be successful in regaining sobriety.[24]

Temptations come from within, not without. "Let no man say when he is tempted, he is tempted by God. For each man is drawn away and enticed by his own desires." My desire was to avoid pain and suffering, to mask my anger and flee from confrontation. Resisting temptation wasn't resisting drugs, it was resisting the temptation to be controlled by fear. Freedom meant dying to habitual patterns of running from pain.

> And the seed which fell among the thorns, these are the ones who have heard and as they go on their way they are choked with *worries*, and *riches*, and the *pleasures of this life*, and bring no fruit to maturity...

Worries, riches, and the pleasures of life all represent value systems which draw us away from God. Anxiety is worry, and worry is fear and unbelief. When we value self more than we do freedom, truth, justice, love, and the will of God, we live in fear. John said, "Love not the world, neither the things of the world... for all that is in the world, the lust of the flesh, and the lust of the eyes, and the pride of life is not of the Father." John is not saying we can't enjoy life or the things God created and intended for our pleasure, but a heart set on pleasure cannot be set on God. When our heart is unequally yoked, that is, tied to Christ *and* to opposing desires and dependencies, we are constantly pulled in opposite directions. This creates inner conflict and double-mindedness, and leaves us at odds with our self. We may *think* we can serve self and Christ, but our *behaviors* oppose such thinking. The result is confusion, inner turmoil, and frustration. Christ said, "You cannot serve both Mammon [material things/riches] and God, for you will end up hating the one and serving the other."[25]

> And the seed in the good ground, these are the ones who have heard the word in an honest and good heart, and *hold it fast*, and bear fruit with perseverance...

Once we align our will with God's, we must hold to it. This is the only difference between victory and defeat. Those who successfully escape addictions hold fast to God's will and to His word. They stand on a belief system rooted and grounded in truth, and they are not moved. Research shows that many who battle addictive behaviors generally succeed on their fourth attempt at sobriety. They try various forms of treatment and fail, but because they never give up they eventually succeed. Perseverance pulls them through. The only time they fail is when they give up trying.

As long as we remain in the race there is always hope we will finish. The minute we drop out, the race is over for us. We must fight for our faith, and remain in the race. Ultimately, faith is confidence in a person, not an ideal or a philosophy. We can be confident that Jesus, who upholds his word and brings all he has spoken to pass, will succeed where we fail because of his unchanging character.

Psychological Warfare

The battle for faith is primarily over *what we will believe* about God, Jesus, self, and others. The battle for sobriety is over *what we will do.* Will we be ruled by our reasoning, our emotions, and what we want, or will we be ruled by God's Spirit? Once we know what to do, *it is always a matter of will* and therefore, choice. True freedom, for which we all aspire, is the right and ability to make choices.

We are never truly free if we will not do what we believe is right, and if we cannot do what is wrong. God put the Tree of Knowledge in the Garden so Adam would be free to choose whom he would serve, himself or God. God's provision was not designed to cause Adam to fail, but to prove Adam's devotion. If all God wanted was obedience from us, He could have created robots. Is this the kind of friendship you would want? Neither did God. He wants to be loved freely. Freedom is required for true service *from the heart.* It is the condition of our heart that makes our service acceptable. Those who would serve God must freely choose to.

When Adam chose independence over service to God, the immediate result was fear. The second result was deception. Adam ran into the Garden to hide. Man has been hiding ever since. The natural man (all we have inherited from Adam) and the old man (and all our beliefs, emotions, vows, and habits) still flee in the opposite direction of God. God confirms that our ways are not His ways. The natural man is also opposed to the spiritual, for the spiritual threatens his authority. God, however, promises to remove both the "veil which lies over our heart" (the self-protective wall around our emotions) and the "hardness in our minds"(the inability to perceive events correctly due to fixed mind-sets), if we will let Him.[26]

Spiritual Warfare

The battle to overcome addiction is not merely psychobehavioral, it is spiritual. Apart from Christ, our spiritual condition is one of enslavement to Satan. Whether we see it or believe it, Satan opposes us.

> You He made alive, who were dead in trespasses and sins, in which you once walked according to the course of this world, *according to the prince of the power of the air, the spirit who now works in the sons of disobedience.* Among them we too all

formerly lived in the lusts of our flesh, indulging the desires of the flesh and of our minds, and were by nature children of wrath...We know that we are children of God and that the rest of the world around us is under Satan's power and control.[27]

God takes believers out from under the dominance and authority of Satan and transfers them into His kingdom, where they come under the authority and protection of Christ. Satan has no power over believers, other than *to tempt or deceive*. Satan's power is delusional. Nevertheless, he resists our becoming free. In the truest sense we are never really free agents, we are either slaves to God or slaves to Satan. However, we are free to choose which master we will serve.

When you present yourselves to someone as slaves for obedience, you are slaves of the one whom you obey, either of sin resulting in death, or of obedience resulting in righteousness.[28]

We are always yoked to someone. Like Bob Dylan said, "It may be the devil or it may be the Lord, but you've got to serve somebody." Satan would yoke us to anything that keeps us in bondage: drugs, alcohol, sex, pornography, religion... whatever keeps us tied to the weight of sin, guilt, and fear. However, Christ's yoke links us to Jesus. We can accomplish whatever task he calls us to because he is right along side of us, carrying us when we tire, and turning us to keep us on the path. His yoke provides the ability to accomplish the impossible.

Relational Warfare

Although we no longer battle against flesh and blood, it doesn't mean that if we change we won't face resistance... even from those close to us. Relationships are dynamic; they are living, breathing, evolving things. When one person in a relationship changes, the relationship itself changes in some way. Our change generally requires some adjustment on the part of someone else.

In all relationships, both individuals are dysfunctional in some way. In addition, each person generally gets something out of the others' dysfunction. A wife may enable her husband to drink, whether she says she likes it or not, so she can continue to be a caretaker, the savior, or the "good guy." If her husband quit drinking she would lose that role, and possibly an important part of her identity. If she is unable to make the adjustment she may sabotage her husband's sobriety just to maintain her own role and identity. Our changes can tap into hidden fears others have. They can bring to the surface issues of rejection, disapproval, guilt, or even abandonment. Change makes some people uncomfortable because life is then no longer familiar. To successfully stand in our freedom, we need to be prepared to face resistance.

Summary

Freedom from addiction comes by knowing our dependencies, ourselves, and God. Change can be miraculous or progressive but it comes from an obedient, faithful walk with God. All good relationships are cultivated by meaningful communication, openness, vulnerability, trust, faithfulness, tireless effort, and time together. A relationship with God is no different. None of us will ever discover all there is to know about God. Our knowledge, experience, and understanding of God comes through a process of revelation and struggle. No tree bears fruit overnight![29]

Freedom from addiction, unhealthy dependencies, and all behavior contrary to truth, requires steady diligence and watchfulness. It is a constant search and destroy operation. Search for the light. Destroy the darkness. We can be cleansed and set free if we are honest with ourselves, acknowledge our lawlessness, and expose the things we keep hidden. God gives us the desire and the power to "put away every detestable thing." We need only ask Him.[30] Keep in mind, addictive behaviors are linked to:

- tendencies to withdraw and isolate,
- feelings of hopelessness and despair,
- unresolved anger, resentment, bitterness, and unforgiveness,
- chronic stress reactions,
- unresolved guilt, condemnation, and self-blame,
- attitudes of futility and cynicism,
- feelings of alienation, and rejection,
- unresolved grief, fear, anxiety, and
- patterns of avoidance, denial, and suppression.

Remember, "It was for freedom that Christ set us free, therefore keep standing firm and do not be subject again to a yoke of slavery." Jesus is our way out! "The Lord is able to make us stand." If we balance trust in God, with our own faithfulness, He will pull us out of the pit we are in. We can be confident in this, "that He who has begun a good work in us will complete it until the day of Christ Jesus."[31]

-Questions-

1. On whom or what do you rely and love more than God?

2. How do these people/things get in the way of your trusting in or depending on God?

3. How does trusting in these people/things prevent you from discovering God's power and his love for you?

4. What will you do differently after reading this chapter?

-19-

The Light at the End
of the Tunnel
[PURPOSE AND MEANING]

"I'm still trying to survive over here but the NVA aren't making it too easy lately. We've just been in contact with them for three days and things aren't looking too bright. When you have bullets cracking right over your head for a couple of days in a row, your nerves begin to frizzle. When you're getting shot at, all you can think about is, try to stay alive, keep your head down and keep shooting back. When the shooting stops, though, you sort of sit back and ask yourself, Why? What the hell is this going to prove? And man, I'm still looking for the answer. It's a real bitch!"

–a Vietnam veteran[1]

"His belief in God was as surely a casualty of the war as his trust in the word of his government. The boy who had gone to mass every morning in Minneapolis could not sustain his faith surrounded by the random and, for him, meaningless carnage of Vietnam; not even his own survival was evidence for him that God lived and cared. 'It's nice to say someone is looking out after me,' he said, 'but the reason I made it was nothing more than blind fucking luck. Why does the mortar hit the guy next to you and not you, if you're in the killing radius? I don't think it's anything that God did, if there was a God. It was just luck...'"

–Mike MacDonald[2]

"The plane out of 'Nam may have touched down at Travis or McChord years before, but full DEROS means achieving peace of mind and heart and soul back in the world."

–Mahedy[3]

In Vietnam, the proverbial "light at the end of the tunnel" was not light, but lies. "The war is just about over." "We are winning." "It will be over any day now." Like carrots on a stick, false hopes were dangled to keep up our spirits. When at the end of the war someone scribbled on a building, "You can turn off the light at the end of the tunnel now," we all knew what it meant. Many of us left Vietnam with the uneasy sense that we had been deceived, and Robert McNamara's disclosures in 1995 only confirmed those beliefs, opening old wounds. Yet in spite of what business, political, or military leaders intended, I believe God had a plan of his own which superseded them all. This chapter examines God's intimate involvement in Vietnam, in the affairs of men. I hope it will provide food for thought. Maybe it will light the way out of your tunnel.

What Was It All For?

Many vets have determined that political or economic reasons were behind our involvement in Vietnam. Others have taken a more philosophical approach. Some have simply resigned themselves to "life as it is," and dodged the question altogether. Since the war was personal for those who fought it, a knowledge of the politics or economics surrounding the war, though beneficial, will never answer questions that are of a personal nature. They may provide an intellectual framework for the progression of events surrounding Vietnam, or they may even provide insight into human behavior, but they will never provide answers to the larger questions of purpose and meaning. Making sense out of Vietnam is important because many vets *may* never experience complete inner peace without discovering its purpose in their life. Yet God, who is all knowing and who understands the purpose behind everything, can help us reach a meaningful conclusion, if we ask.4

If you believe there is no purpose in life and that all things happen by chance, then you have not taken the time to study the world around you. The natural world, from the stars in the heavens to the smallest microbe, is full of order and purpose. Things do not happen randomly, but by highly ordered principle and pattern. If the natural ebb and flow of life reflects order and purpose, and we are a part of it, then our experience in Vietnam was also purposeful.

Research shows that an inability to resolve traumatic personal experiences leads to a sense of unrest and futility, and trauma affects one's general outlook on life. Inner peace occurs in direct proportion to a persons ability to integrate *all* past experiences into a meaningful life pattern. Life without meaning invariably leads to emptiness, cynicism, and despair. Making sense of tragedy is not just a matter of deciding who is right or wrong, or even one of personal reconciliation. Life has moral and spiritual rudiments which undergird all that happens, and we must see beyond the natural senses, for true understanding. Knowledge means little without understanding, and understanding comes from God...generally through personal enlightenment. That is because seeing beyond the natural takes spiritual insight and revelation.

Some experiences force us out of comfortable, familiar patterns and shake long-standing beliefs... sometimes in ways which make us better, sometimes not. Sometimes a gulf is created between us and situations which we once neatly fit into. This, too, can be a part of God's plan. Resolving our experiences, therefore, is linked to obtaining a spiritual perspective. Purpose and meaning ultimately relate to *God's* intention and handiwork in the world, not man's.

An Age-old Question

Our search for meaning is like that of other historical figures. Take

Job and Solomon for example. Job suffered great hardship and sought to find purpose and meaning behind it. Solomon, although the wisest and wealthiest man of his time, did the same. Both men had times when life appeared absurd, ambiguous, two-edged, vague, puzzling, and meaningless. Solomon wrote:

> All things are wearisome; and man is not able to tell it. The eye is not satisfied with seeing, nor is the ear with hearing. That which has been is that which will be...so there is nothing new under the sun.[5]

> I said to myself, as is the fate of the fool, it will also befall me, so why then be wise? It is all vanity, for there is no lasting remembrance of the wise man as with the fool, inasmuch as both will be forgotten. So I hated life, for the work which had been done under the sun was grievous to me, because everything is futility, and striving after the wind.[6]

Both men struggled with the brevity of life, its inequity, and its contradictions. They struggled to make sense of their experiences, their loss, and events outside their control. They too often felt powerless and concluded that life was sometimes profitless.

> For I have taken all this to heart and explain it that righteous men, wise men, and their deeds are in the hand of God. Man does not know whether it is love or hatred; anything awaits him. It is the same for all...I say again, the race is neither to the swift, and the battle is not to the warriors, and neither is bread to the wise, nor wealth to the discerning, nor favor to men of ability; for time and chance overtake them all...Thus I considered all my activities which my hands had done and the labor which I had exerted, and behold all was for nothing, and striving after the wind, and there was no profit under the sun...For who knows what is good for a man during his lifetime, during the few years of his futile life. He will spend them like a shadow, for who can tell a man what will be after him.[7]

I also tried to find purpose and meaning in life apart from God. I rejected God's role in life, refusing to believe He existed. However, my rigid atheistic stance gradually bent in Vietnam, and although I did not come to know God, I did turn toward Him. Eventually I discovered, like Job and Solomon, that all my questions had their answers in Him.

> I know that no plan of yours [God] can be thwarted. You have asked, "who is this that confuses my counsel because they do not have true knowledge?" Surely I have spoke of things I did not truly understand... Up until now what I knew about you was only what I had heard, but now my eyes have seen you. Therefore I also see myself as I truly am and I repent.[8]

Let us hear the conclusion of the whole matter: Fear God and keep his commandments, for this is the whole duty of men. For God shall bring every work into judgment, with every secret thing, whether it be good, or whether it be evil.9

Faith and Understanding

Our natural reasoning, emotion, and physical senses will always leave us short-sighted. Therefore, we must aim for the mark. Without spiritual perception we see life with distorted vision. The way which seems right to us often ends in failure.10 God, however, sees beyond the immediate to the future. He knows the hidden value of each event. That is why He can say we should "count it all joy when we go through different trials or testings." Without a spiritual, eternal perspective, we get stuck in the process as if that were all there was to it... as if the process were an end in itself. Paul wrote, "All things work together for good." All things accomplish God's purpose.11 Even Christ's suffering at the hands of those in authority was in God's control. Peter says, "They did what your [God's] power and will had decided beforehand should happen."12 Seeing the unseen requires faith. Faith opens our lives to the supernatural and gives God an opportunity to involve Himself intimately in our lives. The beginning of faith is believing that there is more to life than what we see.

Whether we choose to believe it or not, God is at work in the world. He works on our behalf and on behalf of His Kingdom. His intent is to reconcile the world unto Himself and to restore whatever was lost or destroyed by sinful rebellion. God sent Christ into the world for this purpose. If all things work together for good to them that love Him, then every troubled situation is a forge through which God works to shape and strengthen those called to Himself. The mere existence of trouble is neither a sign of God's displeasure or of personal sin. In fact, it can be a tool which turns and changes our lives so that we are made better because of it. I believe that our experience in Vietnam was intended as a part of God's blessing.13

Trials like Vietnam are in reality great opportunities. Too often we see them as great obstacles. Our lives would be an inspiration of unspeakable power if each of us would only recognize every difficult situation as God's chosen way of revealing His love and power to us. If we would search for the message God is sending, instead of experiencing defeat, we would soon discover something of His blessing and wonderful nature. Every mountain we face, every hardship we endure, has the potential to become a path of ascension. If we examine our past carefully, we may discover that the very times we strained, struggled, and felt constrained on every side were also the times that God gave to us His richest blessing.

One of the most comforting and revealing scriptures I have read is used in the literature of *Point Man International Ministry*. Each time I read it, I am reminded of God's hand in my tour of duty.

> I think you ought to know, dear brothers, about the hard times we went through in S. E. Asia. We were really crushed and overwhelmed, and feared we would never live through it. We felt we were doomed to die and saw how powerless we were to help ourselves; *but that was good*, for then we put everything into the hands of God, who alone could save us, for He can even raise the dead. And He did help us and saved us from a terrible death; yes, and we expect Him to do it again.
>
> -Paul of Tarsus/Point Man AD 65[14]

Our experiences can make or break us, depending on our perspective. I challenge you to reexamine your experience in Vietnam from God's perspective. See if it wasn't designed for your good. In doing so, you may discover God's intended purpose for your life, and perhaps new meaning and direction.

Seeing Both Sides of the Coin

Every coin has two sides. The whole coin is best known by observing both of its sides. This gives us a balanced perspective. Many of us have trouble letting go of Vietnam because we don't want to let go of the *bad* that happened. Some of us will not let go because of the *good*. We must recognize both the good and the bad to conduct a *realistic* inventory of our experience. Although I have talked a lot about the negative aspects of the war, there were many positive things. Vietnam tested our resolve. It demanded an unprecedented response on our part and, in doing so, provided an exceptional opportunity for our best to come forth. The lessons we learned have stayed with us for life. Consider the following. Vietnam:

- caused us to examine our beliefs, behaviors, and feelings on a deeper level, and solidified those worth keeping;
- exposed our true character and motivations;
- purified and cleansed many of us of a dichotomous lifestyle;
- revealed the results of selfish ambition, greed, and lawlessness;
- helped us discover, exercise, and develop our abilities;
- provided an opportunity to exhibit self-denial, uncommon sacrifice, loyalty, and courage;
- allowed us to see who and what really ruled our lives;
- turned us from old patterns of behavior to new ones;
- provided opportunities to trust and depend on God and others;
- provided an opportunity for God to reveal Himself to us;
- provided an opportunity to exercise and strengthen our faith;
- produced a desire for experiences outside our normal exposure;
- turned us toward uncharted paths of adventure;
- created an atmosphere for hope to flourish; and
- revealed patterns of spiritual warfare.

Personal Lessons

Vietnam was a season of severe stretching for me. Prolonged periods of extreme physical, emotional, and mental exhaustion, coupled with inner conflict and fear, eventually led to a nervous breakdown. The field psychiatrist said I was merely suffering from combat fatigue, but I knew better. Getting healthy forced me to make some decisions I had been avoiding. By the time I finished my tour, I discovered I was capable of doing whatever I put my mind to. If necessary, I could also do it twenty-four hours a day. I discovered potential I had never known. Endurance and perseverance were worked into my life. Because I could not escape responsibility or hardship, a life-long pattern of running from difficulty began to crumble. Personal success caused me to reevaluate beliefs that I was inadequate and worthless... beliefs which had bound me to fear and failure.

The knowledge that every day might be my last caused me to examine the direction my life had taken. Not wanting to die in fear gave me the courage to risk new behaviors. I spoke out. I stood up for myself and others. I gained new-found respect. I learned to distinguish between the important and the trivial. I learned to respect and value life.

Freedom from life's usual distractions, coupled with long periods of isolation and boredom, left lots of time to think and reflect. A year of exile, reflection, meditation, and self-examination, forced me to face things I had spent a life time avoiding. Loneliness made me realize the true value of friendship. Separation from former friends forced me to risk new relationships. I did not want to die unknown, so I began to disclose personal beliefs and feelings I had always kept hidden. Men around me did the same. This created a sense of intimacy and camaraderie I still feel today. I discovered that behind our masks, we were all pretty much the same. This made me feel less abnormal, less disconnected, and less fearful of exposure and rejection. My guardedness and self-preoccupation slowly dissolved. I was forced to focus on others. I learned to listen, and I rediscovered compassion that seemed dead. I realized in a greater sense that love was something you gained by giving, not something you waited around to receive.

Depending on others for survival forced me to reconsider my own independence. I began to see that my independence really came from mistrust and self-protection. In reality, it was a self-imposed barrier that had imprisoned me as much as it had protected me. I saw how empty, lonely, and meaningless my life had become because of it. I began to discover the true satisfaction of helping others. I discovered a sense of belonging that had eluded me most of my life. I learned what it meant to be a part of a team. Trust in others began to be renewed.

Being given a position of authority and responsibility forced me to deal with my irresponsibility and my mistrust and rebellion toward authority. Because I was now *one of them*, I had to learn how to *earn* the loyalty, obedience, and trust of others. This forced me to learn that submission was an inner quality which could not be taken by force, but that it had to be given. I learned to lead by example, to earn loyalty and trust through sacrifice, and to give respect in order to receive it. I discovered that there was a cost for being genuinely concerned for others.

Being betrayed by my country taught me to value honesty and integrity. Having to trust and depend on others taught me the value of a man's word. Some men talked the walk while other men walked it. I learned quickly to discern one from the other. War honed my perception and sense of intuition about who could be trusted.

My forced exile gave me a new appreciation for freedom. Painful losses forced me to get in touch with emotions I had lost through years of suppression, numbing, and callous indifference. As my heart softened toward those around me, I found it softening toward people "back in the world." The changes I experienced in Vietnam made personal reconciliation possible in broken relationships back home.

My attitude toward force and violence changed. My life as a street fighter ended. I saw the consequences of my lifestyle magnified a hundred-fold in Vietnam, and it was a rude awakening. What I did to survive shattered smug assumptions about my own inherent goodness. I realized for the first time that there was little hope for mankind if left on its own. Thus began my search for something outside of myself as a source of salvation. Eventually this led to an encounter with God.

I learned to accept severe privation, to go through periods of restricted gratification, and to be grateful for little things. I discovered what a privileged, comfortable, and rich life I had as an American. I developed a sensitivity to the poor and to the oppressed, and I developed a profound sense of gratitude for other men who suffered and sacrificed on my behalf.

Understanding God's Laws

We reap through experience the consequences of our choices. We are either blessed or cursed by the choices we make. Even when we stumble blindly through life, we set in motion forces which rebound to our detriment. These forces, which fulfill God's laws, are simply a part of God's order in the universe. You may call these laws karma, sowing and reaping, or the belief that "what goes around, comes around." However they are defined, they are still *law*. For the most part we can remain blissfully unaware of them, but our ignorance doesn't stop laws from operating. Our experiences *are* intimately connected to our judgments, attitudes, choices, and behaviors; when we see this it generally compels us to make some corrections. If we make the right corrections our future road becomes less bumpy. Making correct adjustments is called *learning*.

Scientific, moral, and ethical laws govern the universe. These laws, like the principle of gravity, function whether we believe in them or not. Moral, ethical, or judicial laws governing behavior do not exist because man made them up but because they are an expression of God's nature. We cannot escape the consequences of defying them. When scientific law says that for every action there is an equal and opposite reaction, it is simply declaring that stuff just doesn't happen by accident. There is first *cause*, then *effect*. When mathematical law says that both sides of an equation must equal, it merely reflects judicial law which says true justice balances the scales. Life may *appear* to be a series of chance events, but it is only because *we don't see* the forces that are operating behind the scenes (Ecc.1:5-8).

The law of cause and effect, like the Biblical principle of sowing and reaping, enables us to *assign meaning* to events.[15] Understanding the meaning behind things is what enables us to learn and grow. We observe an effect and know that something is causing it. When the temperature drops below zero (cause), water freezes (effect). When water freezes it doesn't take a genius to know *why*; it's because the temperature drops below zero. We may not know the scientific explanation, but we do know a law is at work. Because we see the connection between water and temperature, we can use our knowledge to alter water's shape and condition. Understanding the events that preceded our tour of Vietnam (cause) will help us understand why we ended up there (effect).

Accepting Our Accountability

Brende and Parson give these reasons why men went to Vietnam:
- patriotism
- the anticipated excitement of war
- to develop and refine our masculine identity
- to escape boredom
- to help find direction in our life
- to open avenues to a secure future
- because we felt we had no choice but to serve
- pressure from our family to follow a tradition of military service
- to follow in our father's footsteps by military service
- unconsciously attempting to undo the death of a father, uncle, or brother in World War II, Korea, or Vietnam
- limited options owing to our lower socioeconomic level[16]

Whatever circumstances preceded your service, most of them happened as a direct or indirect result of a series of choices... *your* choices. I had several reasons for entering the service, but none of them were unique. I evaded the draft for nearly a year, but my life was empty; when I finally got tired of going nowhere, I tried to enlist. Like others, I had concerns about our involvement in Vietnam. I questioned whether I wanted to take another human life, but those things weren't foremost on my mind. In all honesty, I just wanted to get my duty out of the way. I would have gone to college, but I didn't have the money. And I was simply tired of my mundane, work-a-day-Johnny existence and thought I could escape the drudgery. After the Air Force and Navy rejected me because of my criminal record, I volunteered for the draft. You know what happened next! It was Basic, AIT, and then Vietnam. Still, each step of the way I was making choices... choices which were determining my destiny. My intentions for military service certainly weren't God's, but God *was* letting me go down a path of my own choosing.

God's Principles for People

I believe that God's purpose in allowing me to go to Vietnam was to turn me from the path I was on in my life. He knew I was a concrete learner. The only way I was going to change was by coming face to face with the consequences of my choices. I had to see the severity of what I was sowing. God's law was at work, helping me to see those areas of my life that needed correcting. Jeremiah wrote, "Have you not brought this on yourself, in that you have forsaken the Lord. Your own wickedness will correct you, and your own backsliding will reprove you." He also wrote, "I know, O Lord, that a man's way is not in himself; nor is it in a man who walks to direct his steps. Correct me, but with justice."[17] True justice corrects. It neither protects or prevents us from reaping the just consequences of our choices. It is impartial in its enforcement, whether reward or penalty. Justice weighs and balances all our actions equally... rich or poor, intelligent or ignorant, black or white.

Because God is just, His laws, whether spiritual or natural, insure that every act balances out. It is only because God is merciful, that our acts are not balanced immediately. However, we cannot escape judgment apart from the cross. God's mercy and justice work to correct us, to turn us from destructive ways. They prevent us from reaping more severe consequences. God corrects and purifies all those He receives into His heart. He deals with us as sons and daughters, correcting us like a father who truly cares. A father who doesn't love his children enough to correct them, treats them like bastards, as if they were not his own. God is not like some of our earthly fathers, He corrects us for *our* profit, not because we're a nuisance to Him.

God's *intent* is to bring every man to a true knowledge of Himself so that we might experience abundant life and true freedom. He involves Himself in our life because of His goodness and love, even when we do not believe in Him or want Him to. Paul says:

> I [God] was found by those who didn't even seek me. I became manifest to those who did not ask for me... All the day long I have stretched out my hands to a disobedient and obstinate people.[18]

God always reaches out, calling to get our attention. Unfortunately, we don't always respond. When we don't, He may reach out to us through circumstances... circumstances often created by our own choices. God doesn't give up easily. If we remain inattentive, He may intervene supernaturally, altering the direction we are going if it is not toward Him.[19] God intervened in Joseph's life through a dream, to keep him from making a wrong decision. God met Saul on the road to Damascus and blinded him, turning him from a path of destruction.[20] God put an ass in the road to block Balaam from going down the wrong path. All these and more illustrate God's intervention. We may not always recognize God's corrective hand for what it is, subsequently trying to go around it, over it, or under it, to stubbornly proceed on our way. Yet if God fixes a fix to fix us, and we fix the fix, then He fixes another fix to fix us. God perseveres!

God's Principles for Nations

Are disasters, grievous events, trials, and reprisals related to God's law of reaping and sowing? Was Vietnam, or the divisive aftermath, an accident? What about America's involvement? I don't think so! God's laws apply to nations, as well as people. This principle is found throughout scripture and history. When we turn from God, allowing sinful behaviors and habits to rule our lives, does this not bring about judgment and retribution (balance) upon our heads?[21] Our founding fathers understood this. At the 1787 Constitutional Convention George Mason said: "As nations cannot be rewarded or punished in the next world, so they must be in this. By an inevitable chain of causes and effects, providence [God] punishes national sins by national calamities."

Ultimately, divine judgments are redemptive last resorts from the heart of our heavenly Father. Judgment always works to restore God's order and purpose and is evidence of His mercy toward us.[22] We may scoff at this, but there is purpose in all that happens. We may believe we ended up in Vietnam for our own reasons, or even as victims of the plans of others, but at any time along the way God could have directed us off the path.

The Book of Acts says that God has made every ethnic group on the earth of one blood, to populate the face of the earth. And that He has appointed beforehand both their times and their boundaries, so that they should seek the Lord and find Him and dwell happily because of it.[23] National and ethnic boundaries are shifted to create upheaval and confusion. Out of instability, people grope for truth. When all we have believed or trusted in gets shaken, then we begin to question everything. *This* is the beginning of knowledge. When we seek to make sense of our confusion and pain, we find meaning and purpose. Our hearts are truly open when we earnestly seek God. This is what He wants! God is wanting a people who will seek Him with their whole heart, a bride who will whole-heartedly love His son. Such a people God can trust to rule with Him.

As it is with nations, so it is with individuals. When God changes our circumstances, situations, or relationships, He is shaking things to bring us to Him. This is a part of God's ongoing discipline and the process He uses to change us. The problem is, we often correlate correction with rejection because of how we were disciplined as children. As a result, we resent God and sulk, thinking He disapproves of us.

Acknowledging God's Hand

Why did we escape death in Vietnam when so many others died? Was it God's sovereign choice? Isaiah says, "Since you are precious in my sight; since you are honored and I love you, I will give other men in your place, and other peoples in exchange for your life." If this is true, then why did God choose us? Does it mean He loved others less? I doubt it. Paul says of Esau and Jacob, twins whose *destiny* had been foreordained by God, that God chose their destiny. For "though the twins had not yet been born, *and had not done anything good or bad* in order that *God's purpose*, according to *His choice* might stand, *not because of works* [performance], but *because of Him* who calls."[24]

There is nothing that happens which we would be better off without. It is not, "that awful event should never have happened, so let's just erase it."[25] God knew it would happen and planned to turn that very event into something good. Everything we go through is designed to help us to be a blessing to others, even as Christ's death was. Divorce, pain, loss, the death of a friend... all our experiences help us to minister to others, if only we learn the lesson God is after in us. As believers we are called to be priests.[26] If our experiences do not make us bitter, they develop strength and compassion out of which we then minister. We must see that our afflictions aren't always the result of personal sin. They may simply be tied to God's plan to make us a source of comfort to others. Paul said he was afflicted for the benefit of others. His suffering, like Christ's, prepared him for ministry. Scripture says:

> Consider the work of God, for who is able to straighten what He has bent. In the days of prosperity be happy, but in the days of adversity consider, God has made the one as well as the other so that man may not discover anything that will be after him... Terror, pit, and the snare are coming upon you. The one who flees from the terror will fall into the pit. The one who climbs out of the pit will be caught in the snare, for I shall bring it.[27]

Sometimes God allows us to be trapped in circumstances from which there is no escape, to make sure we learn our lesson. Vietnam was that pit for me. God works in all things, whether to save us, direct us, teach us, or impart character. All is designed to conform us to Christ's image. Solomon wrote, "In much wisdom there is much grief, and increasing knowledge results in increasing pain."[28] Paul wrote,

> I now rejoice, not that you were made sorrowful, but that you were made sorrowful to the point of turning around; for you were made sorrowful according to the will of God in order that you might not suffer loss in anything through us. For the sorrow that is according to the will of God produces a repentance without regret, leading to salvation; but the sorrow of the world produces death.[29]

Paul's life was an intimate record of suffering. Still, he had a life-long, positive impact on others. Suffering and hardship produce character, endurance, and hope. Hope has as its foundation a full understanding of our limitations, and of the limitlessness of God. If we put our trust in God there will be a day when we truly see that "the Lord binds up the fractures of His people and heals the bruises *He has inflicted.*"[30]

Lessons for Warriors

It was no accident that the prophet Isaiah recorded God correcting

His people through war. God allowed a nation of idol worshipers (vs.10), whom Israel had made a pact with, to trample down Israel's warriors (vs.6). God even sent a "wasting disease" among men He considered to be "stout warriors" (vs.16). He put them through a torturous time of testing and refining, to cause them to return to Him. God wanted them to acknowledge that it was He who "wielded" their lives (vs.15). Out of this process, God saved a remnant unto Himself who would "never again rely on the one who struck them down, but would truly rely on the Lord."[31] Did God intend the Vietnam War to turn us toward Him? Did he allow us to be "struck down," simply to open our eyes to the fallacy of trusting in anything other than Him? Was God looking for "warriors" who would be totally stripped of all other distractions, so that they would only serve His purposes?

The problem with many of us is not that we are warriors, but that we have abandoned our role as warriors. We have strayed from the very path God was trying to set us on. Instead, we have given in to mediocrity and compromise. We have hid out in caves of isolation. We have become self-centered and self-protective. We have abandoned courage and sacrifice and neglected the oppressed and needy.

God's intent for us was that we gain strength and wisdom... not born of age, but birthed through hardship and suffering. This was so we could be used mightily by Him in our generation. God needs an army of men who are free from worldly entrapment, men who know uncommon loyalty, courage, and sacrifice. Men who cannot be bought, compromised or corrupted. Men who can stare into the face of death and not blink an eye because they have "been there... done that!" Men who are intimately acquainted with suffering, who because of their own wounds can identify with the sufferings of Christ, and with the wounds of others. He calls to a lost and dying generation. John Sandford writes,

> Our checkered careers, our utter sinfulness and degradation, our falling into all manner of vain seeking, become by the grace of God on the cross and in the resurrection the inevitable writing of wisdom on our hearts. Our hurts and sins become our schooling and preparation...His mercy is such that He turns the depth of our sin into the strength of ministry...in the end we thank Him for it. Our sins have rather become our training for high calling than our disqualification.[32]

Summary

God not only allowed, but led us into Vietnam to raise up a generation of warriors schooled in courage, discipline, and sacrifice... warriors who would understand the wounds and sufferings of others, and be moved by compassion to become an army of healers, helpers, protectors, and deliverers. Warriors who, having experienced life's losses, would truly understand the value of life... who would stand unafraid and undaunted by any challenge, willing to lay down their lives to follow Christ so that others might benefit.

God "permits every generation to go its own way," and yet "He does not leave Himself without witnesses."[33] Every generation has its moment in the sun, and its impact and importance is best determined by the quality of life it exhibits. Vietnam veterans are an intimate part of this generation, and we must understand the significance of *our* purpose in *this* time. It was no accident that we were born into this generation.

We can do nothing about the past. Neither must we be perpetually tormented by it. Solomon wrote, "A man may ruin his chances by his foolishness and then blame it on the Lord." We often create our own tragedies by foolish behavior. We can blame the resulting losses on God or we can learn from past mistakes and encourage people to trust in God, but only to the extent that we ourselves have trusted. In remembering the painful consequences of our past actions, God has given us a powerful incentive for not making the same mistakes.

> To every thing there is a season, and a time for every purpose under heaven. A time to search, a time to give up as lost. A time to kill, and a time to heal, a time to tear down, and a time to build up... A time for casting stones, and a time for gathering stones together.[34]

The Byrds sang this in the '60s, but it was written in the Bible long before. Take these words to heart! This is a time for healing and reconciliation. We are living stones, fitted together into a building, a habitat for God.[35] Let's stop tearing down one another and start building an Army of Servants that will reach our generation for Christ, for our present behavior best determines our future, not our past.

-Questions-

1. List what you believe were the negative effects of your service in Vietnam.

2. List what you believe were the positive effects of your service in Vietnam.

3. In what ways is your experience in Vietnam now impacting the lives of people around you. Are you having a positive or negative impact?

4. If God had a purposeful hand in sending you to Vietnam, what do think he wanted to accomplish?

-20-

Mirror, Mirror, on the Wall
[IDENTITY]

"It was midsummer in south Georgia, and the humid heat would not relent even though the sun had dropped below the horizon. The low hum of our small window air-conditioning unit helped lull me into a depressed stupor. I felt hollowed out, empty, a carcass of nothing. Day after day for three months I had nothing to do but watch my daughter, Heather, crawl around the apartment. I would feed her baby food for lunch and fry a hamburger for myself; but beyond these minimal demands, I had little to do but daydream and think morosely of Vietnam.

"Susan was lucky, she had a job teaching. I had nothing to do until I began graduate school in the fall, so it was my reasonable assignment to sit at home every day and play house husband. Though I loved my wife and daughter and was glad to be home alive, I was resentful of my daily chores, frustrated at the petty concerns that occupied my time. I felt that something was deeply wrong.

"Like the ex-warrior chieftain who is forced to stay in the village and watch the tents, I was feeling useless and discarded. The crushing intensity of the Vietnam experience was gone. The insatiable demands, the incredible responsibilities, the impossible tasks were all left halfway around the world, unfinished, in the hands of others. I floundered in the vacuum of my new existence, and in the quiet of the evening, I wept.

"I sat there staring out at the fading sunset, tears rolling slowly down my face. As a child uses a security blanket, I wore a faded jungle fatigue shirt that had crawled with me through the sweat and mud and the blood of Vietnam. It was an amulet, a souvenir to remind myself of the valuable and powerful person I once had been. In my heart I called after the departing sun. I yearned to go after it and catch it, to see it rise again on the other side of the world. I thought about 'my' people and wondered how they fared. Had the local Cong struck again? Had the bridge at Phu Tanh village been repaired? Was the rice crop going to be as good as expected? Was soap available in the villages? It hurt deeply to admit that there was really no reason to ask: there was nothing I could do. I sat there in the summer night and harbored a terrible sense of emptiness. I touched the fabric of the old fatigue shirt just to make sure it was real and to prove to myself that all my memories were not simply dreams."

–Once a Warrior King[1]

David Donovan's quote is a revealing example of how difficult it has been for many soldiers to give up their identity as Vietnam veterans. Their inability to shed the uniform has made it hard for many to come home. More importantly, it has hindered them from establishing a new identity. Like changing clothes, you generally don't put on a new identity without taking off the old. If changing identities was as easy as changing clothes, most of us would have done it by now. However, when we become Christians, God's design is for everything to be made new, and that means a new identity in Christ.

> *Do this* knowing the time, that now it is high time to awake out of our sleep, for now our salvation is nearer than when we first believed...*put on the Lord Jesus Christ,* and make no provision for the flesh, to fulfill its lusts...hatred, contentions, jealousies, outbursts of wrath, selfish ambitions, dissensions and the like.[2]

Forever a Soldier

I thought the war was over for me when I left Vietnam, but I soon discovered new battlefields on the streets of America. The anti-war-like atmosphere and the anti-establishment upheaval of the '60's and '70's magnetically struck a chord in my life. My anger, distrust, and sense of betrayal by *the system* drew me into the counter-culture movement. It wasn't long before I became involved in anti-war activities as well, drawn by my desire to prevent any more of my brothers-in-arms from being killed in what I believed was a senseless war. The movement quickly became *us* versus *them,* and the VC became the powers-that-be. For me, the enemy in America was as elusive and often unrecognizable as the VC. Takers called themselves givers. Power brokers called themselves benefactors and servants. Thieves cloaked themselves in respectable titles. I couldn't recognize the enemy by appearance, because even the movement was infiltrated with government agents. I learned to use the discernment I had honed in Vietnam.

Identifying, locating, and confronting the enemy was as frustrating as it was in Vietnam. There was an uneasy familiarity about my struggle. The enemy seemed entrenched in the political, judicial, and socioeconomic system, and like Vietnam, I often found my hands tied by rules which protected them from being exposed. Unlike Vietnam, where I had an incredible array of firepower, technical resources, and manpower behind me, and a license to kill, in America the balance of power had shifted. I couldn't remove the enemy by force. Resources once available to me were now in the hands of the government I resisted. But for years, I wore my fatigue shirt and jungle hat. I remained the dutiful soldier, engaged in battle with society and its values.

In 1990, I bumped into another vet at the university I attended. He too had been diagnosed with post-traumatic stress disorder. He too had fought the Veterans' Administration for years... for recognition, treatment, and compensation. As we talked, he pulled a small business card out of his billfold. It read:

> I suffer from occasional loss of mental stability and become very violent with only slight provocation. The Veterans' Administration has determined that both mental and physical harassment of my person may be hazardous to your health and well being. So stay the hell of out of my face! Thank You.

I laughed! I knew all too well the message. Yet I also felt somewhat embarrassed, because I recognized with sadness that this, in a sense, was his business card. It not only identified his occupation, it identified his preoccupation. It made me stop and think! Was this how I came across to people? Was this the message I was sending? If so, was this the message Christ intended me to send?

My Identity in Christ

Soon after becoming a believer, I discovered that Christ's intent was for me to be his ambassador on Earth. I was to represent him wherever I went, and in all that I did... not just on Sundays. Not only was I an integral part of his body, I was a brother by adoption, his bride, a priest, a servant, and... a soldier. I was a part of an army commanded by Christ. Like other armies, this one also had a battle plan, a chain of command, a uniform, objectives, tactics, and weapons. I had joined this army voluntarily, but with little understanding of the cost. I soon discovered my *standing orders*. It was Paul, who wrote them down:

> And He died for all, that *those who live should live no longer for themselves, but for Him* who died for them and rose again. Therefore, from now on, we regard no one according to the flesh [after his past, his former manner of living/behaving; according to his skin color, ethnic origin, etc.]. If anyone is in Christ, he is a new creation; *old things have passed away; behold, all things have become [or are becoming] new.* Now all this has been done by God, who has reconciled us to Himself through Jesus Christ and *has given us the ministry of reconciliation*...for though we walk in the flesh, *we no longer war after the flesh*; for the weapons of our warfare are not carnal.[3]

These four statements defined my identity and role as a soldier: 1) I was no longer to live for myself, but for Him, 2) I was no longer to live in a manner following my former lifestyle, values, beliefs, emotional responses, or will, but in a new manner, 3) I was given a mission of reconciliation, and 4) I could no longer war after the flesh.

The Battle Plan

God's plan for His people has been the same since the beginning of history. It runs throughout the Bible, from Genesis to Revelations. It's outlined in this statement: I will surely bless you... and through you all nations of the earth will be blessed.[4] God's plan is simple, it is to bless us *in order that we might be a blessing to others*. It is God's blessing... reflected in His nature, character, and love *for us* through salvation, reconciliation, restoration, wisdom, health, mercy, joy, peace, right relationships, understanding, talents, and the provision of finances and needs... that changes us. It is Christ *in us* that draws others to Him.

God has enemies who are opposed to His purposes. Spiritual opposition comes from Satan and an army of fallen angels called demonic forces. Satan's plan is to "steal, kill, and destroy"[5] all that God has created and intends to do and usurp God's rightful place of authority. Wherever there are opposing forces, there are battles. The battle over God's creation takes place in both spiritual and natural realms, in the heavens and on earth. The fight is over who will rule God's creation. The battleground on earth takes place in our body, soul, and spirit, but it is waged most effectively in the heavenlies through prayer.

Ultimately the battle has been decided, for all things in heaven and earth have been given as an inheritance and possession to Jesus.[6] Satan is, in reality, only a spoiler. But regardless of its outcome, the battle is real today and we are conscripted into the fight. We fight not only for our own spiritual fruitfulness, but for the lives of others so that none should fall into Satan's grasp and be destroyed. As we labor to receive God's promised life, our focus is not so much on invading enemy camps as it is on inheriting from God. We fight to receive our inheritance, and we battle on behalf of others so they may receive theirs.

The effects of this conflict are no less damaging than was the war in Vietnam. If we do not understand the enemy's plans, his operative times or location of attack, we will be ambushed. If we are without armor, weapons, and support, we will surely be destroyed. To be unaware of this is sheer suicide. We must understand that every takable territory must first be won in our lives, before we can effectively stand with others in their struggle.

Our Conscription

Regardless of what branch of the military we were in, it was first and foremost a branch of *service*. This is true of Christ's army as well. We are conscripted to become servants, for this exemplifies Christ's role on earth. To live for Christ means we serve Him, not the other way around. A master-servant relationship implies authority, submission, and obedience, and it establishes a clear chain of command.

> I beseech you then brothers, by the mercies of God, to present your bodies a living sacrifice, holy, acceptable to God, which is your reasonable *service*...do not be conformed...be transformed...that you may prove what is the good, and acceptable, and perfect will of God...[7] And do you not know that to whom you present yourself slaves to obey, you are that one's slave...[8]

Not all servants are bondservants. Many who come to believe still go on living for themselves. According to tradition, a bondservant was a slave, who having been set free by his master, freely, willingly, and whole-heartedly committed himself to a lifestyle of obedient service. He chose to serve, no longer counting his life as his own, because of the goodness of his master. The Christian community has historically embraced Christ's gift of salvation, but it has resisted His Lordship. This compromise has left the Church powerless, unchanged, and without a dynamic witness. Our identity as servant-soldiers begins with a determined commitment to live for Christ, our Captain, and to serve Him alone. *Commitment is expressed in one's loyalty and obedience under fire.* How we live during hardship reveals the depth of our commitment.

> For not the hearers of the Law are just before God, but the doers of the Law will be justified...That the proof of your faith, being much more precious than of gold that perishes, though it be tested with fire, will hopefully be found praiseworthy, and honorable.[9]

The charge to live for Christ is challenged! Our commitment is tested and proven! We must not only seek Christ's will. Once we hear His orders we must obey! Discipline is the hallmark of every good soldier and every good disciple. We must say yes to Christ even when it means saying no to self. Discipline is self-denial! Discipleship means we "deny ourselves, pick up our cross (sometimes the cards we have been dealt), and follow after Him."[10] Discipline always requires submission and obedience.

Like every *good* military leader, Jesus never asks us to do what he has not first done. Christ *leads* by example. When Christ gave up his throne and former identity as Lord of the Universe and assumed the identity of a lowly carpenter, it was at great personal cost. He, once the most powerful being in the universe, became a child in a crib, completely dependent on others... powerless. He wasn't forced to do this, he did it willingly. His willing obedience to God eventually cost him his life, the trust of his friends, scorn, contempt, and rejection. Yet none of this deterred Jesus. He laid down his life; no one took it from him. Like Christ, we must be willing to abandon our old identity. To fully fulfill God's call on our life, we must follow in His footsteps. As Christ was himself dependent on God, so must we be.

Once we commit our lives to service, we must be steadfast in our decision. To *believe* means more than to be persuaded. This Hebrew term has its roots in the words *aman, emunah,* and *amen.* Aman means, "lasting, trustworthy, firm, true, and faithful; to stand fast, to be fixed or unmovable." It infers the mental certainty that "something is worthy of full trusting or believing; you can put your confidence in it with full certainty." Emunah means "truth, firmness, faithfulness, honesty, and official obligation." The essential meaning is "to be established, lasting, continuing, or certain." Amen means "truly, genuinely, or so be it." It signifies the voluntary acceptance of the conditions of a contract/covenant. Believing is not just a confession, it is a profession to do… to act in a way which is congruent with our statements.

In Jewish culture a *promise keeper* bound himself to fulfill certain obligations, or subjected himself to the consequences… generally to the terms of a curse. As believers, we bind ourselves to the same conditions Israel did in their covenant to God. God said, "See, I am setting before you today a blessing and a curse. The blessing *if you obey* the commands of the Lord your God… the curse *if you disobey*."11 We, the Church, have been compromised by an easy believism that denies the cost of obedience. We are asleep in our lethargy because of our unwillingness to suffer. We remain in a state of infancy because *we do not apply* what we know. God is looking for a people who will do more than that. He is seeking mature soldiers, servants who will pay the cost. Who better understands this than Vietnam veterans?

Our Uniform

In the world, soldiers wear a uniform which identifies their branch of service. In Christendom, *there is no uniform*. We are identified by behaviors, attitudes, and speech which reflect the life of Christ. We are "clothed" with the character and love of God. Character is an inner issue, not one of religious activity or service. Once we answer God's call on our life, His transforming work in us *begins*. It starts with Basic Training in the principles governing a believer's life, and it is followed by Advanced Training during periods of service and hardship (on the job, so to speak).12 Training is not in *works of service* as much as it is in *character development*. The transformation process is slow but sure. It is paced by the emergence of spiritual fruit (Christlike character). Just as evil is never suddenly eradicated, neither is our old identity. The struggle to become like Christ has many dimensions, of which healing is only one. However, once we gain and sustain each aspect of Christ's life which God promises to give us, we can stand with others. God allows us to be victorious to the same extent that we are fruitful.

To be a blessing, we must become channels of God's mercy, compassion, character, and power. We must allow Christ to live his life through us. We "consider ourselves to be dead… and present the members of our body to God as instruments of right living." Those who let go of their life for Christ's sake discover a truly satisfying life. Whoever protects his life ends up losing genuine life. To the extent we either hang on to or let go of our old identity, we do this.13 The challenge to no longer live after our former ways is, in reality, a choice to live for Him.

Salvation, like conscription, has a beginning and an end. It begins with our spirit being made new, and ends with our bodies being made new.14 In between, the Spirit, which is the Lord, works to save us from our old ways. This process of sanctification, in which specific areas of our life are progressively recaptured and put under Christ's rule, is enhanced by our yieldedness or hindered by our resistance. In the truest sense our souls are not saved, they are put to death. God may choose to restore that portion of our life which was lost or hidden, if it was what

He originally intended us to be, but He must destroy the rest. What is not of Him must be torn down and replaced. In every area we allow this to happen, new life comes forth.

We must fulfill the ancient mandate to "be fruitful, multiply, fill the earth and subdue it."15 This mandate applies to the inner growth of the Kingdom, as well as its outward expansion on the earth. Fruit comes forth by the Spirit which God plants in the form of a seed. Fruit is multiplied as we make room for Christ's life to grow and expand. The Kingdom of God (righteousness, peace, and joy in the Holy Spirit) expands, filling our life in direct proportion to our willingness to confront, subdue, and displace our old ways. Like an old house which is being restored, we may allow the carpenter to rebuild the kitchen, but not let him rebuild any other room. We must let him have it all!

The Bible refers to true believers as *saints*. The literal translation is "holy ones." Many of us are uncomfortable with being called holy ones because of the great lack of holiness in our lives. It puts us in remembrance that we are called to live a life worthy of Christ, one that reflects the righteous character of God. We must keep in mind that our holiness is not always a reflection of *our* performance, but of the performance of Christ. We must keep this in mind as we strive to become like Him. Saints are not just people of exceptional holiness. The term *holy* means to be "set aside or apart for use by God, consecrated for service, sanctified, or made sacred." Christ's robe of righteousness provides our holiness, while His indwelling Spirit simultaneously moves us to embrace a lifestyle which separates us from worldly values, unto Himself.

We *are* in the world. Still, we must set ourselves apart from the belief system and values it represents.16 Since all of us were brought up in the world, and many of us knew nothing of God and His ways until we were saved, this is a challenge. It is not enough just to give up our former or worldly ways, we must learn and apply new ones. To do this, we must first study to discover God's ways. Only then can we make the exchange. To the extent we exchange the old for the new, we reflect the life of Christ and his righteousness. Although the righteousness of Christ is *imputed* (assigned or credited) to us by God when we accept Christ's redeeming work, it also needs to be *imparted*. This impartation results when we die to the old and take on the new. It is then that righteousness becomes an *individual possession*, built into us as a result of our obedience.

God's intent is not just to regenerate our spirit so that we make it into heaven by the skin of our teeth. God wants our whole life to be transformed... body, soul, and spirit.17 God intends for us to experience the Kingdom of Heaven on earth, not just after we die. Being born again is the start of God's plan, not the end. Although God sees the process of salvation as already complete, for us it is ongoing. "For by one offering he *has perfected* for all time those who *are being* sanctified."18 Time does not have the same reality for God as it does for us. He knows full well the outcome of all that He does, and therefore sees His work as finished. We, however, being mortal, experience its working out in "real" time. For us it is still a process.

Our salvation begins and ends with God. He initiates, calls, chooses, carries out, and completes His purpose in us. He gives us both the desire and the power to appropriate our redemption, justification, sanctification, and righteousness. We are predestined to be conformed to Christ's image.[19] It does not depend on us to accomplish God's work, but we do play an important role. We can align our will with God's or set our will against Him. God conspires with willing souls, and our choices either draw the world to Him or cause the world to flee. There is no stronger cause for atheism in the world than Christians who profess one thing, but leave the church on Sunday and do the opposite.

> Those who live according to the flesh [depending on self, their own reasoning, etc.] set their minds on the things of the flesh; but those who live according to the Spirit, the things of the Spirit. For the mind set on the flesh is death, but the mind set on the Spirit brings life and peace; because the mind set on the flesh is hostile toward God; for it does not subject itself to the Law of God, for it is not even able to do so; and those who are in the flesh cannot please God.[20]

Our Mission

We are both the Body of Christ (his representation) and His ambassadors (his representatives) on earth. Our mission is to carry out Christ's ministry. It is ongoing through us. Scripture says:

> God was in Christ reconciling the world to Himself. Now all things are of God, who has reconciled us to Himself through Jesus Christ and has given us the ministry of reconciliation. Therefore, we are ambassadors for Christ, as though God were pleading through us; we implore you on Christ's behalf, be reconciled to God. For Christ Himself is our peace.[21]

Christ completed *His* mission when He died on the cross. He said, "It is finished." He settled accounts between God and all mankind by paying the price of a sinless life. There is no longer anything separating us from God. The road is open for all who would come. Once *we* fully believe and appropriate this message, our mission is to spread it. We are the elect of God, a peculiar people chosen to fulfill a specific mission. We are God's *special forces*. Our mission is to save lives and set captives free. It is not in the Father's heart to see His son's inheritance damaged or destroyed. Our objective, therefore, is to reach out to all mankind in mercy and grace.[22]

Jesus said that even our enemies must be loved and aided. As believers we may be in conflict with social norms and values, but that doesn't mean we are called to take up arms. Our role is not to be an adversary, but a friend. We're not to be against others, we are to be for them. We're not to judge, but we are to identify with their weaknesses.

We're not called to push people away, but to draw them to Christ. We must cleanse ourselves of attitudes and behaviors that *purposely* offend or make people feel unsafe in our presence. The message "leave me alone," must go! We must abandon our self-protectiveness, anger, criticism, hatred, bigotry, hardness, and anything else that prevents us from fulfilling our mission.

Our mission is not just one of reconciliation, but restoration. Reconciliation is first of all a supernatural inclination. It comes from Christ *in us*, reconciling the world to Himself.[23] In like manner, the mission of restoration also springs from the life of Christ in us. It is the character and power of God which enables us to preach the good news, heal the broken-hearted, proclaim liberty to those held in bondage, help the blind recover their sight, and restore those whose lives have been bruised by offenses. We are to be leaves on the Tree of Life, bringing healing now, and in eternity.[24] Christ's ministry was evangelistic, prophetic, and authoritarian in nature, yet none of these can be rightfully carried out apart from His character. In the Kingdom, how we do things is as important as what we do.

Evangelism

Proclaiming the various messages outlined by Christ is perhaps best fulfilled by the life we live, not by preaching at others. That doesn't exclude preaching, for faith comes by hearing, and hearing by the spoken Word. However, we are living books... not written with ink, but by the Spirit of the living God. The law and life of God is written on our hearts and minds. To the degree it is written, we bear witness to Christ. We are witnesses every day whether we want to be or not. We declare our true beliefs in our lifestyle and manner. People read us through their observation. We either testify of faith or of unbelief, not by what we say, but by how we live. If our lives do not line up with what we say, we deceive ourselves and others. If the love of God is in us, it shines through our actions and attitudes though we say nothing at all. In like manner, so does the heart of our old man.[25]

The Prophetic

The prophetic nature of our mission is also best fulfilled in the life we live. God's prophets were those who knew and revealed the heart and mind of God to people. They were recognized as coming from God, because God backed up what they said. We best fulfill our prophetic calling also, by knowing and revealing the nature and character of God. "He that *prophesies* speaks unto men to edification [build up], exhortation [encourage, challenge], and comfort."[26] The words we speak, and the way we present them, should build people up, not tear them down. If our words discourage rather then encourage, we are not speaking prophetically. We are merely criticizing and judging. If our words or demeanor do not comfort, but pierce and wound, we are not speaking prophetically either.[27] Christ's words were spirit *and life*, they brought hope and joy. They only brought condemnation to those who stubbornly resisted His message, and even then it was their sin, not Christ's words which brought condemnation. An effective ministry is judged by its life-changing influence. And, to be effective, we must first be influenced by Christ in a life-changing way.

Christ's Authority

The responsibility of every believer is not just to bring the good news but to demonstrate a lifestyle of authority and power, even as Christ and the prophets did. Christ's nature is that of a ruler. As King over the whole universe, he has both the right and the power to rule. We are to reflect this authority, but not by lording it over others. We are *empowered* through a relationship with God, but if we do not allow that power to rule *our* lives, then we are merely being religious.[28] The Kingdom of God advances in our life through godly behavior.

We might think that the best way to reflect authority is to manifest miracles, or to have dominion over others. This is far from true. The best way to manifest authority is to practice self-government. In other words, we rule our lives by practicing self-control. If we are powerless to rule our own behavior, thought life, or emotions we are not effective witnesses. Christ's authority is seen, or unseen, in every act we perform: in our interaction with others, in how we spend our money, in whether we share or stockpile our resources, or in how we support one another. If we are to model Christ's authority, let us do so by demonstrating self-government, within a model family.

Our Battle and Weaponry

Although we live in the world, we do not battle according to worldly customs. Although we live natural lives, we do not battle using natural strength. Our weapons are not carnal, they are mighty *through the power of God.* The word of truth, the Spirit, the character of God, and the name of Jesus are the effective weapons of our warfare. We use God's word not only to acknowledge and speak truth, but to develop a knowledgeable foundation upon which to stand. We use the power and authority God has given us, not just to stand, but to heal and deliver others. We use the name of Jesus to cast down spiritual strongholds, because it is the name to which every demon must yield. It is the character of God, reflected in our obedience to Him, that keeps us under God's protection.

Paul often defines the believer's life in military terms. Even Jesus is described as a warrior, as one who has broken the yoke of burden off our shoulders, and broken the staff (authority) of the oppressor in our lives. Jeremiah describes Jesus as a *gibbor* (ghib bore') or *geber* (gheh ber'), meaning "dreaded champion." Zephaniah describes him as a "victorious warrior." David says, "The steps of a gibbor are established by the Lord and He delights in his way. When [not if] he falls, he shall not be hurled headlong; because the Lord upholds him with His hand."[29]

In Israel, men were chosen by God because of their warrior spirit, *not their natural strength.* This hasn't changed. When God appeared to

Gideon He said, "The Lord is with you, O valiant warrior." Gideon's response was, *wait a minute Lord, my family is the least among all the tribes, and I am the least among my family.* God often sees us differently than we see ourselves. God sees us as a *"chosen generation,* a royal priesthood, a holy nation; a people for God's own possession who are to proclaim the excellencies of Him who has called us out of darkness into His marvelous light." If we are to battle on God's behalf, and on the behalf of others, we must see ourselves as God sees us.[30]

The battle begins in our own life. It starts by pulling down every stronghold which binds us. We must seek and destroy every speculation which comes from our own immaturity and carnal nature. We must pull down every arrogant conclusion and belief contrary to the Word of God. We must compare our every thought to Scripture, to see if it is true. We must guard our hearts and minds to keep anything but the truth from entering. To do all the above we must maintain vigilant watchfulness, and we must undo every disobedience until our obedience is fulfilled.[31]

Once we secure our own territory, we have a fire-base from which to operate. We can turn our attention outward. This does not mean we have to be perfect to help others, but we should have some level of maturity and accountability lest we enter the battle too quickly and fall. We mature by giving, so we cannot sit around and wait. The wise counsel of mature men will help us to see when we're ready. We are not Lone Rangers. Even *he* had Tonto. We work most effectively when we work as a team.

We need to be acquainted with the strategy of the enemy, his tactics, and his weapons. For "we battle not against flesh and blood, but against principalities, against powers, against the rulers of darkness of this world, against spiritual wickedness in high places."[32] We must not set ourselves against our husbands, our wives, our children, our families, our friends, the brotherhood of believers, nor even those caught in deception and darkness. We battle demonic forces: envy, lies, ignorance, deception, unforgiveness, bitterness, greed, humanistic philosophy, lust, and every evil thing hidden in the heart.

If we clothe ourselves with the whole armor of God, we can stand like godly men and women. We can raise up a standard of righteousness by becoming examples to our nation. Gird your mind with the truth. Walk in honesty and transparency. Put on the breastplate of righteousness, which is faith and love toward God, others, and your enemies. Clothe your feet with the shoes of the gospel. Bring both the good news of Christ's work, and His peace through forgiveness, wherever you go. Serve Him, proclaim Him, and seek to be reconciled in every relationship. Take the shield of faith... holding it firmly to deflect the fiery arrows of the enemy. Put on the helmet of salvation. Hold fast to what Jesus accomplished through his death. Take the sword of the Spirit, which is the word of God, and allow it to inspect and penetrate every area of your life. Let it reveal all hidden motivation. Boldly speak the word which God gives you. In the face of all tribulation, trials, hardship and temptation, stand fast!

Pray for all men everywhere, with hands lifted up like true warriors. Adorn yourselves at all times, with all manner of prayer and entreaty for God's purpose... not only for your life, but for those God has placed under your covering and protection. To this end, keep alert. Remain strong in purpose and perseverance. Intercede on behalf of the brothers for the establishment of the government and kingdom of God. Acknowledge and confess that your power, your ability, your calling, your ministry, and your sufficiency is from God. It is He who has called and qualified you. Draw your battle lines. Take on the true enemy. Become fruitful in the service of our Lord.[33]

It requires great courage, sacrifice, and compassion to follow Christ... to become a soldier in His Kingdom. Yet these are the very characteristics of any great warrior. Be obedient! Be strong and courageous! Seek humility! Endure! Be assured that whatever you need, Christ *in you* will provide. Our best is to become true imitators of Him.

In conclusion, I want to leave you with these words from a vision concerning the last days, and the coming of Christ.

My march to the throne may have taken days, months, or even years. There was no way to measure time in that place. To my considerable discomfort, they all showed great respect to me, not because of who I was or anything that I had done, but simply because I was a warrior in the battle of the last days. Somehow, through this last battle, the glory of God would be revealed in such a way that it would be a witness to every power and authority, created or yet to be created, for all of eternity. During this battle the glory of the cross would be revealed, and the wisdom of God would be known in a special way. To be in that battle was to be given one of the greatest honors given to those of the race of men.

-The Final Quest[34]

END NOTES

Preface

1. Mumford, B. (1993). A prophetic perspective. *Plumbline*, 15(1).

Introduction

1. Bentley, S. (1992). Deja Vu All Over Again. *Veteran*, 12(7/8), 5.
2. Dean, C. (1988). *Nam Vet: Making Peace With Your Past*. Portland, OR: Multnomah Press.
3. Brende, J. O. & Parson, E. R. (1985). *Vietnam Veterans: The Road to Recovery*. New York: Plenum Press.
4. Kulka, R., Schlenger, W., Fairbank, J., Hough, R., Jordan, B. K., Marmar, C. & Weiss, D. (1990). *Trauma and the Vietnam War Generation: Report of Findings from the National Vietnam Veterans Readjustment Study*. New York: Brunner/Mazel.
5. Mellman, T. A., Randolph, C. A., Brawman-Mintzer, O., Flores, L. P. & Milanes, F. J. (1992). Phenomenology and Course of Psychiatric Disorders Associated with Combat Related Post-traumatic Stress Disorder. *American Journal of Psychiatry*, 149, 1568.
6. Washington Times, October 19, 1994, p. A 9.
7. Matsakis, A. (1988). *Vietnam Wives: Women and Children Surviving LIfe with Veterans Suffering Post-traumatic Stress Disorder* . U.S.A.: Woodbine House.
8. Ibid, see Kulka, Ref. 4 above.
9. Alker, J. (1991). *Heroes Today, Homeless Tomorrow: Homelessness Among Veterans in the United States*. National Coalition for the Homeless. Washington, D. C.
   "1 in 3 Homeless Men Seeking Refuge is a Veteran, Survey Says." Fort Worth Star-Telegram, November 10, 1996, Section A., p.16.
   Homeless Veterans (1993). *Veterans News Journal*, National Vietnam Veterans Coalition, November-December, 18.
   Olsen, H. (1988). *Proposal for a Veterans' Shelter* (unpublished grant proposal made in cooperation with the Veterans Council of Tarrant County).
10. Ibid, Brende & Parson, see Ref. 3 above.
11. Kersten III, P. E. (1992). The Human Warehouse. *Veteran*. 12(5/6), 22.
12. Agent Orange: Unclogging the Pipeline, Round II. (1992). *Veterans News Journal*, 65, 11-13.
    Zumwalt, E. R. (1990). *Report to the Secretary of the Dept. of Veterans' Affairs on the Association Between Adverse Health Affects and Exposure to Agent Orange*. U.S. Veterans Administration: Washington, D.C., 2-55.
13. Akqulian, L. (1991). Chemical Warfare: The Government Betrays Agent Orange Victims. *The Texas Observer*, 12, 12.
14. Olsen, H. (1991). *A Question of Service: Healthcare for the Veteran Population in Tarrant County*. (unpublished report for the Veteran's Task Force). University of Texas at Arlington, Texas.
    WACVO Publication, Vol 14, No. 4.
15. VVA Staff Report (1992). *Veteran*, 12(5/6), 3.

16. Jamerson, S. J. (1992). Equal Access to Justice Sought by Veterans. *Bravo*, 8(4), 8.

Chapter One

1. Gabriel, R. A. (1987). *No More Heroes: Madness and Psychiatry in War*. New York: Hill and Wang.
2. Ibid, Gabriel, see Ref. 1 above.
3. Bentley, S. (1991). A Short History of PTSD: From Thermopylae to Hue, Soldiers Have Always Had a Disturbing Reaction to War. *Veteran*, January, 13-16.
    Ibid, Gabriel, see Ref. 1 above.
4. Ibid, Bentley, see Ref. 3 above.
5. Ibid, Gabriel, see Ref. 1 above.
6. Ibid, Bentley, see Ref. 3 above.
7. Ibid, Gabriel, see Ref. 1 above.
8. Brende, J. O. & Parsons, E. R. (1985). *Vietnam Veterans: The road to Recovery*. New York: Plenum Press.
9. Beebe, G. W. (1975). Follow-up Studies of World War II and Korean War Prisoners, II: Morbidity, Disability, and Maladjustment. *American Journal of Epidemiology*, 101, 400-22.
10. Stenger, C. A. (1985). *American POW's in WW I, WW II, Korea and Vietnam: Statistical Data Concerning Numbers Captured, Repatriated and Still Alive as of January 1, 1985*. Washington, D.C.: Veterans' Administration.
11. Goldberg, J. True, W. R., Eisen, S. A. & Henderson, W. G. (1990). A Twin Study of the Effects of the Vietnam War on Post-traumatic Stress Disorder. *The Journal of American Medical Association*, 263(9), 227-33.
12. Kulka, R., Schlenger, W., Fairbank, J., Hough, R., Jordan, B. K., Marmar, C. & Weiss, D. (1990). *Trauma and the Vietnam War Generation: Report of Findings from the National Vietnam Veterans Readjustment Study*. New York: Brunner/Mazel.
13. American Broadcasting Company, 20/20 Program, May 22, 1992.
14. Brende, J. O. & Parsons, E. R. (1985). *Vietnam Veterans: The Road to Recovery*. New York: Plenum Press.
15. Egendorf, A., Kadushin, C., Laufer, R. S., Rothbart, G. & Sloan, E. (1981). *Legacies of Vietnam: Comparative Readjustment of Veterans and Their Peers*. Washington, D.C.: U.S. Government Printing Office.
16. Olsen, H. (1991). *Health Survey of Members of the 25th Infantry Division Association* (unpublished) University of Texas at Arlington, Texas.
17. Gal, R. & Gabriel, R. A. (1982). Battlefield Heroism in the Israeli Defense Force. *International Social Science Review*, 232.
    Ibid, Gabriel, see Ref. 1 above.
18. Ibid, Gabriel, see Ref. 1 above.
19. Dean, C. (1991). *Book of Soldiers*. Mountlake Terrace, WA: Point Man International.
20. Wolfe, J. & Kelly, J. (1993). Following Desert Storm: The Impact on Men and Women. *Clinical Newsletter, National Center for Post-Traumatic Stress Disorder*, 3(1).
21. Persian Gulf veterans: DAV and VA Respond to Unexplained Symptoms, Social and Psychological needs. (1993). *DAV Magazine*, 35(7), 6-10.
22. Ibid, Gabriel, see Ref. 1 above.
23. Ibid, Bentley, see Ref. 3 above.
24. Olsen, H. (1991). *A question of Service: Healthcare for the Veteran Population in Tarrant County*. (unpublished report for the Veterans Task Force). University of Texas at Arlington, Texas.
    Statement of Noreen M. Sommer RN, MSN, President Nurses Organization of Veterans

Affairs Before the House Committee on Veterans Affairs Subcommittee on Oversight and Investigation, (1990, August 28) Washington, D.C.: NOVA.

Statement of Vietnam Veterans of America, Inc. presented by Tim Brown, National Board of Directors, Region VII, and John Woods, Texas State Service Rep. before the House Veterans' Affairs Subcommittee on Oversight and Investigation, (1991). Washington, D.C.: Veterans Administration.

Three VA hospitals Among Eleven on JCAHO Conditional List, (1990). *Modern Healthcare*, 20(14), 11.

25. Ibid, Bentley, see Ref. 3 above.

26. Grossman, D. (1992). Presentation at the National Vietnam Veterans Coalition Leadership breakfast, November 7. *Veterans News Journal*, National Vietnam Veterans Coalition, March-April.

Chapter Two

1. Goodwin, J. (1991). *Readjustment Problems Among Vietnam Veterans: The Etiology of Combat-related Post-traumatic Stress Disorders*. Cincinnati, OH: DAV.

2. Beebe, G. W. (1975). Follow-up Studies of World War II and Korean War Prisoners, II: Morbidity, Disability, and Maladjustments. *American Journal of Epidemiology*, 101,400-22.

3. Dean, C. (1988). *Nam vet: Making Peace with Your Past*. Portland, OR: Multnomah Press.

4. Diagnostic and Statistical Manual of Mental Disorders, Third Edition, Revised. (1987). Washington, DC: American Psychiatric Association.

5. Scott, W. (1990). PTSD in DSM III: A Case of Politics of Diagnosis and Disease, *Social Problems*, 37(13), 294-314.

6. Bentley, S. (1991). A Short History of PTSD: From Thermopylae to Hue, Soldiers Have Always Had a Disturbing Reaction to War. *Veteran*, January, 13-16.
   Caruth, C. (1991). Introduction: Post-traumatic Stress Disorder. *American Imago*, 48(1), 1-12.

7. Scurfield, R. (1990). *Rage, Grief, Fear (and blame) in PTSD*. Presented at the Third Annual Meeting of the Society for Traumatic Stress, Oct. 25, 1987, Baltimore, MD.

8. Kentsmith, D. K. (1986). Principles of Battlefield Psychiatry. *Military Medicine*, 151(2), 89-95.
   Shay, J. (1993). *Achilles in Vietnam: Combat Trauma and the Undoing of Character*. New York: Antheneum.

9. Laufer, R. S. (1985). War Trauma and Human Development: The Vietnam Experience. In S. M. Sonnenburg, A. S. Blank & J. A. Talbott, (Eds.), *The Trauma of War: Stress and Recovery in Vietnam Veterans*. Washington, D.C.: American Psychiatric Press.

10. Ibid, Grossman, see Ref. 9 above.
    Marshall, S. L. A. (1947). Men Against Fire.

11. Breslau, N. & Davis, G.C. (1992). Post-traumatic Stress Disorder in an Urban Population of Young Adults: Risk Factors for Chronicity, *American Journal of Psychiatry*, 149, 671-675.
    Resnick, H. S., Kilpatrick, D.G., Dansky, B.S., Saunders, B.E., & Best, C.L. (1993). Prevalence of Civilian Trauma and Post-traumatic Stress Disorder in a Representative Sample of Women. *Journal of Consulting and Clinical Psychology*, 61, 984-991.

12. Danieli, Y. (1994). As Survivors Age: Part 1. *Clinical Quarterly*, 4(1), 1-5.

Chapter Three

1. Brende, J. O. & Parson, E. R. (1985). *Vietnam Veterans: The Road to Recovery*. New York: Plenum Press.
2. Danieli, Y. (1994). As Survivors Age: Part 1. *Clinical Quarterly*, 4(1), 1-5.

Chapter Four

1. Gabriel, R. A. (1987). *No More Heroes: Madness and Psychiatry in War*. New York: Hill and Wang.
2. Baker, M. (1981). *Nam: The Vietnam War in the Words of the Men and Women Who Fought There*. New York: William Morrow & Company, Inc.
3. O'Brien, T. (1992). Going After Cacciato. In J. T. Hansen, A. S. Owen & M. P. Madden, (Eds.), *Parallels: The Soldier's Knowledge and the Oral History of Contemporary Warfare*. New York: Aldine de Gruyter.
4. Mahedy, W. P. (1986). *Out of the Night: The Spiritual Journey of Vietnam Vets*. New York: Ballantine Books.
5. Ibid, Baker, see Ref. 2 above.
6. Ibid, see Baker, Ref. 2 above.
7. Cole, E. (1993). *Facing the Challenge of Crisis and Change*. Tulsa, OK: Honor Books.
8. Homeless Veterans (1993). *Veterans News Journal*, National Vietnam Veterans Coalition, November-December, 18.
   Post-Traumatic Stress Disorder (1993). *Veterans News Journal*, National Vietnam Veterans Coalition, November-December, 18.
9. Galperin, L. (1992). The Impact of Trauma. *Masters and Johnson Report*, 1(2), 3-8.
10. Parsons, E. (1987). The Reparation of the Self: Clinical and Theoretical Dimensions in the Treatment of Vietnam Combat Veterans-II, In W. Quaytman, (Ed.), *The Viet Nam Veteran: Studies in Post-Traumatic Stress Disorder*. New York: Human Science Press.
11. Proverbs 4:23.
12. Proverbs 13:12.
13. Proverbs 15:13; 18:14.
14. Proverbs 14:13.
15. 1 John 3:14; Philippians 2:4.

Chapter Five

1. Matsakis, A. (1988). Vietnam Wives: Women and Children Surviving Life with Veterans Suffering Post-traumatic Stress Disorder. U.S.A.: Woodbine House.
2. Stouffler, S. A., Lumsdaine, A. A., Lumsdaine, M. H., Williams, R. M., Smith, M. B., Janis, I. D., Star, S. A. & Coltrell, L. S. (1949). The American Soldier: Combat and Its Aftermath. Vol. II. In C. Figley & S. Leventman (Eds.). *Strangers At Home: Vietnam Veterans Since the War*. New York: Praeger Press.
3. Goodwin, J. (1991). Readjustment Problems Among Vietnam Veterans: The Etiology of Combat-related Post-traumatic Stress Disorders. Cincinnati, OH: DAV.
4. Ibid, Matsakis, see Ref. 1 above.
5. Kulka, R., Schlenger, W., Fairbank, J., Hough, R., Jordan, B. K., Marmar, C. & Weiss, D.(1990). *Trauma and the Vietnam War Generation: Report of Findings from the National Vietnam Veterans Readjustment Study*. New York: Brunner/Mazel.
6. Proverbs 15:13, 17:22, 18:14.

7. Cole, E. L. (1992). *On Becoming a Real Man.* Nashville, TN: Thomas Nelson, Inc.
   Galperin, L. (1992). The Impact of Trauma. *Masters and Johnson Report,* 1(2), 3-8.
8. Proverbs 18:19.
9. Parsons, E. (1987). The Reparation of the Self: Clinical and Theoretical Dimensions in the Treatment of Vietnam Combat Veterans-II, In W. Quaytman, (Ed.), *The Vietnam Veteran: Studies in Post-Traumatic Stress Disorder.* New York: Human Science Press.
10. Edelman, B. (1985). *Dear American: Letters Home from Vietnam.* New York: W.W. Norton & Company, Inc.
11. Ibid, Parsons, see Ref. 9 above.
12. Figley, C. & Leventman, S. (1990). *Strangers at Home: Vietnam Veterans Since the War.* New York: Praeger Publishers.
13. Brende, J. O. & Parsons, E. R. (1985). *Vietnam Veterans: The Road to Recovery.* New York: Plenum Press.
14. Sandford, J. & Sandford, P. (1993). Waking the Slumbering Spirit. Arlington, TX: Clear Stream, Inc. Publishing.
15. Ibid, see Sandford, Ref.14 above.
16. Morrier, E. J. (1987). Passivity as a Sequel to Combat Trauma. In W. Quaytman (Ed.). *The Vietnam Veteran: Studies in Post-traumatic Shock Disorder.* New York: Human Science Press.
17. Galperin, L. (1992). The Impact of Trauma. *Masters and Johnson Report,* 1(2), 3-8.
18. Psalms 55:12, 13.
19. Cloud, H. & Townsend, J. (1992). *Boundaries: When to Say Yes, When to Say No, to Take Control of Your Life.* Grand Rapids, MI: Zondervan Publishing House.

Chapter Six

1. Brende, J. O. & Parsons, E. R. (1985). *Vietnam Veterans: The Road to Recovery.* New York: Plenum Press.
2. Hansen, J. T., Owen, A. S. & Madden, M. P. (1992). *Parallels: The Soldier's Knowledge and the Oral History of Contemporary Warfare.* New York: Aldine de Gruyter.
3. Figley, C. & Leventman, S. (1990). *Strangers at Home: Vietnam Veterans Since the War.* New York: Praeger Publishers.
4. Ibid, Brende, see Ref. 1 above.
5. Baker, M. (1981). *Nam: The Vietnam War in the Words of the Men and Women Who Fought There.* New York: William Morrow & Company, Inc.
6. Goodwin, J. (1991). Readjustment Problems Among Vietnam Veterans: The Etiology of Combat-related Post-traumatic Stress Disorders. Cincinnati, OH: DAV.
7. Caputo, P. (1977). *A Rumor of War.* New York: Ballantine Books.

Chapter Seven

1. Kulka, R., Schlenger, W., Fairbank, J., Hough, R., Jordan, B. K., Marmar, C. & Weiss, D.(1990). *Trauma and the Vietnam War Generation: Report of Findings from the National Vietnam Veterans Readjustment Study.* New York: Brunner/Mazel.
2. Goodwin, J. (1991). *Readjustment Problems Among Vietnam Veterans: The Etiology of Combat-related Post-traumatic Stress Disorders.* Cincinnati, OH: DAV
3. Goldberger, L. & Breznitz, S. (1982). *Handbook of Stress: Theoretical and Clinical Aspects.* New York: The Free Press.
   Horowitz, M. J. & Solomon (1978). Delayed Stress Response Syndromes, In C.

Figley, (Ed.), Stress Disorders Among Vietnam Veterans. New York: Brunner/Mazel.

4. Eisenhart, R. W. (1975). You Can't Hack It Little Girl: A Discussion of the Covert Psychological Agenda of Modern Combat Training. In D. M. Martell & Pilisuk, (Eds.), Soldiers In and After Vietnam, *Journal of Social Issues*, 31(4), 13.

5. Baker, M. (1981). *Nam: The Vietnam War in the Words of the Men and Women Who Fought There*. New York: William Morrow & Company, Inc.

   Caputo, P. (1977). *A Rumor of War*. New York: Ballantine Books.

   Goff, S., Sanders, R. & Smith, C. (1982). *Brothers: Black Soldiers in the Nam*. Navota: Presidio Press.

   Olsen, H. (1990). *Issues of the Heart: Memoirs of an Artilleryman in Vietnam*. Jefferson, S.C.: McFarland and Company, Inc.

6. Brende, J. O. & Parsons, E. R. (1985). *Vietnam Veterans: The Road to Recovery*. New York: Plenum Press.

7. Gothard, B. (1992). *Ten Reasons for Alumni to be Encouraged*. Oak Brook, IL: Institute in Basic Life Principles.

8. Figley, C. & Leventman, S. (1990). *Strangers at Home: Vietnam Veterans Since the War*. New York: Praeger Publishers.

   Howard, S. (1976). The Vietnam Warrior: His Experience and Implications for Psychotherapy. *American Journal of Psychotherapy*, 30(1), 121-135.

   Wilson, J. P. (1977). *The Forgotten Warrior Project*. Cincinnati, OH: DAV.

9. Baum, A. (1990). Stress, Intrusive Imagery, and Chronic Distress. *Health Psychology*, 9(6), 653-75.

10. Cannon, W. B. (1932). *The Wisdom of the Body*. New York: Norton.

    Selye, H. (1936). A Syndrome Produced by Diverse Nocuous Agents. *Nature*, 138, 32.

    Williams, R. (1994). Anger Kills. New York. Harper Perennial.

    Health Front. (1996). Anger-oplasty. *Prevention Magazine*. December, 24.

11. McMillen, S. I. (1968). *None of These Diseases*. New York: Spire Books.

12. Green, J. & Shellenberger, R. (1991). *The Dynamics of Health & Wellness: A Biopsychosocial Approach*. Chicago, IL: Holt, Reinhart & Winston, Inc.

    Levy, S. M. & Wise, B. (1988). Psychosocial Risk Factors and Cancer Progression. In C.Cooper, (Ed.), *Stress and Breast Cancer*. New York: Wiley.

    Siegel, B. (1986). Love, Medicine, and Miracles. New York: Harper & Row.

    Simonton, C., Matthews-Simonton, S. & Creighton, J. (1978). *Getting Well Again*. Los Angeles: J. P. Tarcher.

13. Mark 6:37-46.

14. Mark 8:15-17.

15. Ephesians 4:17-31.

16. Nee, W. (1957). *How Does My Spirit Function*. Indiana: Ministry of Life.

17. Mark 2:8

18. Ephesians 4:30, 31.

19. Hebrews 10:29 (NAS).

20. Acts 8:9-23 (paraphrased).

21. Ephesians 4:26, 27.

22. Matthew 21:12-16; Mark 3:5, 11:15-18; John 2:14-16.

23. Matthew 5:21-22; Colossians 3:8; Titus 1:7; Proverbs 15:18; Nehemiah 9:7; Psalms 103:8; Nahum 1:3.

24. Colossians 3:8; Ephesians 4:17-19, 29-31; James 3:14-16.

Chapter Eight

1. Brende, J. O. & Parson, E. R. (1985). *Vietnam Veterans: The Road to Recovery*. New

York: Plenum Press.

2. Cole, E. L. (1992). *On Becoming a Real Man.* Nashville, TN: Thomas Nelson, Inc.

3. 2 Corinthians 7:10

4. Goodwin, J. (1991). *Readjustment Problems Among Vietnam Veterans: The Etiology of Combat-related Post-traumatic Stress Disorders.* Cincinnati, OH: Disabled American Veterans.

5. Bullman, T., Kang, H. & Watanbe, K. (1990). Proportionate Mortality Among U. S. Army Vietnam Veterans Who Served in Military Region I. *American Journal of Epidemiology,* 132(4), 670-4.

   Cleary, D. J. (1979). *Life Events and Disease: A Review of Methodology and Findings.* Stockholm: Laboratory for Clinical Stress Research.

   DelVecchio, J. (1985) Foreword. In J. O. Brende & E. R. Parson (Eds.). *Vietnam Veterans: The Road to Recovery.* New York: New American

   Fairbanks, J., Hansen, D. & Fitterling, J. (1991). Patterns of Appraisal and Coping Across Different Stressor Conditions Among Former Prisoners of War With and Without Post-traumatic Stress Disorder. *Journal of Consulting and Clinical Psychology,* 59(2), 274-82.

   Forcier, L., Hudson, H., Cobbin, D., Adena, M. & Fett, M. (1987). Mortality of Australian Veterans of the Vietnam Conflict and the Period and Location of Their Veteran Service. *Military Medicine.* 152(3), 117-24.

   Kulka, R., Schlenger, W., Fairbank, J., Hough, R., Jordan, B. K., Marmar, C. & Weiss, D. (1990). *Trauma and the Vietnam War Generation: Report of Findings From the National Vietnam Veterans Readjustment Study.* New York: Brunner/Mazel.

   Langer, R. (1987). Post-traumatic Stress Disorder in Former POW's. In T. Williams, (Ed.), *Post-Traumatic Stress Disorder: A Handbook for Clinicians.* Cincinnati, OH: DAV.

   Shatan, C. F. (1973). The Grief of Soldiers: Vietnam Combat Veteran's Self-help Movement. *American Journal of Orthopsychiatry,* 43(4), 640-53.

   Williams, T. (1987). *Post-traumatic Stress Disorder: A Handbook for Clinicians.* Cincinnati, OH: Disabled American Veterans.

6. Romans 12:14, 15.

Chapter Nine

1. Goldman, P. & Fuller, T. (1983). *Charlie Company: What Vietnam Did to Us.* New York: William Morrow & Company, Inc.

2. Norman, M. (1989). *These Good Men: Friendships Forged From Wa*r. New York: Crown Publishers, Inc.

3. Figley, C. & Leventman, S. (1990). *Strangers at Home: Vietnam Veterans Since the War.*.New York: Praeger Publishers.

4. Mintz, J. & O'Brien, C. P. (1979). The Impact of Vietnam Service on Heroin-addicted Veterans. *American Journal of Drug and Alcohol Abuse,* 6, 39-52.

   Nace, E. P. & Meyers, A. L. (1974). The Prognosis for Addicted Vietnam Returnees: A Comparison with Civilian Addicts. *Comprehensive Psychiatry,* 15, 49-56.

5. Jelineck, J. M. & William, T. (1987). Post-traumatic Stress Disorder and Substance Abuse: Treatment Problems, Strategies and Recommendations. In T. Williams, (Ed.), *Post-Traumatic Stress Disorder: A Handbook for Clinicians.* Cincinnati, OH: DAV

6. Bey, D. R. & Zecchinelli, V. A. (1970). Marijuana as a Coping Device in Vietnam. *USARV Medical Bulletin* (USARV Pamphlet 40)(22), 21-8.

7. Samaritan Village Inc. Veterans Study (1982). Unpublished Survey, Samaritan Village

Inc., 118-121, Queens Blvd, Forest Hills, N.Y.

Olsen, H. (1990). *Issues of the Heart: Memoirs of an Artilleryman in Vietnam*. Jefferson, S.C.: McFarland and Company, Inc.

Williams, T. (1980). *Post-traumatic Stress Disorder of the Vietnam Veteran*. Cincinnati, OH: Disabled American Veterans.

8. Wilson, J. P. (1977). *Forgotten Warrior Project*. Cincinnati, OH: DAV.

9. Blank, A. S. (1979). *First Training Conference Papers, Vietnam Veterans-Operation Outreach*. St. Louis, MO: US Veterans Administration.

10. Cloud, H. & Townsend, J. (1992). *Boundaries: When to Say Yes, When to Say No, to Take Control of Your Life*. Grand Rapids, MI: Zondervan Publishing House.

11. Baum, A. (1990). Stress, Intrusive Imagery, and Chronic Distress. *Health Psychology*, 9(6), 653-75.

Blum, K. & Payne, J. (1993). Restoring Brain Nutrition: A Major Factor in Recovery. *Whole Life*, March.

Chapter Ten

1. Brende, J. O. & Parson, E. R. (1985). *Vietnam Veterans: The Road to Recovery*. New York: Plenum Press.

2. Yost, J. F. (1987). The Psychopharmacologic Management of Post-traumatic Stress Disorder (PTSD) in Vietnam Veterans and Civilian Situations. In T. Williams (Ed.). *Post-Traumatic Stress Disorder: A Handbook for Clinicians*. Cincinnati, OH: DAV.

3. Goldberger, L.& Breznitz, S. (1982). *Handbook of Stress: Theoretical and Clinical Aspects. New York*: The Free Press.

4. Selye, H. (1936). A Syndrome Produced by Diverse Nocuous Agents. *Nature*, 138, 32.

_____ (1982). History and Present Status of the Stress Concept. In S. Breznitz & L. Goldberger (Eds.), *Handbook of Stress: Theoretical and Clinical Aspects*. New York: The Free Press.

5. Cannon, W. B. (1932). *The Wisdom of the Body*. New York: Norton.

6. Lazarus, R. S. (1966). *Psychological Stress and the Coping Process*. New York: McGraw-Hill.

Lazarus, R. S., & Launier, R. (1978). Stress-related Transactions Between Person and Environment. In L. A. Pervin and M. Lewis, (Eds.), *Perspectives in International Psychology*. New York: Plenum.

7. Sandford, J., & Sandford, P. (1993). *Waking the Slumbering Spirit*. Arlington, TX: Clear Stream Publishing.

8. Reiser, M. F. (1980). The Psychophysiology of Stress and Coping. *Stress and Coping*, 1(1).

9. Ibid, see Ref. 3 above.

Green, J. & Shellenberger, R. (1991). *The dynamics of Health & Wellness: A Biopsychosocial Approach*. Chicago, IL: Holt, Reinhart & Winston, Inc.

Ornish, D. (1990). Reversing Heart Disease. New York: Random House.

Ibid, see Yost, Ref. 2 above.

10. Hebrews 4:12.

11. Matthew 26:41; Mark 2:8, 8:12; Luke 1:47; John 4:23, 11:33; Acts 17:16, 18:25, 19:21, 20:22; 1 Corinthians 2:11; 2 Corinthians 2:13, 4:13; Ephesians 1:17; Colossians 1:8.

12. 1 Samuel 1:15; Psalms 18:14, 15:13, 17:22; Mark 5:2; Romans 11:8.

13. Ibid, see Sandford, Ref. 7 above.

14. Wasserman, J. (1995). How Children Adapt to Constant Violence. *Fort Worth Star Telegram*, January 15.

15. Janis, I. L. (1951). *Air, War, and Emotional Stress.* New York: Harcourt.
16. Janis, I. L. & Mann, L. (1977). *Decision Making: A Psychological Analysis of Conflict, Choice, and Commitment.* New York: The Free Press.
    MacCurdy, J. (1943). *The Structure of Morale.* New York: MacMillian.
    Rachman, S. J. (1978). *Fear and Courage.* San Francisco: Freeman.
17. Horowitz, M. J. & Solomon (1978). Delayed Stress Response Syndromes, In C. Figley, (Ed.), *Stress Disorders Among Vietnam Veterans.* New York: Brunner/Mazel.
18. Enough is Enough Campaign (1993). Pornography Can be as Addictive as Drugs or Alcohol. *Enough is Enough.* 1(4), 2-3.
19. Monroe, L. J. (1967). Psychological and Physiological Differences Between Good and Poor Sleepers. *Journal of Abnormal Psychology,* 72, 255-264.
20. D'Atri, D. A. (1975). Psychophysiological Responses to Crowding. *Environment and Behavior,* 7, 237-250.
    Kaminoff, R. D. & Proshansky, H. M. (1982). Stress as a Consequence of the Urban Physical Environment. In S. Breznitz & L. Goldberger, (Eds.), *Handbook of Stress: Theoretical and Clinical Aspects.* New York: The Free Press.
    Saegert, S. (1975). The Effects of Spatial and Social Density on Arousal, Mood, and Social Orientation. *Dissertation Abstracts International,* 35, 3649.
21. Averill, J. (1973). Personal Control Over Aversive Stimuli and its Relation to Stress. *Psychological Bulletin,* 80, 226-303.
    Cohen, S., Glass, D. C., & Phillips, S. (1979). Environment and Health. In H. E. Freeman, S. Levine & L. G. Reeder (Eds.), *Handbook of Medical Sociology.* Englewood Cliffs: Prentice-Hall.
22. Ibid, see Green & Shellenberger, Ref. 9 above.
    Ibid, see Ornish, Ref. 9 above.
23. Ibid, see Janis & Mann, ref. 16 above.
24. Breznitz, S. (1972). *The Effects of Frequency and Pacing of Warnings Upon the Fear Reaction to a Threatening Event.* Jerusalem: Ford Foundation.
    Cleary, D. J. (1979). *Life Events and Disease: A Review of Methodology and Findings.* Stockholm: Laboratory for Clinical Stress Research.
    Everly, G. (1989). *A Clinical Guide to the Treatment of the Human Stress Response.* New York: Plenum Press.
    Ibid, see Green and Shellenberger, Ref. 9 above.
    Holmes, T. H. & Masuda, M. (1974). Life Changes and Illness Susceptibility. In B. S. Dohrenwend & B. P. Dohrenwend (Eds.), *Stress Life Events: Their Nature and Effects.* New York: Wiley.
    Lazarus, R. S., & Folkman, S. (1984). *Stress, Appraisal and Coping.* New York: Springer Publishing Company.

Chapter Eleven

1. McDaniel, E. B. (1975). *Scars and Stripes.* New York: A. J. Holman Co.
2. Mellman, T., Randolph, C., Brawman-Mintzer, O., Flores, L. & Milanes F. J. (1992). Phenomenology and Course of Psychiatric Disorders Associated with Combat-related Post-traumatic Stress Disorder. *American Journal of Psychiatry.* 149(11), 1568-74.
3. Luke 2:25.
4. Mahedy, W. P. (1986). *Out of the Night: The Spiritual Journey of Vietnam Vets.* New York: Ballantine Books.
5. Dean, C. (1988). *Nam Vet: Making Peace with Your Past.* Portland, OR: Multnomah Press.

6. Ibid, see Mahedy, Ref. 4 above.
7. 2 Corinthians 12:9.
8. 2 Peter 1:3.
9. Romans 6:6; Ephesians 2:5, 6; Colossians 2:10.
10. Hebrews 3:12, 13.
11. Jeremiah 1:12.
12. John 3:3-7.
13. Hebrews 12:23.
14. Jeremiah 15:19; 30:17; 33:7.

Chapter Twelve

1. Figley, C. & Leventman, S. (1990). *Strangers at Home: Vietnam Veterans Since the War*. New York: Praeger Publishers.
2. Vitz, P. (1995). The Cult of Self. *Cornerstone*, 23(106), 10-14.
3. Ibid, see Ref. 1 above.
4. Adams, J. (1970). *Competent to Counsel*. Grand Rapids, MI: Baker Book House.
5. Ibid, see Ref. 4 above.
6. James 1:13-16.
7. Matthew 16:25.
8. Matsakis, A. (1988). *Vietnam Wives: Women and Children Surviving Life with Veterans Suffering Post-traumatic Stress Disorder* . U.S.A.: Woodbine House.
   Dean, C. (1988). *Nam Vet: Making Peace with Your Past.* Portland, OR: Multnomah Press.
9. Nee, W. (1961).*What Shall This Man Do?* Ft. Washington, PA: Christian Literature Crusade.

Chapter Thirteen

1. Edelman, B. (1985). *Dear American: Letters Home From Vietnam*. New York: W.W. Norton & Company, Inc.
2. Dean, C. (1988). *Nam Vet: Making Peace with Your Past*. Portland, OR: Multnomah Press.
3. Ephesians 4:30-31.
4. Hebrews 12:14-15.
5. Romans 1:28; Ephesians 4:31.
6. John 20:23; Matthew 16:19, 18:18.
7. Matthew 6:14-15.
8. Luke 6:27-38.
9. Hosea 5:6, 15
10. Matthew 18:21-35.
11. Ephesians 4:25-27 *paraphrased*.
12. Proverbs 10:12.
13. Matthew 3:10.
14. Mark 11:19-21.
15. Proverbs 18:19.
16. Ephesians 5:1
17. Matthew 26:24, 25, 40, 56, 59, 60, 65, 67, 68, 74; Mark 15:34; John 1:11; 18:14; Hebrews 4:15; Isaiah 53:3-7.
18. 1 Corinthians 9:12, 17.

19. 1 Corinthians 4:2.
20. Romans 15:3.
21. Psalms 139:23, 24; Lamentations 3:40.
22. Romans 2:1.
23. Matthew 18:21-22.
24. James 4:7-10.
25. 1 John 1:9.
26. Acts 3:19.
27. Romans 8:1, 24, 30, 33.
28. Romans 6:6.
29. Ezekiel 1:19.
30. Isaiah 61:1; Psalms 51:10.
31. 2 Corinthians 10:3-5.
32. Romans 1:18-28, 12:12; 2 Corinthians 10:3-6.
33. John 8:32, 17:14-19; Romans 8:6, 7.
34. *National Geographic*, January 1965
35. *America Ambushed! The Unseen War*. (Oct. 1990). Point Man International Ministries.
36. Colossians 1:13; 1 John 3:8.
37. Proverbs 25:28; Matthew 12:43-45; Ephesians 4:25-27.
38. Matthew 12:29; 2 Corinthians 10:3; Galatians 5:1; Ephesians 6:12.
39. Matthew 11:12.
40. Romans 10:9.
41. Matthew 8:8-10.
42. Matthew 16:19; Mark 1:27; Luke 9:1; John 17:2, 11, 12; Acts 3:16, 4:12; Ephesians 1:22; Philippians 2:9, 10; 1 Peter 3:22.
43. Ephesians 6:11-13.
44. John 8:36.

Chapter Fourteen

1. Norman, M. (1989). *These Good Men: Friendships Forged from War.* New York: Crown Publishers, Inc.
2. Brende, J. O. & Parson, E. R. (1985). *Vietnam Veterans: The Road to Recovery.* New York: Plenum Press.
3. Deuschle, T. (1993). *Breaking the Bonds of Iniquity.* Dallas: Hear the Word Ministries.
4. 1 Peter 1:18.
5. Philippians 3:10-14.
6. Jeremiah 6:44.
7. John 11:35.
8. James 5:10; Ephesians 4:25.
9. Psalms 51:6.
10. Ephesians 5:11-13.
11. 2 Timothy 2:19-26.
12. James 5:13-16.
13. Romans 10:10; Hebrews 12:1.
14. Proverbs 14:10.
15. Matthew 5:3.
16. Isaiah 61:1, 2; Luke 4:18 Amplified.
17. Isaiah 53:3.
18. Hebrews 4:14-16.

19. Psalms 34:17, 18.
20. Jeremiah 17:5-8, 30:17, 33:3-8, 39:18.
21. 2 Corinthians 1:3-5.
22. Philippians 4:7.
23. 2 Corinthians 7:6.
24. Matthew 5:4.
25. John 8:31, 44 NIV; Genesis 32:24-30.
26. Philippians 2:13.
27. Jeremiah 30:17.

Chapter Fifteen

1. Sonnenberg, S., Blank Jr., A., & Talbot, J. (1985). *The Trauma of War: Stress and Recovery in Viet Nam Veterans.* Washington D.C.: American Psychiatric Press, Inc.
2. Hersh, S. M. (1970). *My Lai Four: A Report on the Massacre and Its Aftermath.* New York: Random House.
3. Cloud, H. & Townsend, J. (1992). *Boundaries: When to Say Yes, When to Say No, to Take Control of Your Life.* Grand Rapids, MI: Zondervan Publishing House.
4. Luke 13:2-5.
5. Sandford, J. & Sandford, P. (1977). *The Elijah Task: A Call to Today's Prophets and Intercessors.* Tulsa, OK: Victory House, Inc.
6. Cole, E. L. (1982). *Maximized Manhood: A Guide to Family Survival.* Springdale, PA: Whitakeer House.
7. Matthew 26:28
8. Luke 22:54-62.
9. John 21:15-17.
10. Psalms 34:22; Romans 8:21.
11. Romans 5:8-9.
12. Romans 3:24-26 Living Bible.
13. Nee, W. (1957). *The Normal Christian Life.* Bombay: Gospel Literature Service.
14. Hebrews 9:11-14, NAS
15. John 1:29.
16. 1 Peter 1:18-19.
17. Hebrews 10:22, 11:6.
18. Revelations 12:10.
19. Matthew 5:25.
20. 1 John 1:8.
21. Ibid, see Nee, Ref. 12 above.
22. Acts 20:32; 1 Corinthians 3:9-10; Ephesians 2:22.
23. 1 Corinthians 3:11.
24. Isaiah 1:18, 44:22.

Chapter Sixteen

1. Brende, J. O. & Parson, E. R. (1985). *Vietnam Veterans: The Road to Recovery.* New York: Plenum Press.
2. Cole, E. L. (1992). *Nothing But the Truth.* Dallas: Christian Men's Network Video.
3. Psalms 138:2; John 3:33.
4. Genesis 26:3; Jeremiah 1:12.
5. Numbers 23:19.

6. John 1:1-2, 14:6.
7. John 8:31-32, 17:7.
8. Hebrews 13:8; James 1:17.
9. John 3:16-18; Romans 5:8, 8:33-38.
10. John 3:19-21, 10:38, 14:9.
11. John 15:14-16.
12. John 2:24-25.
13. Ecclesiastes 9:3.
14. Psalms 118:8-9; Jeremiah 9:4, 17:5-7; Micah 7:5.
15. 1 Samuel 16:7; Isaiah 11:13; Matthew 5:22, 28, 7:1-3.
16. Matthew 7:1-5 paraphrased
17. John 8:15; 1 Peter 2:23
18. John 10:10, 12:24, 25.
19. Hebrews 12:2, 15; 2 Timothy 2:13.
20. Romans 8:28-30; Colossians 1:21, 3:9-10; Philippians 3:21.
21. Colossians 3:12-13.
22. James 5:19-20; 1 Peter 4:8.
23. Deuteronomy 23:21-23.
24. John 15:15.
25. Ecclesiastes 4:9-12.

Chapter Seventeen

1. Saperstein, R., & Saperstein D. (1993). The Invisible Wounds of War. *The Retired Officer Magazine*, May, 32-36.
2. Jeremiah 27:22, 30:17.
3. Leserman, J., Perkins, D., & Evans, D. (1992). Coping with the Threat of AIDS. The Role of Social Support. *American Journal of Psychiatry*, 149, 1514-1520.
4. John 17:15.
5. Ornish, D. (1990). *Reversing Heart Disease*. New York: Random House.
6. Psalms 139:23, 24, 141:4.
7. 1 Corinthians 13:11.
8. 1 Corinthians 13:12.
9. Proverbs 16:25.
10. Matthew 6:23.
11. Philippians 2:5.
12. Isaiah 55:8, 9.
13. James 3:13-17.
14. Psalms 101:3.
15. Romans 1:28, 8:7; 2 Corinthians 4:4; Ephesians 4:17, 18; Colossians 1:21, 2:18.
16. Romans 8:6; 1 Peter 1:13.
17. Isaiah 6:10; Ephesians 4:17, 18; Philippians 4:8.
18. Mark 14:33; Isaiah 26:3; Acts 2:25-28.
19. Nee, W (1957). *The Normal Christian Life*. Bombay: Gospel Literature Service.
20. Philippians 4:17; Ephesians 3:19.
21. Galatians 5:22.
22. Luke 17:21; Romans 14:17.
23. Hebrews 13:5.
24. 2 Corinthians 4:7-9.
25. 1 Corinthians 2:16.

Chapter Eighteen

1. Lutes, C. (1988). *What Teenagers are Saying About Drugs & Alcohol.* Wheaton: Tyndale House.
2. Ibid, see Lutes Ref. 1 above.
3. 2 Corinthians 3:17, 4:7.
4. Jeremiah 2:20, 27, 28, 37, 25:6.
6. Jeremiah 2:21, 25, 3:1, 9; Deuteronomy 6:4, 5.
7. Isaiah 30:1-12.
8. Philippians 2:13.
9. 2 Corinthians 4:2.
10. Isaiah 30:15.
11. Ibid, see Ref. 9 above.
12. Matthew 5:3, 8.
13. Isaiah 50:10.
14. Jeremiah 3:8, 22.
15. Psalms 86:15; Jeremiah 5:1-3 NAS.
16. Romans 12:3.
17. Matthew 13:14.
18. Romans 1:14, 17; 2 Corinthians 3:18.
19. Isaiah 14:12-15; Genesis 3:1-19; Romans 8:28.
20. Isaiah 21:3, 4.
21. Jeremiah 17:9, 10.
22. Luke 8:4-8.
35. James 1:8.
24. McGrady, B. (1986). Alcoholism. In David H. Barlow (Ed.). *Clinical Handbook of Psychological Disorders.* New York: Guilford Press.
25. 2 Timothy 2:25; Matthew 6:24.
26. 2 Corinthians 3:14-16; Matthew 6:52.
27. Ephesians 2:1, 3; 1 John 5:19 TLB.
28. Romans 6:16.
29. Exodus 23:29, 30; Luke 10:22.
30. Jeremiah 7:24; Deuteronomy 2:26-37; 1 John 1:9.
31. Galatians 5:1; Romans 14:4; Jeremiah 2:6-8, 3:12-15, 17, 22, 8:4, 15:19-21; Psalms 40:1, 2; 1 Corinthians 12:9.

Chapter Nineteen

1. Edelman, B. (1985). *Dear American: Letters Home From Vietnam.* New York: W.W. Norton & Company, Inc.
2. Goldman, P. & Fuller, T. (1983). *Charlie Company: What Vietnam Did to Us.* New York: William Morrow & Company, Inc.
3. Mahedy, W. P. (1986). *Out of the Night: The Spiritual Journey of Vietnam Vets.* New York: Ballantine Books.
4. Acts 3:14 NIV; Hebrews 5:9, 12:2.
5. Ecclesiastes 1:8-11.
6. Ecclesiastes 2:15-17.
7. Ecclesiastes 1:13-15, 2:11, 22, 6:12.
8. Job 42:2-6.
9. Ecclesiastes 12:13, 14.

10. 1 Corinthians 13:2; Proverbs 16:25.
11. James 1:2-4; Romans 8:28; Hebrews 11:6.
12. Acts 4:28 NIV.
13. 1 John 3:8; Acts 3:17-26; Romans 8:28.
14. 2 Corinthians 1:8-11 LB.
15. Galatians 6:7.
16. Brende, J. O. & Parson, E. R. (1985). *Vietnam Veterans: The Road to Recovery.* New York: Plenum Press.
17. Jeremiah 2:17-19; 10:23, 24.
18. John 3:16, 10:10, 8:31-36; Romans 10:20, 21.
19. Matthew 10:16; 1 Thessalonians 5:24; Romans 8:28-20.
20. Matthew 1:20; Acts 9:1-19; Numbers 22:21-35.
21. Proverbs 6:27; Ezekiel 22:31; Romans 2:1-11, 6:23; Galatians 6:7.
22. Psalms 119:156, 101:1, 105:7; Isaiah 26:9,10.
23. Acts 17:26, 27.
24. Proverbs 16:9; Isaiah 43:4; Romans 9:11; 2 Timothy 1:9 (NIV)
25. Sandford, J. & Sandford P. (1977). *The Elijah Task: A Call to Today's Prophets and Intercessors.* Tulsa, OK: Victory House, Inc.
26. Acts 4:28; 1 Peter 2:9.
27. Ecclesiastes 7:13, 14; Jeremiah 48:42-44.
28. Ecclesiastes 1:18.
29. 2 Corinthians 7:9, 10.
30. Isaiah 30:26.
31. Isaiah 10:3-21.
32. Ibid, see Sandford, Ref. 25 above.
33. Acts 14:16 & 17.
34. Ecclesiastes 3:1-7.
35. 1 Peter 2:5.

Chapter Twenty

1. Donovan, D. *Once a Warrior King: Memoirs of an Officer in Vietnam.* New York: McGraw-Hill Book Company.
2. Galatians 5:20.
3. 2 Corinthians 5:15-18, 10:3,4.
4. Genesis 12:2, 3.
5. John 10:10.
6. Psalms 2:8 NAS, 110:1, 2; John 3:35.
7. Romans 12:1, 2.
8. Romans 6:16.
9. Romans 2:14; 1 Peter 1:6, 7; 2 Corinthians 2:9, 8:24, 13:3; Philippians 2:22; 2 Timothy 4:5.
10. Mark 8:34.
11. Deuteronomy 11:26-32.
12. Hebrews 5:12-14.
13. Romans 6:13, 8:13; Luke 17:33.
14. John 3:3-8; Philippians 3:21; 2 Thessalonians 1:10.
15. Genesis 1:28, 9:1,7.
16. John 17:6-17.
17. 1 Thessalonians 5:23.
18. Hebrews 10:14.

19. Galatians 5:13; 1 Peter 1:1, 2; Colossians 1:13, 2:10, 4:12; Romans 3:22-28, 4:16, 8:2, 11, 29, 30, 9:28; Psalms 23; 2 Thessalonians 2:13; John 4:34; Hebrews 12:2; Philippians 1:6, 2:13.

20. Romans 8:5-8, Colossians 3:2.

21. 2 Corinthians 5:17-20; Ephesians 2:14-16.

22. John 19:30; Romans 5:10, 8:33; Colossians 1:22; Isaiah 65:9, 22; 1 Peter 1:2.

23. 2 Corinthians 4:12.

24. Revelations 22:1-3.

25. Romans 10:17; Hebrews 11:2-6; 2 Corinthians 3:3; 1 John 1:6-10.

26. 1 Corinthians 14:3 paraphrased

27. 2 Corinthians 1:3-6.

28. 2 Corinthians 4:7.

29. Isaiah 9:3-7; Jeremiah 20:11 NAS; Zephaniah 3:17 NAS; Psalms 37:23.

30. 1 Kings 12:11; 2 Chronicles 11:1; Judges 6:12; 1 Peter 2:9.

31. 2 Corinthians 10:3-6.

32. Ephesians 6:12.

33. Psalms 34:14; Ephesians 2:14, 6:11-14; John 17:7; 2 Corinthians 3:5, 6, 10:4; 1 John 4:4.

34. Joyner, R. (1996) *The Final Quest.* Charlotte, NC: Morning Star Publications.

Your Opportunity to Respond

Wounded Warriors, Chosen Lives

has been written and published as a labor of love in hopes that those who read it may be helped to achieve healing in their lives and reconciliation in relationships that have been damaged through years of pain.

If you found this book helpful, we hope you will want to obtain additional copies to share with friends and family members, or to help in our effort to make gift copies available to Vietnam veterans who would not otherwise obtain a copy. The *Response Form* below is provided for your convenience in making a contribution or for ordering additional copies. Please make a copy of the form, or clip it from this page. Complete the appropriate information and send with check or money order to:

Clear Stream Publishing   Phone 817-265-2766
Wounded Warriors Project   Fax   817-861-0703
Box 122128
Arlington, TX 76012

We would also appreciate any comments you have after reading *Wounded Warriors, Chosen Lives*. Let us hear from you by letter or Fax.

Wounded Warriors Response Form

___ I want to make a contribution to the **Wounded Warriors Project** to help cover the cost of providing gift copies of Howard Olsen's book to Vietnam Veterans. Amount Enclosed: $ _____

___ I received *Wounded Warriors, Chosen Lives* as a gift and want to respond in gratitude by contributing $12.95 so another person will receive a gift copy.

___ I want to order additional copies of *Wounded Warriors, Chosen Lives* to share with friends or family.
_____ # of individual copies desired ($12.95 each)   Total $ enclosed: _____
_____ # of 5-Book discount packages ($60.00 each)   Total $ enclosed _____
Postage included for U.S. and Canada. For overseas delivery, please add $3 per book

Name _____ Vietnam Vet? ___ Yes ___ No

Address _____

City _____ State _____ Zip _____

Make checks payable to: *Clear Stream, Inc. W.W. Project*
Send to: Clear Stream, Inc. Wounded Warriors Project, Box 122128 Arlington, TX 76012

Other books by
Clear Stream Publishing

Waking the Slumbering Spirit
by John & Paula Sandford and Norm Bowman

Lack of loving nurture, extended periods of emotional stress and patterns of sinful behavior can cause a person's God-given personal spirit to be dulled into what the authors call spiritual slumber. The slumbering spirit results in a dulling of the personal conscience, inability to learn from mistakes, difficulty in maintaining relationships, lack of spiritual focus, and other debilitating problems.

Waking the Slumbering reveals ways to discover the extent to which the personal spirit may be slumbering and what can be done to restore lost spiritual vitality. Helps are given to more effectively nurture children to full vitality of their personal spirits and help adult friends and family members to renewed vibrancy through love, encouragement, and the power of prayer. A study guide for personal evaluation and small group interaction is included at the end of each chapter.

Choosing Forgiveness
by John & Paula Sandford and Norm Bowman

Inability to forgive is the most common issue that destroys relationships and is the most common problem for which people seek help through counseling. *Choosing Forgiveness* is a very readable and practical book which explains the necessity for Christians to live a lifestyle of forgiveness. Scripture-based and packed with illustrations, it provides insights on how to respond appropriately to personal woundings, how to keep bitterness from lodging in the heart, and how to receive healing and restore unity through the power of God's Holy Spirit.

Guides for personal evaluation and group interaction are included at the end of each chapter. *Choosing Forgiveness* also features a 31-day Scripture-based devotional guide to help individuals on the journey toward forgiveness.

241

The Jesus Principle
by Charles R. Wade
with Norm and Carol Bowman

Dr. Charles Wade, pastor of the dynamic and influential First Baptist Church of Arlington, Texas, shares from a wealth of wisdom gained from over thirty years in the pastorate. With great insight and spiritual maturity, he helps individual Christians, church lay leaders and ministers focus on what it means to be the Body of Christ, courageously doing God's work in the world today

Wade identifies how the character of Jesus is reflected in the five basic functions of the church: Christians are to worship, evangelize, disciple, minister, and build fellowship. He gives valuable insights on understanding the church's mission, discovering a vision for the church's role in the community, and exercising leadership consistent with the character of Jesus Christ.

The Jesus Principle calls Christians, both individually and corporately, to seek the mind of Christ and to follow the example of Jesus in every attitude, decision, and course of action. This is an important book that challenges all Christians to look beyond their differences and unite in a recommitment to the mission of Jesus Christ. Study guides are included for individuals and small group interaction.

Books may be ordered direct from Clear Stream Publishing

___ Copies *Waking the Slumbering Spirit* ($12 ea.)   Total $_____

___ Copies *Choosing Forgiveness* ($13 ea.)   Total $_____

___ Copies *The Jesus Principle* ($14 ea.)   Total $_____

Postage & handling included within continental USA   Total Order $_____
Make checks payable to Clear Stream, Inc.

Name _____

Address_____

City _____State_____ Zip _____

Send to Clear Stream Publishing   Box 122128   Arlington, TX 76012
